urban
reflections

narratives of place, planning and change

mark tewdwr-jones

Gateshead Millennium Bridge

For my parents,
Peter and Marilyn Jones

First published in Great Britain in 2011 by

The Policy Press
University of Bristol
Fourth Floor
Beacon House
Queen's Road
Bristol BS8 1QU
UK

t: +44 (0)117 331 4054
f: +44 (0)117 331 4093
tpp-info@bristol.ac.uk
www.policypress.co.uk

North American office:
The Policy Press
c/o International Specialized Books Services
920 NE 58th Avenue, Suite 300
Portland, OR 97213-3786, USA
t: +1 503 287 3093
f: +1 503 280 8832
info@isbs.com

© 2011 Mark Tewdwr-Jones

British Library Cataloguing in Publication Data
A catalogue record for this book is available from the British Library.

Library of Congress Cataloging-in-Publication Data
A catalog record for this book has been requested.

ISBN 978 1 84742 841 7 paperback
ISBN 978 1 84742 842 4 hardcover

The right of Mark Tewdwr-Jones to be identified as author of this work has been asserted by him in accordance with the Copyright, Designs and Patents Act 1988.

The statements and opinions contained within this publication are solely those of the author and not of the University of Bristol or The Policy Press. The University of Bristol and The Policy Press disclaim responsibility for any injury to persons or property resulting from any material published in this publication.

The Policy Press works to counter discrimination on grounds of gender, race, disability, age and sexuality.

Cover design by Qube Design Associates, Bristol.
Front cover and all other images: © 2011 Mark Tewdwr-Jones.
Printed and bound in Great Britain by Hobbs, Southampton.
The Policy Press uses environmentally responsible print partners.

FSC
www.fsc.org
MIX
Paper from
responsible sources
FSC® C020438

Contents

About the author

Mark Tewdwr-Jones is Professor of Spatial Panning and Governance at University College London's Bartlett School of Planning and Architecture and the UCL Urban Laboratory. He is a recognised authority on urban planning, the politics of the city and the use of land. His previous books include *The planning polity: Planning, government and the policy process* (2002, Routledge), *Planning futures: New directions for planning theory* (co-edited with Philip Allmendinger) (Routledge, 2002), *Second homes* (with Alan Mace and Nick Gallent) (2005, Ashgate), *Territory, identity and spatial planning: Spatial governance in a fragmented nation* (co-edited with Philip Allmendinger) (2006, Routledge), *Decent homes for all: Reviewing planning's role in housing provision* (with Nick Gallent) (2007, Routledge) and *Urban and regional planning* (with Sir Peter Hall) (2011, Routledge). He is a Visiting Professor at University College Dublin and Adjunct Professor at the University of New South Wales. He lives in London.

Acknowledgements

This book has been a long time in the making. In truth, it was subject to fits and starts over a 10-year period, although the ideas and thoughts behind it go back much further. The way it has developed conceptually, the interests it has precipitated during the course of research, and the urban reflections represented in its pages, reflect the support of a great many people.

Much of the book was researched and written while I was a film student at Birkbeck College London and I wish to thank my mentors there – particularly Ian Christie, Mike Allen, Laura Mulvey and Amy Sargeant – who reawakened my passion for film and photo graphy and who had to endure endless discussions and tutorials devoted to my hobby horse – place, landscape and setting in film. It was a challenging period, not least because I was also attempting to hold down my full faculty position at The Bartlett and teach and publish work on spatial planning, governance and policy matters simultaneously. I am also grateful for the new friendships that developed there, particularly with Alistair Wardill.

For assistance during the course of research, I am immensely grateful to the British Film Institute librarians and the custodians and archivists at BBC Caversham Park who enabled me to access so many original sources and historical material relevant to my interests. A number of people deserve special attention for their participation or for being subjected to long interviews, notably Edward Mirzoeff, Anne Marie Carty, Stephen Games, Alan Powers, Stephen Ward, Peter Hall, Robert Freestone, Michael Hebbert, John Goddard, Iain Borden, Adrian Forty, Jonathan Hill, Phil Steadman, Nick Phelps, James Throgmorton, Leonie Sandercock, Donald McNeill, Kim MacNamara, John Pendlebury, Geoff Vigar, David B. Clarke, Mark Goodall, David Bell, Geraint Ellis, Michael Short, Ben Clifford, Claire Colomb, Matthew Gandy, Ben Campkin, Johan Andersson,

Raul Diaz, Marco Bianconi, Elena Besussi, Sonia Arbaci, Nikos Karadimitriou, Michael Edwards, Judith Hillmore, Ian Scott, Andrew Hoolachan, Olivier Sykes, Lawrence Napper, Indi Sihra and Ole Jensen. I would like to thank Ben Clifford and Nick Phelps for permission to use ideas from jointly authored papers and I am especially grateful to Rob Seaman, Gary Farrer, Piotr Lanoszka and Rui Guerra Figueira for their friendship and for allowing me to subject them to long photographic jaunts through the modern city across the UK, and also because I learned so much from them about photography and the places we visited.

An original version of Chapter Seven was published in *Planning Perspectives* (2005), vol 20, no 4, pp 389-411. Thanks to the journal editors and the publishers, Taylor & Francis, for permission to reproduce aspects of this work.

I would like to acknowledge the excellence of The Policy Press and the support of Emily Watt, and Laura and David for their first class work, who took the decision to run with publication of the book, and I am grateful to the original proposal referees and to the typescript reviewers who provided critical but insightful comments on the draft work. All errors, blunders and oversights, if any remain, are of course, my own.

Ultimately, it has been my family and friends who have made it possible for me to bring the project to completion. Robbie has done more for me than he knows to keep me sane when the book seemed to be going nowhere. Our friends Robert and Matthew have been so supportive and interested over the years and a fantastic escape from the rigours of writing. Above all, I wish to publicly thank my parents, Peter and Marilyn Jones, for their lifetime support. I owe them my deepest and heartfelt thanks and it is as a small gesture that I wish to dedicate this book to them.

Preface

The eye does not see things, but images of things that mean other things. (Calvino, 1974 p 13)

I can recall vividly as a child in the early 1970s my surprise and awe at visits with my family to Cardiff, our nearest city, on shopping expeditions and days out. Cardiff, unlike the small Welsh village where we resided, was quite different. It was vast, or at least so I thought, with grids of streets and terraces of shops and houses that seemed to go on as far as the eye could see, many of these – built in Victorian or Edwardian times – in severe decay or covered in grime and the after-effects of a long declining industrial age. Adjacent to these, and in some cases set between them, were a handful of gleaming high-rise office buildings that looked distinctly futuristic in comparison. The street pattern was different too, with dual carriageways meandering through the city centre, some still under construction, while other roads were empty or seemed to lead to dead-ends. It had a castle that conjured up thoughts of the Welsh princes in battle, but in reality was less than a 100 years old. It was most certainly in Wales but curiously most of the street names seemed Scottish in origin. There were crowds, more people than I had ever seen in one place, which added to the excitement of visiting somewhere different, but also posed a danger. My mother would say to me as we stepped off the train, "Now don't let go of my hand, there's a good boy", as if foretelling my natural desire in later life to wander off inquisitively to explore parts of the urban realm in a fairly absent-minded way. Above all, being fascinated with all things motorised, one feature of Cardiff that really demonstrated its difference was that the city possessed brightly coloured *orange* buses! And to a six-year-old, these looked much more exciting than the dreary and archaic municipal red double-deckers from back home.

Conversely, occasional daytrips to Bristol and Weston-super-Mare confirmed the fact that to me we really were in strange territories simply because all their buses were green liveried.

Could it have been these early experiences of visiting Cardiff and other towns that encouraged a desire to learn more about places, their history and geography, in my later years at school and university? A deep-seated passion to learn more about history combined with a stronger geographical awareness, together with an upbringing in a solidly working-class and socialist society, perhaps inevitably fuelled my longing to study more critically. At 16, Advanced Level subjects of Geography, History and Politics were followed by the choice of Urban Planning – an examination of cities, city planning and the urban political landscape – at degree level and beyond. As time passed, I soon realised that although trained and professionally qualified in town planning, my real interests remained rooted in place and space – how they were, how they changed, why they changed, who was responsible for them and, importantly, how other people felt about change as it was occurring. And these questions have preoccupied me in my professional and academic career in the 20 plus years since graduating. But there have been another series of questions and problems concerning the urban environment that has beset my mind over this time. And they relate more to matters of how my ideas of the city, and those of others too, have been influenced by the image and representations of urban planning and of urban change, predominantly in film, photography and cultural media.

As a child of the 1960s, it would come as no surprise to learn that television and film played an increasingly prominent role in my leisure time. My fascination with real places was often mirrored by a fascination for the places I saw on screen, some of which I recognised, or thought I recognised, while others were somehow different. Television and film offered a unique laboratory of learning, one that I did not fully recognise, admittedly, at the time, about how people lived and co-existed in places, how they coped with change, or even opposed it. Above all, film provided a unique lens through which to analyse contemporary change or urban histories in a way that was not necessarily thought of academically at the time I was viewing them. Some of these depictions were fictional, narrative story lines involving crime capers, car chases, the noir side of urban life; others were set within suburbia, gentle family comedies involving ongoing light-hearted tensions between different values of members of the same family or circle of friends; and others were documentary or realist in tone, that revealed in a much more graphic way, perhaps, the consequences of change, the inadequacy of the state, or the exclusion of societies in particular settings.

Over the last 10 years I have given a considerable amount of thought to ways that I could combine my interests in urban planning, place and space, and filmic representation that would provide a new perspective, literally an alternative lens, on a subject matter that we all have become used to analysing. I started writing this book in 2001, just as I commenced a part-time Master's in Film History, but it has taken the years since for my ideas to start to coalesce. In the interim, ongoing academic work in Cultural and Urban Geography, Film Studies, Anthropology and Architecture, to name just a handful of disciplines, have used film prominently in studies of city, society and change. But curiously, my own discipline, Urban Planning, has not embraced the cultural turn with anything like the same degree of enthusiasm. Exactly why this remains so is a matter of conjecture – is it a belief that the discipline should remain true to its realist parameters of place-based interventions, procedural efficiencies and political-governance questions? Or is it a desire to keep the professional concern of planning to narrow, discrete concerns and not become subsumed under what may be regarded by some as non-planning subject matters? It is my contention that planning and place and people's perceptions of planning and of places are indecorously bound together, and using images, stories and film from cultural sources is a highly effective way to reflect not only on different perceptions of place and urban change, but also on the role and status of urban planning itself.

We all have prior perceptions of places, even if we have never set foot in the place in question. These perceptions have been formed from the media, from literature and film, from historical developments, from chance encounters and from a suspicion that somehow the people from other places *are not like us*. These perceptions of places continue to be peddled, not least by popular media representations of people and urban planning. Culture itself has assisted people in thinking about places and the perception of places, even if these depictions are not absolutely accurate. Consider film, for example, and the use of major cultural projects as locations in some of the most recent *James Bond* films – the Millennium Dome, the Guggenheim Museum and the Eden Project. Or think of the depiction of parts of Montemarte, Paris, in *Amelie*. Think of Vienna in *The Third Man*, San Francisco in *Vertigo*, Rome in *La Dolce Vita*, Turin in *The Italian Job* or Venice in *Death in Venice*. These depictions are both representative of the place, and are fictional characterisations of actual places, but the important point is that they communicate ideas of places that can sit heavily on people's emotions and sense of attachment to locations and their own ideas about the identity and meaning of a place. Similar to maps, films are just another way of looking at the world, but evoke matters concerning power and contestation.

Society attaches significance to notions of place. Some of these notions are erroneous, whereas some are genuine forms of affection. What we mean when we talk and think about place matters a great deal. And how those multiple perceptions of places (sometimes of the same place) have been coloured by cultural or historical experiences needs to be considered. The difficulty for urban planners, charged with the task of considering possible courses of future intervention into the real landscape as opposed to mere analysis, is how to embrace these notions of culture and place meaning within harder decisions concerning land, development, resources and strategy. There is also a further problem over the extent to which planners should extol the existing cultural attributes of a place or impose new cultural meanings within places. Stamping out all traces of the older values of cities and regions, even if they are unpopular, would be detrimental.

How we, as urban planners, perceive of a place and what, in turn, people try to cling on to in their perceptions of a place, are issues that need to be considered fully within the urban planning realm. Planning has to become more sensitive to notions of place and meaning if it is going to perform a key role in helping shape distinctive places of the future that society and the market find appealing. Above all, educators need to place themselves in the position of their student audiences. Individuals enter planning programmes because they have an interest in a vocational discipline and (usually) want to make a difference to the built environment. But we need to develop new ways to engage with and communicate ideas to them.

A growing element of teaching at University College London's (UCL) Bartlett School of Planning, a laboratory of social science and design research, is occurring through the humanities, and this has engendered greater responses from the students, who are beginning to understand what places mean to people and what they represent. This is a first critical step before we even begin to consider any form of urban planning intervention. Students are well aware of the problems of towns and cities and rural areas, and of the political dilemmas surrounding intervention. They are not naive individuals living in a vacuum. They are the users of places – travelling on poor transport services, using shops, fighting to secure full- or part-time employment, living in inadequate housing or socially diverse communities, and perhaps longing for further leisure and entertainment places. They are aware of design and the aesthetics of place; they recognise economic competition between spaces; they are at the forefront of using new technological developments; and above all, they are media savvy. And they are already versed in aspects of environmentalism and conscious of issues concerning health, safety and security. Planning educators need to inspire them, give them confidence, develop their critical capacities and provide mentoring. This does not mean teaching the same modules that have always been part of an Urban Planning curriculum; it means looking to Geography, History, Architecture and Art degrees, for example, to develop modules that analyse critically notions of place and space and how these are represented.

This book concerns place and the urban landscape and political attempts to shape and control urban spaces since the introduction of formal urban planning in the early 1900s to the present day. It provides a series of narratives that examine our perception of place and change, both through official town planning accounts and through literary, cinematic and social depictions and reactions to urban change and development. It attempts to provide a multidisciplinary story of the UK's love–hate relationship with modernisation and city building drawing an imagery from the period 1930 to 1979, but with implications for the present day. Uniquely for this subject matter, the book draws on cultural sources, as well as geographical, political, cinematic and photographic readings to provide a meta-narrative of urban topographical change. The work is written from the perspective of an urban planner, but one sensitive to and aware of media and public perceptions of planning. To some extent, my objective in undertaking this work has been to get under the skin of urban planning and to reveal some home truths. I have already discovered, in presenting aspects of this work at academic conferences and in research seminars, that some members of the academic planning community have not only failed to recognise the broader place-sensitive context for planning, but also in a small number of cases have been outright hostile to my ideas. This has only confirmed to me that I must be heading in the right direction.

My inspirations for the book originated from a diverse range of sources, some academic, some practical, some cultural, some observational. In the key thinkers bracket I would single out Doreen

Massey, Leonie Sandercock and John Gold, for their comprehensive discussions of space, place and planning; filmic works of the Ealing Studios, the British documentary movement and the British new wave, while specific films such as Vertov's *Man with a Movie Camera*, Tati's *Playtime*, Patrick Keiller's *Robinson in Space* and Terence Davies' *Of Time and the City* communicated as much to me about towns and cities as reading half a dozen academic works; the photography of Martin Parr and John Davies reveal so much about our urban landscape and the people within it; the historians Peter Ackroyd and David Kynaston always provide a refreshing interpretation of recent and not-so-recent events; while works by the authors and poets J.B. Priestley, George Orwell, W.H. Auden and John Betjeman enabled me to stand back from the observable to see hidden aspects of everyday life; finally, television series by Edward Mirzoeff and Jonathan Meades always capture and represent the take-it-for-granted everyday places in revealing and subtle ways. Their role and influence in this project have to be set on record.

The title of this book, *Urban reflections*, is meant to evoke the real and imagined perspectives of both place and planning, and photographic and textual narratives of place and change. These reflections can be accurate portrayals or distorted images, but all serve to tell a story of how cities experience change, a process that is forever enduring.

City of London

PART ONE

Between recreated past and threatening future:
The modern planning project

ONE

Introduction

THE (HI)STORY OF URBAN PLANNING

> ... after 100 years debate on how to plan the city, after repeated attempts – however mistaken or distorted – to put ideas into practice, we find we are almost back where we started....That does not mean, of course, that we have got nowhere at all ... it does mean that certain trends seem to reassert themselves; perhaps because, in truth, they never went away. (Hall, 2002, pp 11-12)

Urban planning within the UK, as in so many other countries, has undergone mixed fortunes over the decades. The establishment of a modern planning process in the early 20th century to combat poor public health, inner-city squalor, bad housing development and high densities, led to a belated political acknowledgement of the need for some form of state intervention in the future form and planning of places. The grand 17th-century architecture of Christopher Wren and the bold Georgian designs for Bath and Brighton, for example, in the 18th century, paled into insignificance compared to what happened to British towns from the mid-1800s.

The Industrial Revolution, dramatic increases in the population and a shift from an agrarian to an urban society had rapidly transformed previously small towns into large urban areas. In West Hartlepool, County Durham, the town grew from a population of 4,000 in 1851 to 63,000 by 1901. The population of London doubled, from approximately one million to about two million between 1801 and 1851; it doubled again to four million by 1881, and then

Originally the second largest Medieval city in England, shades of Italianate, Moorish, Deauville and Dutch vernacular, but essentially English: Norwich

added another 2.5 million to reach 6.5 million in 1911. Towns and cities had only the most elementary arrangements, if indeed any, for providing water, clearing refuse or for sewage treatment, while there was no system of mass public transport. With water supplies lacking, personal hygiene was very poor, epidemics became commonplace, and overcrowding grew steadily worse. Medical treatment, and public health controls, were almost completely lacking until the closing years of the 19th century. Life expectancy in Liverpool in 1841 was 26; in Manchester in 1843 it was just 24.

As the condition of towns and cities was revealed, principally by social reformers, journalists and authors rather than politicians, so recognition grew about the need for some form of intervention. Even in these early days, there was a great deal of uncertainty as to whether such high political intervention was warranted. But by the first decade of the 20th century the first elements of an organised process of urban planning for improved housing and conditions was initiated. Visionary individuals put forward proposals for 'garden cities' that combined the best features of towns and countryside as future design frameworks for new development. Progress was slow, particularly in the provision of new and better quality housing. British Prime Minister David Lloyd George's promise in 1918 to provide 'homes fit for heroes' was followed by a decade of debate between the political parties on the need for public housing, subsidised rents and finding sufficient amounts of land for new house building. Almost 100 years later, rather depressingly, the debate is still raging.

In the interwar years, the process of planning for new housing advanced rapidly. The implementation practically of an urban planning movement did not have the effect of transforming the

Relics of a great port: ferry crossing the Mersey

worst inner central areas of towns and cities, as had been desire in the latter part of the 19th century, but rather the outward expansion of urban areas in the form of suburban growth and decentralisation. It was always so much easier to build out 'in the sticks', where landownership and the existing built form posed no problem, and where land was relatively cheap. The forces driving this suburban movement were partly economic, partly social, partly technological. People began to aspire to buy a house of their own with the aid of a mortgage. Railway companies and speculative builders saw an opportunity to buy cheap land for housing adjacent to roads, railways and underground lines. In the 1920s, the General Manager of the London Underground, Frank Pick, even launched a successful marketing campaign in London to 'live in metro-land!', encouraging Londoners to buy homes in the countryside, able to travel speedily and easily by fast transport to their work in the city. Developments in transport technology extended commuting possibilities. London's area extended up to four or five times its previous limits. Suburban housing also developed along major road corridors into and out of cities, even along dual lane highways, and sprawled in a form that became known as 'ribbon development'.

As the years passed, and public and political reaction started to voice concern over the effect on the countryside of new housing in suburban locations, the urban planning process was expected – and indeed, was reshaped – to champion protectionist interests. As Peter Hall remarked, 'a small, but powerful and vocal movement' built up to limit urban growth through positive planning (Hall and Tewdwr-Jones, 2011, p 25). It represented a working coalition between people interested in urban planning and rural preservationists but was, in essence, intent on halting planning in its tracks. Urban planning had not set out deliberately to sprawl over the countryside – it was, after all, intended to improve conditions in central urban areas. But, through a combination of new mass transport opportunities, the availability of mortgages and cheap land, it had indirectly fostered urban expansion, with developers preferring edge-of-town sites to inner-city locations. Planning, or perhaps the absence of planning, was not only creating housing development in the countryside, but also the accoutrements of mid 20th-century urban living out in rural areas such as petrol pump stations, garages and advertising hoardings. The proactive role for planning – creating better places for people in the interests of better housing, improved public health, 'green lungs' (plenty of fresh air and wide open space) and community well-being – was shadowed by a reactive role intended to control, stop or regulate development interests in the name of rural protection. Planning from the 1930s had to henceforth undertake both roles simultaneously. In the UK town planning became 'town and country planning', two processes with somewhat different rationales rolled into one legislative commitment. This fragile relationship remains in place in the urban planning system today, and lies at the heart of growth/anti-development public and media sentiment: to plan ahead with housing and economic development to accommodate the long-term needs of our towns and cities, while controlling development pressures that might affect the countryside.

New plans produced after the 1930s therefore had to embody a vision to accommodate the development pressures of towns, while being pragmatic to channel growth into designated areas. This dual policy regime has been an enduring feature of our way of managing land use change through the planning system: to allow development while protecting the environment. Both policies have created their own legacies where the market and regulation may be in conflict. As the town and country planning process attempted to achieve a balance in delivering growth in particular patterns of development while protecting the best landscapes and agricultural land in the 1930s, cities were simultaneously undergoing rapid physical change due to the changing economic base, the decline of heavy industry and the growth of the service sector. These changes created their own impacts and demands on the land and on land use patterns. In some larger urban areas, rising car ownership and the desire to accommodate the car was achieved through trunk road building programmes and ring roads around city centres. People began to be more mobile and could live and work in locations some distance from each other. This made the planning of new patterns of land use activity much more difficult to achieve. Individuals could live and pay taxes in one administrative area, but work and use the services and facilities of a different administrative area.

The impact of the Second World War on countries' economies and the need to rebuild towns and cities physically in the aftermath of war devastation necessitated a new central role for planning, in coordinating change, improving economic growth and organising space. One third of the total housing stock was damaged or destroyed by enemy action by 1945, and other buildings such as factories, schools and hospitals had also been targeted. Many of Britain's cities had been blitzed. The postwar government implemented a process of public ownership of services and industry and was committed to introducing a welfare state. The Bank of England, civil aviation, coal, transport, electricity, gas and iron and steel were all nationalised under the control of the government. A National Health Service (NHS) was created, providing free health treatment. There was an urgent need to replace bomb-damaged homes and, between 1945 and 1951, over one million public sector (council) houses were built. In 1947, a new planning system was created, allowing individual towns and cities to draw up development plans for their area and allowing local authorities to control new developments.

Postwar planning and architecture created a legacy for British towns and cities that is being contested today as part of a discussion about the failure of the modernist movement and of planning in particular. The comprehensive redevelopment of city centres, dehumanising landscapes caused by strict single-use zoning, urban motorways, high-rise tower blocks, large housing estates and the widespread use of exposed concrete as building material helped to create visionary futuristic landscapes for cities, but have long been unpopular with the public and commentators. This period of modern planning could be characterised as urban geometry, a symptom of the welfare state and top-down planning, and the dehumanising of cities. The 1950s and 1960s modernist movement in planning and architecture

Finsbury Health Centre, designed by Bertold Lubetkin and Tecton in 1938, a prototype for the NHS and an attempt to lift the urban poor out of disease and squalor

received a backlash, politically and publicly, from the 1960s onwards, as new development projects wiped away elements of Georgian and Victorian buildings, and later in the 1980s, as attempts were made by urban growth coalitions to re-image cities in support of economic growth and commercial interests. What we have remaining in British cities today, architecturally and structurally, are the layers of previous planning attempts to intervene, interspersed with a continuing recycling of land and buildings, as part of what David Harvey (1989) refers to as waves of capital accumulation, new urban forms and land use patterns caused by changing mobility.

To a significant extent, the postwar modern vision of the role of urban planning became a dominant policy instrument and continues to have a significant impact on aspects of policy towards land use in the 21st century. However, during the 1960s the negative impacts of some aspects of the policy framework had begun to be recognised. Significant increases in population, greater mobility, higher levels of car ownership and greater traffic movement and economic rejuvenation had given the country new prosperity. Between October 1951 and October 1953, wages had risen by 7.2 per cent; there was a reduction in the official working week; affluence was measured in the acquisition of consumer durables, with 88 per cent of households possessing a television by 1965 and 98 per cent

Twenty-first-century spaces of contention – base or sublime? Birmingham Central Library, a brutalist structure from 1974 and under threat of demolition

refrigerators, while the number of cars on Britain's roads increased from 2.25 million in 1951 to 8 million in 1964, and homeownership rates doubled during the same period. The motorway network, planned and development by the government outside the new 1947 planning framework, created new conditions and contexts for development patterns that had localised effects and allowed people to live and work in different locations, thereby undermining some of the assumptions behind development planning. The expansion of airports and the rise of air travel led to major patterns of new growth in the urban periphery, not just for land for runways and terminal buildings, but also for airport services and logistics.

These trends meant that socioeconomic conditions and changing infrastructure began to outstrip the 1947-style development plans and their projections. Town planning was criticised for its over-optimism and its inability to update plans quickly, perhaps partly because the visions were not realised in the way people had imagined, and also because economic and social prosperity beyond expectations had been achieved. Even under the relatively restrictive postwar regime, development outside urban centres continued. Growth around existing urban areas was supplemented by the creation of a series of 'garden cities' and 'new towns' on land that had previously been agricultural, in rural locations around Britain. Even policies for which there was often very strong local support, such as greenbelts around major conurbations, began to see creeping development on either side of these 'green bands', which were also cut through with major transport infrastructure. In respect of the social impacts of postwar development, there was also growing criticism of the often poor quality of urban and peri-urban housing design and its impact on communities.

In terms of the impact on the land caused by employment changes, UK manufacturing decline reached its most extreme in older industrial regions in the 1970s. A subsequent wave of industrial and service reorganisation led to movement of activities to the regions, to metropolitan cores outside London, and subsequently to global locations. Critically, face-to-face activities continue to be concentrated, both in absolute and in relative terms, in London. The South East has had a massive effect on national labour markets as it has drawn in regional migrants. Some of these migrants have returned to the regions as part of the 'escalator' effect; however, London continues to be a net beneficiary of the regions, and international migration. At an aggregate level the population has become wealthier (although the social and spatial distribution of wealth is little changed). Thus, the population has more disposable income and this, in turn, has had major impacts on other sectors, notably a growth in retailing and personal transport. The number of cars on the roads has increased dramatically, creating pressures on transport infrastructure and a massive modal split in favour of the car.

Interwoven in this process has been the reorganisation of retailing and distribution. The first supermarkets emerged in the 1960s and out-of-town superstores, located at edge-of-centre locations and at major road intersections, arrived in the 1980s. Big-box retailers have been facilitated by changes in logistics; namely, as in manufacture, the adoption of just-in-time systems and regional and national warehouse hubs. In spatial terms this has led to the progressive abandonment of city centre locations first of 'big-box' goods, then of major city centre retail stores. In part, this has led to a further 'hollowing out' of city centres, and pressure on motorway intersections to take on the role of new employment hubs. Both processes have created new challenges for the land use system that has emerged in the last 25 years as a consequence of taking policy decisions in other fields. On a national scale, warehouse development has been concentrated

The insatiable demand for mobility has caused new urban spatial forms and new ways to navigate the city

in the main English motorway corridors and strategic hubs such as London, Bristol, Leeds and Manchester, since the 1970s. These developments have occurred despite the continued existence of elements of a postwar policy regime aimed at urban containment, greenbelt protection and a concentration of services. London is one of the main centres for warehousing development in the UK and has around 10.5 per cent of the total warehouse floor space in England and Wales. More recently, the focus for logistical and distribution services has been towards the provision of intermodal freight terminals, large hard-standing areas adjacent to rail sidings for short-term holding and transhipment of intermodal units. These terminals are also becoming a strategic location for distribution centres, receiving and despatching a proportion of their throughput by rail. Several of the intermodal terminals were set up in the early 1990s to handle Channel Tunnel freight traffic at places such as Daventry, Wakefield, Trafford Park and Mossend near Glasgow.

In the face of these new economic locations outside traditional urban areas, since the 1990s there have been attempts to revive towns and cities with a relaxation of regulatory controls in favour of 'mixed land use'. Mixed land use planning responses have attempted to bring employment back into towns and city centres through the provision of new retail spaces, cafes and restaurants, leisure and tourism developments and new residential apartments. This policy

Optimism at the urban fringe: Kingsway Business Park, near the M62

has also attempted to respond to desires for economic development within urban areas, and created a renaissance for cities. A net effect of this has been the replacement of inner-city manufacturing with (mainly) single-person housing; however, new jobs have not often been co-located – these are commonly found out of town.

During the last 60 years, housing has been under extreme pressures at a regional scale, and within London in particular. However, it is important to note the structural changes in housing supply, namely the shift from public to private, and from rental to ownership. Whereas the state was able to manage labour supply and minimise transport problems through housing supply in the postwar period, this is no longer possible. There has been a change in employment participation rates, which is also in lock step with rising house prices (especially in the South East). Thus, households increasingly require multiple incomes. In practice, the turnover rate for jobs and locations means that home and work have little relationship, aside from the use of a car to mediate it. New build housing has fallen below demand, in part due to lack of building land, especially in London. These processes have been mixed with social change, alongside female participation in the workforce and multi-earner households, but smaller family sizes, the end of extended families and the rise of single-person dwellings. In short, the existing building stock is also out of sync with demand; added to this is that over the last 50 years people have sought more space in their homes. Of course, all of these issues have a regional dimension, trends led by London and the South East, but by no means confined to it. Moreover, there is considerable vacancy and oversupply of housing in the North.

There has been a strong tendency for development to be concentrated within urban areas, which, over recent years, has not been entirely confined to existing footprints or to existing urban areas. London's greenbelt has restricted such development around the capital, with greenbelt having a similar effect around Birmingham. But 'belts' of greenfield development are identifiable between West Yorkshire and the West Midlands, within the Mersey Belt and in the North East.

These historical drivers of change to the landscape and to the way the urban planning process attempts to mediate between conflicting land uses have given rise to new patterns of development and growth. If anything, the pressure on the urban planning process has intensified over the last 30 years to accommodate ever more complex societal and business needs. Government, inheriting an urban planning process that once possessed a clear ideological central control rationale, has been uncertain about whether to lead or follow trends, and which level of democracy should have the most say in shaping urban futures.

THE FORM OF URBAN PLANNING TODAY

> We are disinclined to trust anyone who says they can predict the future, and with good reason. The desire to know what happens next is nothing new, and the kind of people who until recently have set about fulfilling this need – necromancers, gazers into crystal balls, science-fiction fantasists, not to mention town planners – don't inspire much confidence. (Collard, 2003, p 22)

The urban renaissance in British cities has been predominantly dependent on credit card usage: Bristol

The emergence of the political New Right in the 1980s questioned not only a central role for planning as a state function but also whether the public sector should be expected to determine the future shape and form of urban space. The death (or at least mortal wounding) of modernism only contributed to the undermining of planning, as the public started to react against modernist architecture, the concept of new towns and the unfortunate perception that planning was removing community rather than supporting community development. The 1980s witnessed an ideological conviction from some quarters that planning had had its day. An ideological swing towards the market and supporting financial services was accompanied by Margaret Thatcher's viewpoint that there was 'no such thing as society', thus undermining the case for planning to exist in order to represent the wider social good.

The origins of planning, to assist in the creation of better housing and urban areas for the benefit of communities, started to appear archaic to say the least. But even the New Right recognised the value of planning, even if its proponents' perceptions about its usefulness were focused more on the reactive role it performed in protecting individuals' property rights and property prices against development externalities. Looking back, the idea of state planning was virtually killed off in the 1980s together with the notion that you can ever have a state-organised, medium to long-term vision for the development of towns and cities as property-led urban regeneration came to the fore. The consequence of increasing globalisation and the desire for pragmatic responses, together with rapid social and economic changes on the domestic front, completely confounded the idea of proactive urban planning. What was left over for public sector planning was little more than a neighbourhood protection service.

Even under New Labour, planning as a component of government continued in much the same ideological vein as that existing in the early to mid-1990s. The government still faced dilemmas about promoting domestic economic growth, wrestling with the aftershocks of globalisation, protecting the environment, supporting infrastructure developments that possess high aesthetic externalities, delivering houses, encouraging community development and declaring that urban planning – that sits in the midst of all these dilemmas – is a function of central, regional and local government, developers, communities and the public.

Despite all these changes and political reactions against planning, it is perhaps surprising to think that we still possess an urban planning system today within which professional planning experts are employed. The problem is that the wider socioeconomic and political changes of the last 60 years have created a problematic legacy for planning and professional planners to deal with. The planning profession has long recognised the fact that the planning service is prone to attack; professional planning has been squeezed by political

A global economic space and a world heritage site: London Docklands from Sir Christopher Wren's Hospital/Royal Naval College, Greenwich

convictions against the nation state, against the welfare state, against public sector service delivery, against modernism and by a continued questioning of professional expertise. To some, even within the built environment professions, the very notion of urban planning now appears archaic, perhaps lost in the sands of time alongside socialism. How can planning exist within an increasingly globalised world, governmentally fragmented landscapes, encompassing diverse societies that possess a myriad of demands, one of the most notable of which is individualism and freedom? The public, fuelled by a suspicious and negative-centric media, have chastised planners for the creation of a modern world that has failed to live up to expectations and to provide something better.

In the meantime, professional planners have continued to work unfailingly against the political, public and media criticism. One wonders whether these criticisms are, in point of fact, the outpouring of legitimate claims against change generally, a focusing on the very professional personnel charged with making sense of ongoing deep-rooted and inevitable processes of change and renewal within landscapes that are familiar and cherished. Planners still believe that they are just as valid a group of experts in coordinating spatial change now as they were in the postwar era. They have concentrated on improving their process, on their administrative efficiency, of protecting neighbourhoods. The more visionary duties for and of planning – making bold plans and decisions for future generations, through vision and ingenuity – have been watered down, however, as a consequence of the external criticism, the transformation of urban planning into a reactive property protectionist system and a suspicion of professional expertise.

The late English poet Sir John Betjeman called planners bureaucrats and small-minded men from the ministry. Developers, enterprising business people and even national politicians have harangued planners for being impediments to growth. Michael Heseltine, a former Deputy Prime Minister, supposedly accused planners of locking jobs up in filing cabinets. The public have, for some time now, mocked planners (on the back of modernism) for their toy-town mentality and obsession for frustrating ordinary people's lives. Mention to anyone in casual conversation within the UK roundabouts, concrete tower blocks, new shopping centres, house building and the threat to the greenbelt, or some of the more notorious modernist developments in the UK of the last 50 years, and you will usually spark a list of derisory remarks about town planners.

Despite the public ridicule, continued promises by politicians to change the urban planning process for the better and everyone's wish to see something created that is useful for their own desires, town planners remain an ever-present group of choreographers in the changing landscape, responding to constant requests from politicians to meet certain global demands and local challenges. Concern over sustainable transport provision, economic growth, urban regeneration, commercial viability, housing need and housing development, protecting the natural environment and the best features of the built environment, encouraging tourist and leisure facilities, protecting and supporting communities, creating social inclusion, providing people with a voice in landscapes of rapid change, and designing urban places and spaces for people, all indicate that there has never been a more important time for planning, even if it is politically and publicly unacceptable to say so.

Britain has always been uneasy about grand city planning: Eduardo Paolozzi's sculpture at the British Library

GRASPING THE PLANNING NETTLE

> Modern town planning sprang … from two different worlds, far removed in time and space: the one embracing ideal cities and finite visible utopias … the other composed of documents, manifestos, pamphlets and blueprints for new social orders. (Rose, 1984, p 33)

This overview of urban planning's transformations is necessary at the present time because here in the UK we are embarking on a continual cycle of urban planning change and reform. Since 2001 there have been four pieces of primary legislation that have revised the planning system markedly. Why do politicians nationally continue to have problems with planning? Hardly a year goes by without a desire politically for planning reform. John Prescott, the then UK Deputy Prime Minister, announced in the summer of 2002 that he was determined finally to make the town and country planning system 'work', and a new Bill on the future of planning was introduced in 2004. Within four years, another Act of Parliament had been passed; a year later, a further piece of legislation removed aspects of the 2004 changes and, under the Coalition government in 2010-11, another Bill is intended to amend both the 2004 and 2008 laws. Do these reforms indicate problems with planning or with the governmental process within which planning resides?

The answer is both, to some extent but, despite the changes, the problems of the shortage of affordable housing, the growth of cities, social exclusion, the protection of the countryside and the need to take action on climate change remain ever-present matters that require addressing. These issues sit alongside much localised concerns, about neighbourhood protection, community support, public involvement and site-by-site projects. So the reforms to the purpose and mechanisms of urban planning are always attempting to strike a balance between national and local matters, economic and environmental matters, strategic and community matters, and long-term and short-term interests. Add to the equation party politics, entrenched political loyalties and constituency interests, and one begins to recognise the difficult task that planning has to resolve. Urban planning remains in place despite the fact that it will never placate all those who expect it to deliver for themselves: this is the crux of the problem. In a society that is used to its freedoms, that is no longer a socialist state, that does not like big government, and is used to the edict 'an Englishman's home is his castle', the idea that in the 21st century every citizen still has to ask the state's permission to change his or her property beforehand, seems outright bizarre. The property classes, developers and the right-wing press may resent an urban planning process that remains a socialist leftover, but equally they often recognise the need for planning at certain times. Those occasions may be to exercise their democratic right to oppose other people's development projects, or to demand the provision of local public services, or simply recognition that since planning constrains the supply of new land for building, individual property prices remain protected and high. It is all beautifully ironic.

Within the UK, government ministers over the last 15 years have already recognised the pain of grasping the nettle. If they continue to provide businesses and developers with a planning system they want, the government could be accused of ignoring local concerns, of not doing enough to protect the environment and stamping central authority on local democracy. If they protect all the green land around existing towns and cities, they would show support for the rural lobby but they would have difficulty finding space for the homes the country needs. If they do not allow for the occasional airport, port or railway expansion, the economy may be affected and the country will lose out to other regions, competitively, in Europe and beyond. Politicians at the national level may resent occasionally the workings of the planning game, but they are equally reluctant to keep their sticky fingers off the system. After all, they know only too well what they themselves could win or lose in the political world of promising the earth. Town planners may still occasionally be the butt of jokes with the public and the media, but the unique political and strategic skills within planning to resolve conflicting dilemmas and directions are constantly called on.

Urban planning, whether it is addressing national needs or local desires, ploughs on through a torrid political landscape and an ideological context that looks incredibly different to that of the early 1900s. Planning, in the UK and elsewhere, seems to be in a continual state of flux. Changes are being enacted within government and planning right across the globe at the present time that are intended to assist in the creation of what are considered to be 'more distinctive places', and to make urban planning more relevant, more responsive and more inclusive in the years ahead. After over 100 years of its existence, urban planning in many western countries has undergone mixed fortunes as a proactive tool of political ideology, as a central plank of the modernist movement, and then, in the latter 20th century and early 21st century, as a subservient enabling process to an all-persuasive market. And so this

Planning's rollercoaster ride over the last 100 years: Southend on Sea

new spirit of positive planning seems a highly unlikely reawakening, particularly as it is being pushed by the very governments that have long sought to deregulate, abandon or ignore large tracts of urban planning, especially if it had been configured to serve community or non–economic growth agendas.

This positive stance towards urban planning centres round the creation of three distinct features: the promotion of 'spatial planning'; enhanced public involvement; and a focus on place-based governance. All three features flirt with either regionalism or localism as the preferred policy delivery scale, depending on which political party is in office. This is not the place to explain and critique each of these proactive planning tools. But to advocates of urban planning, it appears to be a story about creating a new belief – an ethos – for planning among those inside the planning profession, within government, and those who have high expectations about what urban planning is expected to deliver for cities and regions in the future. To sceptics, it may appear to be another example of state interference, bureaucratic meddling or the retention of an urban planning process that should have been abandoned a long time ago. The positive stance, promoted as we would expect from inside the planning profession, tends to be that we should not view the subject of planning as an isolated, alien or outdated process – the dream of utopian men and women in the mid 20th century about creating in an ideological and practical sense the cities of the future. Urban planning, they maintain, is as vital today as the time it was created in its modern guise more than 100 years ago. It is about meeting the challenge of our ever-changing urban and regional spaces and of responding to the needs and demands of economies and of our societies.

In a 21st century of continual and rapid change, planning needs to be a fluid process. Indeed, urban planning has demonstrated its remarkable resilience by surviving and transforming itself over successive decades. To some extent, this has always been the case: 'Urban planning, *qua* a historical series of empirical events, is a markedly changeable, and even, in some cases ephemeral phenomenon' (Scott and Roweis, 1977, p 1100). What Scott and Roweis were pointing to here is the need to understand planning in relation to the enduring social phenomena to which it is concretely related. In this respect, it is quite tempting to interpret the evolution of planning thought in ways that stress its intimate relationship to the functioning of capitalist economies. Thus for David Harvey, 'the role of the planner ... ultimately derives its justification and legitimacy from intervening to restore that balance which perpetuates the existing social order' (Harvey, 1985, p 177). This is not to say that planning and planners inevitably defend the status quo or that planning does not attempt to be progressive. However, it does mean that 'The planner's world view, defined as the necessary knowledge for appropriate intervention and the necessary ideology to justify and legitimate action, has altered with changing circumstances' (Harvey, 1985, p 178). As Phelps and Tewdwr-Jones (2008) point out, the evolution of planning thought and practice may have become at least partly detached from its role within capitalist economic systems. Thus, as Reade noted, 'planners appear to abandon particular ways of working, and to adopt new ones, not on the basis of empirical evidence, but in accordance with changes in professional fashion' (Reade, 1983, p 160); we might also add to that, political fashion.

In the language of the 21st century, urban planning has to adapt and change to the conditions within which it is supposed to operate. It is not only about physical development and urban renewal; it is pausing to think about the meaning of places, about how people use and think about places and how places can capitalise on their own identities and distinctiveness, to deliver development and create better quality places to live and work within. These are the challenges facing planning globally at the present time. Cities have been rebuilt continuously, sometimes spectacularly, and at other times disastrously. The key question here is whether urban planning politically and professionally can really adapt to the place-based sensitivities of 21st-century cities without a central guiding philosophy. As Leonie Sandercock has pointed out, there is one undeniable fact: planning has not been so careful to see how places are used and viewed by the people who live and work within them. It has failed to see cities as living places, places of work and of homes, of interactions and communication, because during the 20th century planning '... turned its back on questions of values, of meaning, and of the arts (rather than science) of city-building' (Sandercock, 2003, p 221).

So to what extent can we rely on urban planning to assist in the promotion of place-based governance and localism when it lacks an ideological core? Surely this goes to the heart of Sandercock's concern about the ability of planning to think of cities as living places. More pertinently, this role would award urban planning with a much more proactive role at a time when public attitudes toward planning remain largely sceptical. History has shown that when imbued with a degree of reliance in past times, with a strong ideological component, the results of proactive urban planning have often been met with hostility from the public or media, or subject to criticism from politicians nationally. Can we learn from previous eras of proactive planning? How do cities and towns change physically and architecturally as planners manage processes of change? And if

Cities as diverse places and unique identities: Manchester

we expect more from urban planning in the years ahead, what can history teach us about how planning has reconfigured space and territory?

CONCEPTUALISED AND REPRESENTED SPACES

> If space is rather a simultaneity of stories-so-far, then places are collections of those stories, articulations within the wider power-geometries of space. (Massey, 2005, p 130)

The spatial turn in the social sciences has been a growing phenomenon in recent years. Awareness of space as an organising category, and of the usefulness of spatialisation in social and cultural theory in modern and postmodern times, has influenced a number of authors over the last 25 years, including Henri Lefebvre, Michel Foucault, David Harvey, Edward Soja and Mike Davis. The spatial turn in the social sciences has assisted us in understanding 'how relations of power and discipline are inscribed into the apparently innocent spatiality of social life, how human geographies become filled with politics and ideology' (Soja, 1989, p 7).

Henri Lefebvre, in his *The production of space* (1974 [1991]), identifies three different types of space within his spatial triad. Spatial practice is the perceived space, which embraces production and reproduction, the particular locations and set characteristics of each social formation. Representations of space, by contrast, encompass conceptualised space, 'the space of scientists, planners, urbanists, technocratic subdividers and social engineers' (p 39), the dominant space in any society, intellectually worked out and tied to the relations of production. The third type, spaces of representation, are lived spaces, those of the inhabitants and users, of writers and philosophers, who aspire to do more than describe. It overlays physical space, making symbolic use of its objects and is alive: 'It embraces the loci of passion of action and of lived solutions, and thus immediately implies time ... and is essentially qualitative, fluid and dynamic' (p 42). This distinction is especially relevant here because the call by Sandercock, Massey and others for a greater appreciation and understanding of space and place suggests that planners and those used to boundaried views of space will have to make a mental jump to another focus of space altogether. Lefebvre is cynical of such a transformation, and views it as an anathema: 'Surely it is the supreme illusion to defer to architects, urbanists or planners

as being experts or ultimate authorities in matters relating to space'
(Lefebvre, 1974 [1991], p 95).

When urban planning is viewed in its totality, over 100 years of
intervention as part of the project of modernity, it is easy to agree
with Massey's (2005, p 64) belief that there has been a hegemonic
understanding of space itself, and of the relation between space and
society. Urban planners devoted most of their energies to constantly
making the case for planning as a grand totalising project within
robust legal and governmental frameworks in the face of ideological,
political and capitalist opposition. The deeper components of space
were never really considered in any meaningful way. In Sandercock's
parlance, not only was the city of memory and desires neglected, but
space was also viewed within the confines of narrow administrative
boundaries, in a uniform way. The public were either largely excluded
from discussions about the use of space and place (there was no such
thing as formal public consultation within urban planning in the UK
until the early 1970s) or else were treated as one undistinguishable
cohort. If, according to Massey (2005), space really does comprise
of three elements – the product of interrelations, the sphere of the
multiplicity and is always fluid or under construction – then clearly
urban planning does have some significant challenges to face, even
more so if future political expectations are for it to embrace place
distinctiveness.

The biggest challenge is to reconcile an historic desire for spatial
fixedness on the one hand, with recognition of space as a sphere of
multiplicity and flows on the other. Spatial fixedness not only relates
to viewing geography and location in a one-dimensional way; it also
involves the planner's desire to legitimise and politicise intervention
which, by its very nature, requires space to be conceptualised and
pinned down. Here, then, is the paradox of planning and space –
urban planners may recognise the city of emotion, of desires, of
interconnections and of flows, but may not feel they can translate
this awareness into a conceptualised and legitimate form without
dismantling the very confines of conceptualised space they rely on
to work within. Urban planners are caught between order and chaos,
the natural desire for ordered spatial patterns, layouts and behaviour
against a space of movement, flows and interconnectedness. The
history of planning, as normally told by the planning historians
themselves, is a story of spatial politics, the ordering of chaos and of
regulation and deregulation. But what is more revealing, and now
required within urban planning, is a discourse on spatial change and
space-place characteristics as discovered through other stories and

spatial representations. Only with this awareness can urban planning truly perform a more significant role in place-based governance contentions fit for the 21st century.

SPACE, PLACE AND FILM

> … An essential ingredient of planning beyond the modernist paradigm is a reinstatement of inquiry about and recognition of the importance of memory, desire, and spirit, as vital dimensions of healthy human settlements, and a sensitivity to cultural differences in the expressions of each. (Sandercock, 2003, p 227)

The remnants of empire and pride: the site of the rebuilt 1851 Great Exhibition building of Sir Joseph Paxton, Penge Place, Crystal Palace, destroyed by fire in 1936

This greater sensitivity to space and place has assisted in interpreting the concept of space within particular cultures and geographies, and one of the most ideal formats through which this understanding can be developed is cinema. Film often provides a unique sense of place that is unavailable to other media. Film can be highly personal. Film observes, captures emotion, personality, motivation, reactions and conflicts, and allows these emotions and experiences to be translated to an observer in a more immediate and personal way, providing more focus on events and providing closer insights into events. Film can also capture changing environments over time and changing human behaviour, and allows time for the viewer to analyse and interpret. It can often communicate a visual presence, impact and development in an immediate way, and can be used subjectively to illustrate place. We may consider the use of how evocative filming of physical places deepens audiences' impressions of the subjective experience, while providing a good spatial sense of environmental change and development, by allowing reflection and a perspective on the interpretation and representation of places.

Like urban planning, cinematic film is a product of modernity and, interestingly, is about the same age. The urban has long been a feature of motion pictures and the use of urban landscapes for the setting of films has taken varied forms since the dawn of the cinema more than 100 years ago. What is purportedly to be the first moving picture ever made has an urban focus, the Lumière Brothers' short 50-second silent film of 1895, which shows workers leaving a factory at the end of their shift in Lyon. The urban has been ever-present in film since this time but takes on varied forms. There are the studio urban landscapes, possibly employing special effects and popular with film noirs, that serve to represent everything that is dark and dangerous about city living, and there are the location urban landscapes, where places are recognisable either by setting and/or by name. This typology is a little simplistic, however, since one can additionally think of the use of specific places to falsely represent other geographies, and the use of specific places to represent more anonymous urban industrial or post-industrial landscapes that are symbiotic of wider socio-political issues. The urban landscapes form part of the narrative text to these films since they serve to represent and promote a discourse on particular social conditions of urban existence that appear to be unified. This (selective) construction of the city in turn leads to discourses concerning the lives and portrayal of personal identities and interpersonal communication between family, friends, work colleagues and fellow urban habitants, and the social relations between them.

Although outside shots, the development of film sets and the use of CGI (computer-generated imagery) have enabled a degree of authenticity in the representation of places, it does not mask the fact that these cinematic geographies have often been completely manufactured. In some cases, this has been intentional from the outset, but in other cases, built environments have been recreated for film sets but have often appeared false in comparison to the real. These varieties of film locations – both actual and unreal – have helped create a perception in the minds of audiences about places, how places are, how they seem and what the audience imagines to be somehow 'appropriate'. Such perceptions often generate what may be thought of as irrationalities on the part of the public, as to how places are, how they should be protected from development, what is unique and special about them and indeed whether they are recreated realities. It is right for urban planners to dip into culture and filmic representation and become familiar with these

Symbols of redevelopment: the gasometers at King's Cross railway lands

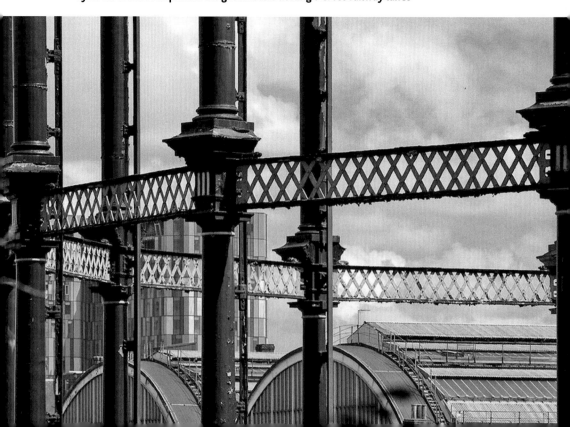

real and imagined place perceptions, since the perceptions of places are often translated into strong public emotions about places. These perceptions provide clues about the unique features that people regard as 'good' places to be, what they feel passionate about in our built environment, and in turn, whether professional planning is assisting in shaping similar or completely contrary landscapes.

My argument in this book is that the camera lens is well positioned to provide an holistic interpretation of materially substantial interventions in the urban environment. The eclecticism of planning – associated with a growing body of theory on place identity, on placeness and spatial awareness, on the interrelated linkages between place, space, people and politics, with a long-standing interest in urban form and city life, and with an understanding of the use of urban space and arrangement – provides an opportunity for an alternative critical perspective, gleaned from celluloid representation, that might explain the prevalence and significance of people's perceptions of places that often planners feel remote from or unable to discern. For me, film could provide a prompt to consider representations of space alongside spaces of representation.

When considering perceptions of the urban – how it is planned and designed, how it has evolved historically – it also has to be acknowledged that a considerable amount of the best work has been undertaken in other disciplines to planning. Here, I make a call for planners to take a fuller interest in place image and representation,

Thoughts of Michael Caine in *Get Carter*: Trinity Square car park, Gateshead, prior to demolition in 2010

through three main bodies of work: first, the literature on cultural geography which opens up a number of perspectives on place identity and place emotion; second, the relationship between the 'city' as an identifiable place with its own identities, histories, myths and collective place narratives; and third, a discussion of the real and imagined worlds associated with place, or what Donald McNeill has referred to as 'the plasticity and multidimensionality of the urban experience' (McNeill, 2005, p 43). Film may be viewed as a technique or tool within these bodies of work that can assist those in urban planning to reinterpret places and understand emotional attachments to places. Much of the work referred to here originates from outside planning, including History, Architecture, Urban Studies, Film Studies, and – of course – Geography. Many of these fields have strong interdisciplinary relationships to Urban Planning and further attempts to bring together these parallel paradigms could enrich planning writing by a greater sensitivity to place. Sandercock (2003) has been one of the few academic planners lately who has identified a need for this greater sensitivity: 'In the postwar rush to turn planning into an applied science much was ignored – the city of memory, of desire, of spirit; the importance of place and the art of place-making; the local knowledges written into stones and memories of communities' (Sandercock, 2003, pp 2-3). Contemporary cities are sites of spatial struggles coping with dilemmas of identity and difference (Sandercock, 2003; Massey, 2005), and planners need to understand the 'noir' side of planning in organising hope and mediating collective memories of urban belonging.

Shiel (2001) states that cinema is the ideal means through which to understand increasing spatialisation organised both culturally and territorially, since it deals with the organisation of space. This entails analysis of how space is treated, interpreted and portrayed in film and how film is treated in space through the shaping of human spaces. The space within which a film is shot, the place and landscape of a narrative setting and the differing geographies between different sequences within a film are as important as the spatial setting of film production with its unique production, distribution and screening. My interest here is how we may utilise film to depict the multiple meanings of places, and how the city represents the difference and distinctiveness for people, places and various territorial cultures. My contention is that the public often possess attitudes towards notions of difference and distinctiveness, particularly when forces of globalisation appear to create uniformity in the streetscape (the repetition of the same chainstores and coffee shops, for example, city to city), as they cling on to real or imagined perceptions about the stories, memories, traditions and cultures of individual places. Cinema and photography can be a useful medium through which to record and represent these distinctive places and to locate and position narratives within built environments.

Spatial analyses of a variety of different forms of culture and landscapes have assisted in our understanding of the concept of space within particular societies and geographies. A deeper reading of filmic representations may not only assist in our reading of the urban, but can also assist in how observers and professionals might learn and understand how particular people and communities possess attachments to particular urban landscapes. This understanding has also helped us in interpreting the concept of space within particular cultures and geographies. Culture itself has assisted people in thinking about places and the perception of places. The problem is that the meaning of places, and how planners should take into account notions of place in 'place-shaping', is a rather nebulous concept. Place is and should be distinctive; it is difficult to pin down

College Street, London

and planners have often been accused over decades of ignoring the unique features of places.

STRUCTURE OF THE BOOK

The book is divided up into a series of parts and chapters that take the reader on a journey, showing the uneasiness people feel towards urban places, highlighting features we take for granted and others that people criticise. A series of photographic narrative chapters illustrate graphically the changes to cities and the architectural and planning legacies that subsequent generations feel emotional toward. The book attempts to be alternative for the way it seeks to provide an interdisciplinary emphasis on discussions relating to urban change, place and planning, but uses film, photography and literature as a means of communicating ideas and stories. There is a strong emphasis on providing theoretically informed chapters, alongside imagery, drawing on empirically robust texts drawn from several years of research into filmic genres and productions that serve as story lines of change and representation in the period 1930 to 1979. It is diverse in its contents and perhaps ambitious, but has been set up deliberately as an attempt to engage diverse disciplines and to capture the complexity of urban change and attitudes towards it in new and challenging ways.

At the start of optimistic times for urban planning and the modernist movement, a large banner was draped over the bottom of Nelson's Column in Trafalgar Square, London, in 1945 that read, 'The time for war is over, the era of reconstruction begins. HM The King.' Chapter Two examines the birth of modern development and reconstruction for cities after 1945, the initiation of the town and country planning process and the era of comprehensive development, slum clearance, urban motorways, housing estates and high-rise blocks and shopping precincts, alongside public, cultural and professional reactions to modern city living. It is not only a chapter repeating historical detail, but one that draws on literary, filmic and political sources to tell the story of change and modernisation of urban conditions in the period since 1940.

Chapter Three is a photographic narrative that serves to represent the physical manifestation of change to British towns and cities from the 1940s to the 1960s. The images are intended to capture the type of developments constructed at this time, from new housing to civic and public buildings and the new opportunities for public space, as well as illustrating the form of architecture and planning.

The path towards a modern society and the modernisation of infrastructure and services can best be told and illustrated through the advances in transportation during the 1950s and early 1960s. Transport has always radically altered our landscape and cities and the antiquated public transport services of rail, bus and tram demonstrated a need to use technology and new forms of communication to move the country into the 20th century, thereby creating the integrated and well-connected cities of the future. Capturing this immense period of change was the government's British Transport Films (BTF) Unit that made over 1,500 short documentaries on the process of change and promoted the new services to the general public. The story told in Chapter Four is of optimism and coordinated public services in and between our urban areas, run to the benefit of the public.

With Chapter Five, an examination is provided of the changing industrial urban landscape through British social realism films of the late 1950s and 1960s. Films such as *Room at the Top* and *A Taste of Honey* were considered innovative when released for their revelation of the British working class at a time when the working classes had been largely excluded from cinematic depictions, and their depiction of community, urban landscapes and an attachment to place. Comparison is drawn with British films from the immediate postwar era, and the argument put forward is that there are both continuities and differences between the uses of urban place in the narrative as locations for action that have been depicted in cinema for decades. The story concerns the clash between a 19th-century landscape in decline and the onset of modern and sanitised industrial and housing places and people's positions in the midst of these changes.

There is a memorable black and white news clip from the 1960s showing an interview with an elderly lady, her hair in curlers, wearing an apron, sat in an armchair in a new flat in the Park Hill Estate in Sheffield. The interviewer asks her how she feels about moving in to these very modern facilities and away from the dilapidated terraced housing she used to call home. Without pausing she states, "Oh it's like living in heaven up here!" And given the fact she was on the top floor of the new blocks that overlooked the city, that was probably exactly how she felt. Chapter Six provides an illustrative tour of the form of architecture and planning that emerged in the mid-1960s, where a humane form of modernism gave way to more high-rise buildings and the rise of the car in determining urban form.

Chapter Seven outlines the onset of the conservation movement and the initial reaction against modern architecture, comprehensive development and the desire to preserve and protect older buildings and areas of cities. It focuses on the life and work of Sir John Betjeman, his poetry, prose, humour and irony, and his involvement in architectural conservation movement, enacted through film and television, to campaign against modern development in the 1960s and 1970s.

Chapter Eight Illustrates the public fascination with physical change of the landscape and the desire for television material showing the urban. We are now used to television series showing aerial footage of the landscape, including *Coast*, *Britain from Above* and Andrew Marr's *History of Modern Britain*. This chapter considers physical change in the 1960s and 1970s through a case study of a pivotal television series from 1969-71, called *Bird's-Eye View*. The series, filmed aerially and entirely from a helicopter, allowed the audience to witness at first hand the dramatic changes to Britain caused by the legacy of the Industrial Revolution, urban motorways, nuclear power stations and the decline of agriculture. *Coast* and *Britain from Above* are, of course, more recent television series that seek to provide an alternative perspective of geography and change. This chapter explores modern development as television subject matter and using film to make a landscape argument.

The Prince of Wales accused planners and architects of ripping out the hearts of towns and cities in the 1960s and 1970s, and of finishing off the job started by the German blitzing of British cities in the war. Chapter Nine considers the form of cities after this time, with the development of more brutalist forms of modern buildings, the clearance of large parts of city centres to make room for road improvements and cars and public consternation at the 'planning disasters' emerging.

Chapter Ten tells the story of how the process of modernising our urban landscapes has left a legacy today for professionals and the public. Places possess multiple meanings and have multiple characters that give rise to different contentions and demands for either change or the resistance to change. The concern with urbanisation and urban sprawl is discussed with reference to films and literature of more recent times in an attempt to assess the extent of public unease with change and development, with the urban planning process charged with managing change. The public, the media and even planners often look at space and place as singular entities, whereas the urban can be characterised today as comprising liminal spaces, fluid and diverse, aesthetically good and bad, that together make up place character.

Chapter Eleven offers an illustrated narrative of British towns and cities today, by looking at the mix of architectural and planning styles co-existing, and spatial layering, the historic features of places that have become part of the built environment and the public's use of places. The postwar planning minister's desire to create places that possess 'a sense of beauty, culture and civic pride' (Lewis Silkin, 1946, see Chapter Two) has been created to some extent, but in a guise that he probably would not recognise and one that continues to create place-space contentions.

Finally, Chapter Twelve considers what has happened to our cities after 80 years of planning and design. Has optimism and vision returned for our urban places? And if so, whose visions are we talking about: architects, planners, politicians, communities, or those of the global market? Why does the public and developer perception of urban planning remain so poor? This chapter closes with a no-holds barred critical look at planning and development today, the inadequacy of politicians and the state to determine visions for our landscapes, and the control wielded by economic interests to standardise and commodify towns and cities.

John Wood of Bath designed
the town hall railings: Liverpool

TWO

"This new fangled planning doctrine"

INTRODUCTION

In this chapter I explore how urban planning has been represented in a range of British media between the Second World War and the present day. I assess perceptions and representations of planning, development and of the planning profession in the immediate postwar period when planning was in its modern ascendancy. I explore the image of town planning and town planners in literature, film and television, and discuss how this image is embedded with powerful symbolism that links to a particular discourse surrounding the activity of planning in Britain. The chapter's overall purpose is to identify the perceptions of urban planning and development since the interwar period, with the aim of working towards identifying why representations of British urban planning are stereotypical and monolithic.

The town and country planning process in Britain, through its management of development, is responsible for much of the contemporary cityscapes and landscapes that form our environment (Hall, 1992). The planning process attempts to reconcile the benefits of development with the costs they impose. Founded in its current comprehensive statutory form in 1947, according to recent government policy planning exists to promote optimal uses of land in relation to environmental management, social welfare, cultural conservation and economic development objectives. While these broad objectives are an enduring feature of the British planning system, the exact orientation of planning to these broader purposes has changed according to the various underlying socioeconomic, environmental and political objectives put forward by governments over time (Bruton, 1984; Tewdwr-Jones, 2002). Thus while the very basic *principles* of town and country planning remain the same as those first championed in the late 19th century by philanthropists, environmentalists and individuals concerned with healthy environments in towns and cities (cf Howard, 1898; Ward, 2002), the context in which the system operates and the expectations of what it should achieve have changed dramatically since its inception (cf Ashworth, 1954; Reade, 1987; Allmendinger and Haughton, 2007).

This continuity is illustrated in recent times where, after 1997, the Labour government made concerted efforts to 'modernise' the planning system in Britain as part of a political programme intended to modernise various public institutions and policy areas (Allmendinger and Tewdwr-Jones, 2000). This programme attempted to improve the effectiveness, efficiency and relevance – and to some degree, ownership – of the planning process to a range of stakeholders that extended beyond simple notions of the public and the private (Healey, 2006a). These reforms culminated with radical planning overhaul from 2004 onwards with the adoption of spatial planning (Tewdwr-Jones et al, 2010; Nadin, 2007), the introduction of regional and sub-regional spatial tiers of policy making (Haughton and Counsell, 2004), and a strengthening of local planning and community strategy making (Raco et al, 2006).

Simultaneous to the political motives for modernising planning, the professional planning body – the Royal Town Planning Institute – has also attempted to reform the professional purpose and role of planning and planners, through the adoption of a new vision (RTPI, 2003), and to establish culture change among professional planners (NPF, 2007). This reform has been thought necessary to reposition professional planning in the 21st century, and to promote the role of a modernised planning process in broader place making and through partnership activities.

A further interesting development over the last 10 years or so is that, increasingly within a complex policy sector and fragmented state, planning is seen by central government as a key vehicle for 'spatial coordination' and 'local delivery' across a range of policy areas (Healey, 2006b; Morphet et al, 2007; Morphet, 2010). Twenty-first century planning therefore provides an alternative role alongside that of land use planning – namely, joined-up governance. This is one reason why governments and the professional planning body have both been concerned about achieving the right skills and culture change within the planning profession (Egan, 2004), about the relationship between planning and economic growth (Barker, 2006), and concern about crises in the recruitment and retention of planners (Audit Commission, 2006). Durning and Glasson (2004) link these ongoing recruitment problems to the image and representation of planning in popular media and among the public in Britain, a subject that has also been the subject of more 'internal' concern within the planning profession itself (Sutcliffe, 1981; Tewdwr-Jones, 1999).

So while the planning system and the planning profession have undergone an immense amount of reform, it remains unclear whether wider audiences have noticed such reforms. One concern is that planning continues to suffer from low social standing, a poor public image and mistrust within the community (Davies, 2001; Clifford, 2006; Swain and Tait, 2007). There appears to be a disjuncture between the way in which the wider community sees planning and the way planning is changing proactively. This remains a largely unresearched area, although it is acknowledged as being important to current academic and policy debates (Campbell and Marshall, 1995).

It is contested that the public image and identities of planning exert powerful influences on levels of trust of planning. Indeed, the understanding of the current public image and professional identities associated with UK planning is of critical importance to both the practice and theoretical underpinning of spatial planning. The type of planning undertaken in the postwar period, particularly the new towns and associated redevelopments of the 1950s and 1960s, have left a legacy for the planning profession that may also be part of the root cause of public discontentment. For many, the only other work planners do is giving out, refusing or putting 'unnecessary' conditions on planning permissions for householders to build garages or houses in the countryside (Tewdwr-Jones, 1999). As the catalyst for more reactionary responses from a right-wing press, town planners are continually lambasted for their overt bureaucracy, their 'toy-town' outlook and for their destruction of Britain's heritage (Clifford, 2006). But this tendency for the public to criticise town planners for the state of the nation is not a recent phenomenon in Britain; in fact, such sentiments can be traced back to the origin of the 1947 planning legislation when the National Coalition government attempted to get people thinking about reconstruction and the shape of cities once the war was over (Sharp, 1940). But there remained a great deal of scepticism on the part of the British people to step unknowingly into such a future, partly out of fear of change and a desire to return to pre-war values, and also because the idea of planned change was indecorously bound up with socialist political agendas. Despite leading a government that embarked on introducing a modern planning system, the wartime Prime Minister Winston Churchill perhaps summed up more widespread feelings when he commented to his colleagues in Cabinet in typical Churchillian terms, 'All this stuff about planning and compensation and betterment. Broad vistas and all that. But give to me the eighteenth-century alley, where foot-pads lurk, and the harlot plies her trade, and none of this new fangled planning doctrine' (cited in Kynaston, 2007).

At a time of constant destruction, such a longing for order and familiarity may be natural. But these sentiments continued after the war right through into the late 20th century and early 21st century. Take, for example, Peter Hall's book *Great planning disasters* (Hall, 1978) that catalogued some of the biggest failures of the modernist movement. More recently we have witnessed the publication of the popular and populist book *Crap towns: The 50 worst places to live in the UK* (Jordison and Kieran, 2003), followed by *Crap towns II: The nation decides* (Jordison and Kieran, 2004) that reported the public's vote on their reconstructed towns and cities. Or the television series *Demolition* in 2006, which encouraged the public to vote for the buildings and developments across the UK they considered the ugliest and warranting demolition. This may seem bewildering to an international audience and scholars in other countries where urban planning may be accepted, established and viewed as a necessary governmental activity. A key issue here is that the successes and achievements of planning have not necessarily been promoted positively and loudly simultaneously. The reactions in the UK reveal an ongoing love–hate relationship between planners and politicians, businesses and communities that masks a range of contradictions and deficits between values and actions on the part of the public and others. Regardless of these contradictions, the subject itself has become, to all intents and purposes, something of a national pastime, even if these dualisms in perceptions towards planning have rarely been reported or discussed academically.

This pastime is itself continually framed by cultural milieux which frame the beliefs and values that people hold in relation to the planning system, to places, to state intervention and the ways in which urban and natural environments are produced and shaped. This chapter seeks to explore these interactions and the ways in

Architecture for a new technological age: the Barbican

which the city has been undeniably shaped by representation of it in the media (Clarke, 1997). The concern here is not with cities per se, but with the image of town and country planning which, it is argued, is indecorously bound up with the representations of a cultural few. The representations of the interwar and immediate postwar period, when the system itself was born and expectations for its role in rebuilding Britain were high, are of particular relevance. This is especially so given that in an age that predated the media explosion of the 1990s, such views attained a far more dominant voice than would be the case today.

This chapter attempts to assess the perceptions and representations of planning, development and of the planning profession over the last 70 years, and begins with the interwar period. This is achieved by examining the image of town planning and town planners in British newspapers, in literature, film and television. Popular media provide ideal reference points for more immediate and public assessment of planning that may reflect contemporary debate and thoughts.

We begin with reference to a selection of cultural works and their depiction of the country and, by implication, planning within the country at certain moments in time. This is intended to provide a context for the more detailed assessment that follows, and concentrates on the modernist period. A final section offers some conclusions of more general trends, on the role of the media and cultural elite in leading debates about planning.

PLANNING FRAMED BY CULTURAL MILIEUX

Depictions of urban and rural change, and of the form of planning, development and redevelopment and its affect on the environment, are not a recent phenomenon. The works of Charles Dickens, for example, provide both fascinating and lurid accounts of the spread of urban disease – and lack of planning – in 19th-century London. By contrast, in his book *Anticipation* from 1900, H.G. Wells looked forward to the new patterns of transport and development likely in the following decades:

> ... the whole of Great Britain south of the Highlands seems destined to become an urban region....Through the varied country the new wide roads will run, here cutting through a crest and there running like some colossal aqueduct across a valley, swarming always with a multitudinous traffic of bright, swift (and not necessarily ugly)

Increasing urban paraphernalia

mechanisms; and everywhere amidst the fields and trees linking wires will stretch from pole to pole....The old antithesis will indeed cease, the boundary lines will altogether disappear; it will become, indeed, merely a question of more or less population. (cited in Sharp, 1940)

Throughout the 20th century, several authors used novels and travelogues to communicate both a real sense of what Britain was like to certain sections of society and also to promote a utopian vision of what (somewhat unusually beyond built environment professionals) a future predominantly *urban* Britain could look like.

In a sketch written in 1929, D.H. Lawrence described English towns as 'a great scrabble of ugly pettiness over the face of the land'. The English, he stated:

... are town birds through and through. Yet they don't know how to build a city, how to think of one, or how to live in one. They are all suburban, pseudo-cottagy, and not one of them knows how to be urban....The English may be mentally and spiritually developed. But as citizens of splendid cities they are more ignominious than rabbits. (cited in Sharp, 1940)

The starting points for J.B. Priestley's views, in turn, were his experiences of England documented in his *English journey* of 1934 (reprinted in 1979) where he describes a country of:

> ... arterial and by-pass roads, of filling stations and factories that look like exhibition buildings, of giant cinemas and dance-halls and cafes, bungalows with tiny garages, cocktail bars, Woolworths, motor-coaches, wireless, hiking, factory girls looking like actresses, greyhound racing and dirt tracks, swimming pools, and everything given away for cigarette coupons. (p 401)

George Orwell's writings also display a fascination with a changing country and changing social patterns. Writing during the Second World War, he reflects not only on the social and cultural changes underway, but also on the new urban patterns that generate further behavioural change:

> The place to look for the germs of the future England is in the light-industry areas and along the arterial roads. In Slough, Dagenham, Barnet, Letchworth, Hayes – everywhere, indeed, on the outskirts of

Lacking the character of Sir Giles Gilbert Scott's K2 red telephone box, even these replacements are largely obsolete, thanks to the rise of mobile phones

great towns – the old pattern is gradually changing into something new.... It is a rather restless, cultureless life, centring around tinned food, *Picture Post*, the radio and the internal combustion engine. (Orwell, 1941, reprinted 2001, p 273)

In more modern times, this view compares strikingly with other, more contemporary, representations:

... no matter how many times I criss-crossed through its heart, all I seemed to encounter was a vast, glossy new shopping centre that was a damnable nuisance to circumnavigate and a single broad endless street lined with precisely the same stores I had seen in every other city.... British towns are like a deck of cards that have been shuffled and endlessly redealt – same cards, different order. (Bryson, 1995, p 346)

J.B. Priestley statue, Bradford

In both these representations there is an implicit criticism of planning, or its absence. However, Charles Jennings, in *Up North* also of 1995, is more explicit:

> What is England, really? If you want to be brutal about it, England is shopping malls, staggeringly thick-witted and insensitive road schemes, lousy architecture, supermarkets, theme pubs and crowds of people wandering around, looking puzzled and disgruntled.... North to south, you find the same chainstores, the same eateries, the same cretinous planning fuck-ups. (pp 229-30)

I suggest that such recent descriptions derive from a historically determined cultural milieux and may thus be inaccurate stereotypes. What is interesting here is that these representations focus not just on the 'England' of village greens, as emphasised in much postwar rhetoric (Paxman, 1998), but implicitly that 'England' has become more urban, and that to some degree, urban problems arise from interventions, or non-interventions, in constructing (or not constructing) built environments. The importance of such statements is that they are also likely not merely to represent a particular view, but to further one. Thus, it is possible to suggest that if these sorts of comments are more representative of a wider opinion evident in British popular culture and media, it is hardly surprising that the general public do not have a particularly favourable view of the planning process, especially where awareness of the (often rather small) role town planning actually plays in these processes is limited (DoE, 1992). Furthermore, there may arise policy implications from the media reporting as a consequence of the complex, symbiotic relationship that politicians have with the media (Kaniss, 1991).

A key issue here is thus the power of the media and of culture, and even using popular media, to construct particular narratives. This power comes both through the selection of which events the media gives coverage to and through the preferred readings of reality given by the media in their interpretation of those events (Allen, 1999). Indeed, Hay and Israel (2001) argue that the media is intimately linked to the projection and production of 'imagined worlds'. In other words, 'media communications may actually be theorized as a circuit of cultural forms through which meanings are encoded by specialist groups of producers and decoded in many different ways by the groups who constitute the audiences for those products' (Burgess, 1990, p 139). It is possible to say that places are physical constructs, but the social construction of place is a vital element in how people see the environments that surround them (Lefebvre, 1974 [1991]). Representations evoke the real and the imagined.

PLANNING AT THE HEIGHT OF MODERNISM

The creation of modern town planning in the postwar era

The Second World War had a profound impact physically, economically and socially on Britain and the British population. The 1939–45 period not only witnessed the destruction of Britain's towns and cities through German bombing but also a changing, and possibly quite frightening, new social and economic order. This was a time when the postwar Attlee government was elected with a landslide electoral majority to rebuild the country and to

Mixed materials, levels and vistas and the avoidance of spatial symmetry: Liverpool One bridges and shops, from 2008

implement a radical socialist programme of renewal. This renewal included, inter alia, the creation of the NHS, a national education programme, the establishment of the nationalised industries, the continued decentralisation of manufacturing industries to the regions, and the legislative birth of town and country planning (Childs, 2001).

Simultaneous to the political and economic changes occurring through the creation of the modern welfare state, there was an urgent need for postwar rebuilding of the bombed towns and cities, focusing in particular on the reconfiguration of British industry, the provision of new housing, particularly in greenfield locations decentralised outside core urban areas, and the development of transport infrastructure. At the time, despite postwar austerity, rationing and shortages, these factors led to a determination for Britain to look in a modern, confident and progressive way towards the future, an attitude illustrated perfectly by the Festival of Britain Exhibition of 1951 (Hennessey, 1994). These factors and the visions of modernist architects such as Berthold Lubetkin, Denys Lasdun, and Geoffry Powell, were large influences on the town planning profession and are reflected in many of the design solutions of the time (Gold, 1997; Bullock, 2002). Later modernist developments

Virtually all of the buildings in this vicinity were blitzed in December 1940

in London such as William Holford's 1960s Paternoster Square, adjacent to St Paul's Cathedral, and the South Bank complex were criticised for their designs by a relatively small cultural elite throughout the 1950s and 1960s. Simultaneously, the conservation movement started in earnest and became politicised (Gold, 2007; Pendlebury, 2009) as battles were fought and lost in London over the future of Euston Arch and the Coal Exchange, while the Houses of Parliament, the Foreign Office, the Tate Gallery, Tower Bridge and St Pancras station were all perceived to be under threat from redevelopment. Engineering-led solutions to urban restructuring and traffic movements in towns also became the norm following the publication of the Buchanan report in 1963, to accommodate the large-scale increase in car ownership (HM Government, 1963).

The nationalisation of land development rights and the introduction of statutory development plans and planning control was created by the Attlee government through the Town and Country Planning Act 1947. This Act effectively witnessed the birth of what we can identify today as the town and country planning process in Britain that was charged with the task of coordinating development and managing development change. *The Times* identified the legislation as radical: 'The British people, almost without knowing it, are embarking upon one of the greatest experiments in the social control of their environment ever attempted by a free society. In the process they are putting old individual liberties in trust for the common good' (cited in Kynaston, 2007, pp 168-9). The 1947 Act, together with the New Towns Act of 1946, placed planning as a central task of Labour's welfare state credentials. The task was deliberately ambitious and utopian; as Lewis Silkin, the minister for town planning, stated in the House of Commons during the passing of the new towns Bill, the aim of the legislation was not simply to create a planning framework: 'We may well produce in the new towns a new type of citizen, a healthy, self-respecting dignified person with a sense of beauty, culture and civic pride' (cited in Mullan, 1980, p 42). This broader social agenda points to the political turmoil that the government faced at the time and in the period afterwards; Silkin was accused of social engineering and attempting to control people's lives through the new towns programme, and he received a hostile response when he attended a public meeting in Stevenage to announce details of the designation of the first new town:

> I want to carry out in Stevenage a daring exercise in town planning.... It is no good you jeering: it is going to be done....The

project will go forward, because it must go forward. It will do so more surely and more smoothly, and more successfully, with your help and co-operation. Stevenage will in a short time become world famous. (cited in Kynaston, 2007, p 161)

The crowd shouted 'Gestapo!' and 'Dictator!', boys deflated the tyres and put sand in the petrol tank of his official car, and protestors

Millbank, formerly Vickers Tower, London, constructed in 1963 and previously the campaign headquarters of the Labour Party

changed the name of the railway station to Silkingrad, with a deliberate reference to the Soviet Union and centralised control (Hall and Tewdwr-Jones, 2011; Kynaston, 2007).

There were other problems with the new planning process as it began to be rolled out (Docter, 2000). First, the system rarely attained stability with regard to the full range of tools with which it was envisaged to operate. Thus, public sector finances were such that public sector-led planning was never implemented in the ways initially conceived, and the loss of betterment provisions further undermined the potential finance available to public authorities. Second, while the introduction of new statutory land use planning processes was hailed as the way to ensure the physical rebuilding of towns and cities in the aftermath of war, the resultant developments were not completely viewed by the public as the sort of solutions they craved for. Both of these factors, given the flexibility inherent within the British system, have arguably influenced the way the planning system is today configured, with its central concerns for regulating the impact of development on 'neighbours' and its role in protecting the countryside from development (the latter a legacy of 1930s campaigns to protect the countryside, ironically enough, from planning, urban encroachment and sprawl).

This latter issue concerning the perceptions of the postwar planning solutions was taken up by prominent figures in the literati and the public, concerned that their pre-war existence was being violently swept away. 'Turf wars' developed in the popular media between protagonists espousing modernist architecture, such as Sir Nikolaus Pevsner, and conservation figures such as Sir Clough Williams-Ellis and Sir Patrick Abercrombie through the Council for the Protection of Rural England (CPRE), and Sir John Betjeman through the Georgian Group and The Victorian Society (Mowl, 2000). This perception of what the planning process was creating in the eyes of these members of the literati, articulated through travel writing, prose, poetry, film and television during a period of immense political, economic and social change, would have far-reaching implications and a legacy that today's planning profession still has to cope with (Green, 1997).

The first new town and
the first purpose-built
traffic-free shopping area
in Britain: Stevenage

The development of pro-community/anti-change sentiments in British culture

The postwar Labour government's radical agenda was felt necessary for a country emerging from the destructive trauma of a world war, and certainly emphasised newness and rebirth. A large banner draped over the bottom of Nelson's Column in Trafalgar Square, London, quoted the King: 'The time for war is over, the era of reconstruction begins. HM The King.' Lord Latham, the Leader of London County Council, also remarked directly to camera in the pro-planning film *Proud City* of 1946: 'Planning is, in many ways, the continuation of war by other means, against poverty and decay and inefficiency.' But the era was also associated with the loss of the old, recognition on the public's part that things would never be quite the same again.

This loss–of–something view seems to have been widespread among the literati at the time, and since town planning was at the centre of facilitating this newness, it was the one profession most readily identifiable in causing physical change. Such a view seems to have been adopted by wider cultural communities in the subsequent period, even among those who may have been

Plaques to the planning authority and planning minister: Stevenage

thought of as possessing a more enlightened and 'modern' vision, as Finnegan (1998) demonstrates in her analysis of new town residents. Mowl (2000) suggests that prominent cultural figures were able to champion their nostalgia views on a largely unsuspecting public through film, television and writing because, during the middle of the 20th century, there was no consensus of what constituted a 'British style' for architecture and planning. The public's concern about town planning started to occur both as a reaction against inevitable change, but also in recognition of the literati's view that planning was the process sweeping the old away and causing social disorder. In reality, it was the bombing of British cities, the need to revitalise British manufacturing, the immense population changes of the postwar period and car ownership that proved to be the catalysts for change. But since planning was the profession charged with coordinating restructuring at this time, certain sections of the public protested against town planning itself.

The writings, poetry and cinema of some of Britain's most respected cultural icons reflect this lament at the loss of the pre-war existence, the perceived loss of community and the birth of state planning. Between the 1940s and the 1970s, for example, the

A total of 930 people died in the air raid bombings of Portsmouth in the Second World War; the city centre was reconstructed afterwards

poet Sir John Betjeman ridiculed town planners for their idealised worlds in his poems, including 'Inexpensive progress', 'The town clerk's views' and 'The planster's vision'. Through his poetry, his weekly columns in periodicals and newspapers on architecture and conservation matters, his membership of conservation bodies and his work for BBC radio and television over 50 years, including the production of over 100 television documentaries, many of which focused on British towns and cities, he usefully managed to awaken a conservation movement at the grassroots level in the 1950s and 1960s, at a time when the modernist movement was in full swing, much to the annoyance of the planning, architecture and development professions at the time (see Chapter Seven).

Author and playwright J.B. Priestley was not so tinted by a desire to 'preserve and conserve'. In fact, Priestley was a socialist committed to common ownership of land and industrial resources, but he nevertheless identified the emergence of 'two nations' in Britain, between the pre-war thatched cottage, cricket pitch and village green community and the industrialised, planned and modern image associated with restructuring and development (Priestley, 1979). These two nations arguably exist in more recent representations of England and Englishness despite having a population that is 90 per cent urban. E.M. Forster criticised the designation of Stevenage new town in 1946, suggesting the new plan would 'fall out of a blue sky like a meteorite upon the ancient and delicate scenery of Hertfordshire' (cited in Mullan, 1980, p 49). George Orwell attempted to chart what it meant to be English in the mid–20th century. In 'The road to Wigan Pier' he paints an exaggerated bleak picture of urban life and the drudgery of a life at slave to a capitalist bourgeoisie in ways reminiscent of Priestley. In an essay entitled 'England, your England', he raised a further theme concerning the 'privateness' of British life and people's aversion to the erosion of their local communities through inevitable change (Orwell, 1941). Both Priestley and Orwell differ from Betjeman in their identification of a new nationhood in the postwar period; Betjeman specifically pinpointed town planners and developers as the root cause of a loss of community, whereas Priestley and Orwell were more interested in identifying how a community copes with change and should be shaped for the greater good of all. This is an important distinction to make, for an implied criticism of planners may, in actuality, be nothing more than a lament at the loss of pre-existing community living, and the two may be separate matters.

Within film, some of the celebrated British Ealing Studios' films of the 1940s and 1950s are similar to Betjeman's poems in their desire to look backwards for comfort during immense socioeconomic change. The Studios' producer, Sir Michael Balcon, installed a plaque on the building when they were sold to the BBC in 1955 that read, 'Here during a quarter of a century were made many films projecting Britain and the British character.' Many of the most successful Ealing comedy films possessed one particular common characteristic: a story of one small community's desire to break free from overt bureaucratic control (Chapman, 2006).

The 1949 film, *Passport to Pimlico*, bases its whole plot within a small London residential area and the people's desire to escape postwar restrictions while coping with physical change and the loss of community. Within the film, the people are divided in deciding on what sort of development to permit to be built on a derelict bombsite in the heart of their community: a commercial centre (progressive, economic and necessary but portrayed as 'harsh') or a swimming pool 'for the local kids' (social, community-centred and 'nice'). The dilemmas of choosing which type of development for the area reflect the two nations phenomenon identified in Priestley's writings; both are intended to be pro-community and people's attempts to get on with their lives by creating something new. But the swimming pool dream is portrayed as the more heartfelt response, because it is something the whole community could become involved in.

Ealing Studios' 1953 film, *The Titfield Thunderbolt*, uses a similar theme in telling the story of a rural community's protest at the closure of their local railway line (the community's lifeline) and their attempt to take over the railway themselves to avert the operation of a rival bus service (the operators, 'Pearce and Crump', are portrayed in the film as shifty, corrupt, greedy and anti-community, eager to turn the village of 'Titfield' into 'Pearcetown'). In one interesting scene – a public inquiry into the community's application to run the local rail service – the lead character turns to the assembled public gallery and pleas with the audience for support against Pearce and Crump:

> Don't you realise you're condemning our village to death! Open it up to buses and lorries and what's it going to be like in five years time?! Our lanes will be concrete roads, our houses will have numbers instead of names, there'll be traffic lights and zebra crossings. And that will be twice as dangerous!

Site of the bullion van robbery in Ealing Studios' *The Lavender Hill Mob*, 1951: Queen Victoria Street, London

The view from Mrs Wilberforce's house, in *The Ladykillers*, 1955: Argyll Street, London

Charles Barr's authoritative work on the Ealing films excellently portrays this almost pro-community/anti-change sentiment in the film scripts of T.E.B. Clarke, by referring to the 'polarisation' displayed in the films 'between recreated past and threatening future, between the dynamism of acquisitiveness and the static nature of community', and a tendency to increasingly portray 'Something nice and wholesome and harmless, quaint and static and timeless' in the films as change unfolded at the time (Barr, 1983, p 106).

During the 1940s and 1950s Britain probably did comprise two nations: one of a people looking backwards for community stability, and one of a people longing for reconstruction, improved conditions, economic prosperity and better housing. For many, including some members of the literati, these two nations were viewed as being at opposite ends of the spectrum; unfortunately, we might say that town planning was caught in the middle. What is of concern in some media at the time is the portrayal of town planning as a force against the community, whereas planners themselves were attempting to coordinate change for the benefit of community building. This is possibly the fault of planning at this time; instead of planners ensuring place connectedness (through the recognition of, and importance attached at this time to, geographical propinquity in relation to environments and neighbours), planners categorised community into something that could equally be reconstructed. It was never going to work in quite this way (Gans, 1972; Goodman, 1972; Pahl, 1975).

These discussions are useful for they place the birth of statutory town and country planning in an historical context. It is possible to identify the alienation some of the people of Britain felt towards the onset of radical change promoted through a new town planning process, but simultaneously to recognise the need to organise such a process in postwar restructuring. But the debate is also necessary to understand how the British desire to continually lambaste, or at least be suspicious of, town planning has always existed. It emerged in the austerity years of the 1940s and people's agitation with the loss of their pre-war communities (more directly through the ravages of war than planning), and continued through into the 1950s and 1960s as the public continually lamented at the loss of their pre-war existence and vented their frustrations with the professionals who were charged with the task of physical rebuilding. The dream of improved housing, economic prosperity and planned communities was realised but not in the way people had imagined (Hopkins, 1964). In cinematic representations, the British film industry eagerly portrayed the changing conditions of the country, but was tarnished by a desire to look backwards nostalgically and continue the wartime machinery of reasserting the pre-war spirit and community of Britain (Murphy, 1989; Higson, 1997; Richards, 1997).

Reactions to bulldozers and bureaucrats

The tendency to cope with physical change by recreating a golden era image of pre-war Britain only served to fuel the public's dismay at the postwar town planning developments. It is doubtful whether the sort of romanticised images of community one-nation Britain portrayed in the films of the 1940s and 1950s actually existed. The works of Orwell and Priestley suggest that they in no way reflected northern urban life. They are rather middle-class visions of a Britain comprising scenes of English identity (Easthope, 1999), features that the public appeared to be more comfortable with than the visionary/modernist new developments being provided in rebuilt towns and cities across the country.

Certainly the spirit of much media appeared to change in the late 1950s and 1960s. First, in film, a number of projects very much still in the tradition of the 'David' of the individual or community against the monolithic 'Goliath' of the planning system, depicted most blatantly in the Ealing comedies, exposed the conflicts arising from community redevelopment (Barr, 1993). Then the social realism 'kitchen sink' dramas of the late 1950s and early 1960s, such as *Room at the Top* (1959), *Saturday Night and Sunday Morning* (1960), *A Taste of Honey (1961)* and *This Sporting Life* (1963) reflected a more realistic sense in a 'documentary style' (Higson, 1986) of what living in England meant for the vast majority of an urbanised land (see Chapter Five). While cinema went the way of gritty urban realism, in literature and television the preconceived image of town planning as a 'threat' to community and heritage was further expressed.

The oldest recorded town in Britain has experienced various planning impacts over the years: Colchester

Thanks to the likes of Betjeman and others who captured, framed and perhaps led, the public imagination, town planners were increasingly criticised for what were perceived to be their utopian visions. The criticisms only reinforced a belief that town planners were more interested in physical rebuilding rather than with the people using the buildings (Jacobs, 1962; Dennis, 1970; Gans, 1972). Such concern with a perceived lack of concern for people and community among planning professionals can be seen as part of a decline in the postwar consensus that 'the values of society could be safeguarded by the judgements of professional planners and democratically elected politicians' (Davies, 2001, p 194), and prompted the government to commission a committee to investigate 'public participation in planning'. The committee, chaired by A.M. Skeffington, reported in 1969 and suggested that planners should be much more proactive in their consultations with the public (Skeffington, 1969).

And yet despite such remedial measures, the era of the planning professional in his (as it usually was) ascendancy was over. The literati's pronouncements toward town planning during the modernist era had captured the public's imagination and had stuck. More recently, since the 1980s, such attitudes have been picked up by a number of travel writers and prominent individuals. Indeed, Lucinda Lambton's television series for the BBC and her accompanying book *A-Z of Britain* (Lambton, 1996), and the 1990s BBC current affairs programme devoted to conservation issues, *One Foot in the Past*, are both very much in the Betjeman style.

The Prince of Wales, too, in several speeches and in his *Vision of Britain* television documentary and book for the BBC (The Prince of Wales, 1989), pointed out examples of perceived poor and good architecture and planning in the mid-1980s, again in language not dissimilar to Betjeman. In a radio broadcast of 1943, Betjeman had made a link between planning and the war:

> Planning is very much in the English air now. Let the planners be careful…. In a single week of our planning, centuries of texture can be brushed away. Is all to be replanned?… I do not believe we are fighting for the privilege of living in a highly developed community of ants. That is what the Nazis want. For me, at any rate, England stands for the Church of England, eccentric incumbents, oil-lit churches, Women's Institutes, modest village inns, the noise of mowing machines on Saturday afternoons…. (John Betjeman,

'Coming home, or England revisited', BBC Home Service, 25 February 1943, cited in Games, 2006, pp 138-9)

In a speech marking the 150th anniversary of the Royal Institute of British Architects in 1984, the Prince of Wales criticised Sir James Stirling's proposed extension to the National Gallery in London: "What is proposed [for Trafalgar Square] is like a monstrous carbuncle on the face of a much-loved and elegant friend." Three years later, he made a more profound attack on the modernist movement in planning and development in a speech at Mansion House:

> At least when the Luftwaffe knocked down our buildings, it didn't replace them with anything more offensive than rubble. We did that … planning turned out to be the continuation of war by other means … large numbers of us in this country are fed up with being talked down to and dictated to by an existing planning, architectural and development establishment…. This is the age of the computer and the word-processor, but we don't have to be surrounded by buildings that look like such machines. (The Prince of Wales, 1987)

In the ensuing outcry in the media over the Prince's remarks, criticisms were all framed with respect to the architectural profession. Planners escaped the attention of the media and the public (possibly because both media and the public did not recognise an obvious difference between the professions), although it is noticeable that the Prince had blamed both disciplines for the onset of the modernist movement in cities. More recently, the Prince has become embroiled in a dispute and has been accused of high intervention concerning the redevelopment of Chelsea Barracks in London, designed by the international architect Richard Rogers. Planners themselves, in response, have tried to reclaim the argumentative high ground through their own use of media but this has frequently only served to further their image as being remote, technocrats or bureaucrats (Gold and Ward, 1997; cf the Channel 4 television programmes *Cream Teas and Concrete* [1991] and *An Inspector Calls* [1996]). Indeed, since the late 1970s, television representations of planning or the planner have been predominantly technocratic and bureaucratic; see, for example, how the planner is portrayed in David Nobbs' *Reggie Perrin* and Tom Sharpe's *Blott on the Landscape* and *Restoration* for the BBC, and *The Secret World of Michael Fry* and *Demolition* for Channel 4.

Site of a controversial London planning battle in the 1980s: the Mappin and Webb listed building was demolished and replaced with Sir James Stirling's No 1 Poultry

It is also possible to identify a shift in the representation of town and country planning away from the threat to community portrayal of the period between 1945 and the 1980s, to one over the last 25 years where the town planner was not only a threat to the community but an overt bureaucratic – a 'paperclip pusher', strictly following laws and policies, but with little regard for people or places. What is apparent, however, is that there remains little in the way of hard evidence to substantiate the media claims that planning today is a curse on the private sector and on communities, and also fails to deliver what it is expected to politically. Perhaps as a little piece of leftover socialism that, amazingly, still exists, the planning system will remain an anachronism in 21st-century Britain, and one that will attract the venom of the right-wing press, the development industry and politicians who are more than content to repeat the scathing accusations and, pertinently, to establish constant reviews and reforms of planning in an attempt to 'do something about it' (see, for example, DTLR, 2001; Barker, 2004, 2006; Lyons, 2004; Conservative Party, 2010). In the final analysis, it is worth highlighting that despite the reforms and criticism, planning remains a valid political tool even if it is electorally unpopular to say so.

CONCLUSIONS

Hopes were high with the foundation of the statutory town and country planning system in Britain in 1947. Visionary plans, such as Abercrombie's *Greater London plan* (Abercrombie, 1944) would be implemented, large new towns would be constructed, slums cleared, urban problems eliminated and urban sprawl prevented, issues that had persisted since the 19th century (Hall and Tewdwr-Jones, 2011). Indeed, the Town and Country Planning Act 1947 was one part of a host of measures, including new towns and national parks that formed part of the socialist, welfare state.

But the planning system envisioned the majority of development (particularly housing) being conducted by the state, and:

> The founders of the postwar planning system foresaw modest economic growth, little population increase ... little migration either internally or from abroad, a balance in economic activity among the regions, and a generally manageable administrative task in maintaining controls. (Cullingworth and Nadin, 2002, p 22)

Unfortunately, many of these conditions and the postwar consensus did not last. Nevertheless, in the 1950s, 1960s and 1970s, planners were closely involved in building, reconstructing and visioning, trying to realise predominantly modernist goals. While 'planning wizards' (see Gold and Ward, 1997; Tewdwr-Jones, 2005) tried to promote such schemes through visual media, others – a cultural elite using similar media – attempted to resist them. At times, the two came to co-exist. In Milton Keynes, public participation resulted in traditional house design in an essentially modern spatial framework so that it 'is a futuristic city which goes in for collective nostalgia' (see also Bendixson and Platt, 1992). But in the majority of cases, the two visions of Britain were at odds, and media representations of planning were strongly critical.

Such commentary may be linked to a number of underlying themes. At one level, deep concern began to emerge in the 1960s about how many of the great planning schemes were being 'imposed' on communities without adequate consultation about how and where people actually wanted to live. This led to the Skeffington report at the decade's close yet, arguably, the damage to planning's reputation had already been done.

A deeper theme, for the literati at least, was probably anti-urbanism. This has had a powerful hold on the English psyche since the urban problems of the 19th century, with rural dwelling seen as healthier but also, with the English countryside seen as a feature of national identity (Lowe et al, 1995). Since the modernist developments of the immediate postwar decades were decidedly pro-urban, and planning was the profession most closely associated with this, it is unsurprising that it should come under such attack.

Furthermore, by its foundation and very name, 'planning' possesses strong socialist overtones. Thus, with the breakdown of the postwar consensus in the 1970s and 1980s and the rise of the 'New Right', planning was a natural object for derision and criticism for interfering with the market. Such attitudes may have fed into critical imagery of planning, particularly in the right-wing press. Nevertheless, even during the Thatcherite 1980s, the right wing's policy towards town and country planning was somewhat ambivalent given that market-oriented Tories detested planning but rural 'Shire Tories' liked a system that protected their property rights (Allmendinger and Tewdwr-Jones, 2000). Such pro-property interests may, however, now be more weary of planning given the contemporary role of planning in attempting to deliver new housing in South East England.

The early criticisms of the literati appear to still have a powerful impact on the framing of planning in the media and, through this, the imagination of the general public. Therefore, we can still see planning depicted in a postwar modernist movement frame, and the planner arraigned as ignoring community views in modern coverage, a figure akin to that caricatured by Everlsey: 'a monster, a threat to society, one of the most guilty of the earth-rapers' (1973, p 14). Such coverage draws heavily on stereotypes, many of which may be years out of date given the longevity of stereotypical images (Burgess and Gold, 1985).

And yet, while an imagery of planners as those imposing their will on society and space continues to be seen, ironically an image of the planner as an almost bumbling bureaucratic paperclip pusher has also arisen in recent decades and sits alongside the earlier imagery. Such framing may be linked to a discourse of declining trust in professional expertise. In the postwar period, there was a feeling that the public sector professions could manage the creation of a new Britain, but such opinion no longer holds sway today.

The renaissance for planning has materialised but it is, to some extent, embedded within local participatory mechanisms and within the political process, and concerns itself more overtly with policy development, policy and agency integration and strategy development, and is therefore often working behind the scenes, hidden from public and media view. It also manifests itself in urban contestations on individual sites and development projects that say so much about attitudes towards enduring forms of the postwar planning machine. These include, for example, mixed emotions surrounding the perceived threat to the greenbelt by a proposed new housing complex, or dilemmas over the protection and conservation of a postwar brutalist-designed listed building (While, 2006, 2007). It is possible to suggest here that planning has 'lost out' to media stereotypes, and yet perversely remains heavily utilised by those who wish to exercise their democratic right to voice an opinion about change generally. It is also a popular profession, given the continued over-subscribed demands from (predominantly Geography) students for postgraduate planning programmes, and rising salaries at the present time within both the public and private sector for planning employment across the UK. Nevertheless, the policy implications of a negative media image continue to be an issue, as does the question of whether this image will improve in time or whether planning will continue to be a behind-the-scenes process, unloved and unappreciated by much of the public and by business leaders alike.

Commonwealth Games symbol, but a victim of health and safety concerns: Thomas Heatherwick's B of the Bang sculpture, East Manchester, 2002-09

THREE

"The era of reconstruction begins"

Bath Spa

Council House, Bristol, 1956

The Spa Green Estate, London, 1946-50

Bevin Court, Clerkenwell, 1951-54; the architect Lubetkin originally wanted to name the building Lenin Court

The bus station in the heart of the shopping area: Stevenage new town

Centrepiece of the Festival of Britain 1951

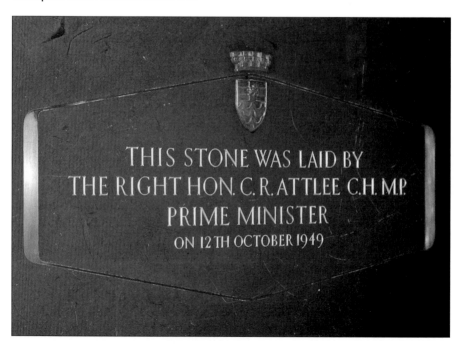

THIS STONE WAS LAID BY
THE RIGHT HON. C. R. ATTLEE C.H. M.P.
PRIME MINISTER
ON 12TH OCTOBER 1949

Sir Frederick Gibberd's Liverpool Catholic Cathedral, 1962

Royal Festival Hall by Sir Leslie Martin, a symbol of modernity

Golden Lane Estate by Chamberlin, Powell and Bon, 1957-62

New Zealand House of 1959, only
built after the British Cabinet
approved of the plan

Crystal Palace National Sports Centre, a Grade II* listed building

Some of the remaining postwar 'pedways' in the city of London, separating pedestrians from traffic

Exposed concrete and urban walkways:
London's South Bank developed from
Abercombie's Greater London plan of 1944

The desire for the modern world: Narratives of change for cities and planning 1930–1979

FOUR

Poetic realism: filmic planning in an era of transport modernisation

INTRODUCTION

The British documentary film movement embraced modernity wholeheartedly. The filmic works of Robert Flaherty, John Grierson, Arthur Elton, Basil Wright, Paul Rotha and Humphrey Jennings sought to capture and depict a radical period of British history, from the 1930s onwards. A radical political period, alongside economic depression, scientific and technological discovery, cultural innovation and rapid urbanisation, had created new conditions. The documentary film movement sought to contribute democratically to social reform and national renewal, by creating new communication mediums that reflected the Britain that was changing rapidly while additionally fostering a sense of national identity. The urban planning process broadly was an integral purpose to this social movement that could be captured on film, depicting industrial development, housing conditions and the pattern of land use across the country. Many of the film directors were from the political left and had forged close relationships with leading intellectual figures of the time, including W.H. Auden, J.B. Priestley, H.G. Wells and T.S. Eliot, who were also writing, as noted in Chapter Two, about changing conditions and social renewal.

The government of the day had also been persuaded of the merits of sponsoring and establishing state film units with the express purpose of documenting social and economic change. The Empire Marketing

Board (EMB) Film Unit started to make short documentary films
for distribution in Britain and overseas including making films on
such subjects as industrial Britain, children, heavy industry workers,
community development and housing needs. Within a short space
of time independent film units had also been set up by the General
Post Office (GPO) and some of the railway companies: the London
Midland and Scottish Railway's *Night Mail* of 1936, a 23-minute film
of the London to Glasgow overnight mail train with a commentary
by W.H. Auden and music by Benjamin Britten, is still one of the
most well known and celebrated film outputs from this period. The
films were unique because they focused on real life situations and
uniquely for cinema, concentrated on members of the working class
at home and in employment, allowing them a voice in cinema for the
first time. With the outbreak of the Second World War, the expertise
of the film units that survived had been brought into the Ministry
of Information, responsible for propaganda, but the documentary
work continued through the war and into the postwar period, with
the Crown Film Unit. This survived until the early 1950s when the
British documentary film movement ceased to exist in the form it
had in previous decades, although it created a legacy in the style of
film output that has continued to this day.

   An interesting fact about the documentary film movement is that
it celebrated change and modernity in all its guises. This positive
depiction was justified since change was seen as contributing to
social advantage and cultural identity, a celebration of achievement.
There was no attempt to halt progress or to dwell too much on
the past, but rather to concentrate on the present and to look
forward optimistically to the future. This chapter looks at transport
modernisation from the 1940s and the work of one of the
documentary film units as an illustration or narrative of the positive
portrayal of change in Britain at the time. British Transport Films
(BTF) was established in May 1949 with Edgar Anstey (1907–87) as
its first producer. Anstey was a protégé of John Grierson, the leading
documentary filmmaker of the 1930s, and widely regarded as the
founder of the British documentary movement. The nationalisation
of the four privately owned railway companies – the Great Western
Railway, the London Midland and Scottish Railway, the London
and North Eastern Railway and the Southern Railway – together
with a number of other transport undertakings relating to road
transportation and canals, occurred on 1 January 1948 when the
British Transport Commission (BTC) was formed. Both the
London Midland and Scottish Railway and the Southern Railway

had operated film units, and, on nationalisation, these units were amalgamated into a new filmmaking arm of the BTC, the BTF Unit. The purpose of the BTF Unit was threefold:

- to make travelogue films, that promoted destinations in town, country and seaside resorts throughout the British Isles, and promoted rail or associated transport as the best means for people to travel to the destinations represented on screen;
- to depict the transport workforce and the part they played in transport operations; and
- to provide training films, to explain complicated operational aspects of transport undertakings (these were made not for general release but rather for training schools) (Reed, 1990).

Although normally associated with railways, the BTF output covered all aspects of a modern transport process under the BTC, including London Transport, buses, inland waterways and seaports and general travel promotion features and natural history. The Unit's production arm functioned from 1949 until 1982, and produced over 1,500 films. During the functioning of the Unit, the films received 202 film industry awards, including an Academy Award, several Academy Award nominations, three BAFTAs, the Golden Lion of Vienna and several first prizes at international film festivals.

Films from the BTF are captivating for their depiction of the modernist movement. They are somewhat nostalgic today, but they are acclaimed pieces of British filmmaking. The very best creative and artistic talents of the day were used to make the films, and included poets, actors and composers, among whom were Sir John Betjeman, Sir Michael Redgrave, Sir Arnold Bax and Ralph Vaughan Williams, John Piper, Robert Shaw, Anton Rodgers and Hubert Gregg. The names of film crews and directors employed by the BTF Unit are equally impressive, including the director John Schlesinger and the cinematographers Robert Paynton, David Watkin and Billie Williams, all of whom went on to work on acclaimed major Hollywood film productions.

The trajectory and development of the BTF Unit was very much bound up with government policy towards public transport and its funding, and it was eventually wound down under the Thatcher government. But the fortune of the BTF Unit could be allied to the fortune of short cinema documentary films and the cinema newsreel more generally. As short films were abandoned as a prelude to main features in British cinemas in the 1980s, the outlet of the BTF Unit similarly waned. Despite this uncertainty, by the early 1980s, the BTF Unit still produced features for a professional transport audience and for exhibitions at local film societies. This latter outlet depended heavily on voluntary participation and interest from a specialist audience, and involved the leasing of not only the film but also the projection equipment from the BTF Unit directly.

Despite this commercial vulnerability, the release of features for a specialist audience and as short documentary films for general release is very much in keeping with the broader social, educational and entertainment value of the films, and reflects both Edgar Anstey's and John Grierson's faith in the documentary feature that extends beyond mere frivolity. This chapter charts the development of the BTF Unit from the British documentary movement of the 1930s, presents an overview of the output of the Unit, charts its success and recognition, comments on the distribution of the films and considers a number of films in more detail. It is recognised that the output of the BTF Unit comprises a significant and under-rated contribution to the history of British cinema and the depiction of a changing Britain that deserves credit alongside major cinematic features of the period. The film output should be reassessed for its geographical,

The old clock at platform 8, King's Cross station, demolished in 2008

educational and entertainment contribution to cinematic audiences in the postwar period, since the films offer a significant historical record of not only a changing transport system across the UK, but also a valuable depiction of the modernist movement in architecture and design in the 1950s to 1970s, and of a changing British landscape.

Research material was drawn from the BTF Unit output, held at the British Film Institute (BFI) Archives and at London Transport. At the time of writing, almost 100 of these short films are now available on BFI-produced video and DVD, having been released over the last 10 years. Research material in the form of the BTF Photographic Archive was also scrutinised from its home at the Picture Library of the National Museum of Science and Industry. Written archive material was gleaned from papers held at the BFI, including Edgar Anstey's papers and a series of recollection papers authored by past employees of the BTF Unit and brought together by John Legard, the former chief editor at the BTF Unit.

THE DOCUMENTARY FILM MOVEMENT IN BRITAIN

The emergence of the documentary movement occurred as a reaction to a belief held by John Grierson, among others, that the educational and public service role of film could not be provided by the private sector and required government sponsorship. Enticknap (2000) highlights Grierson's consternation at the 'Woolworth intentions' of the commercial film industry at the time, and the possible effects such output would have for British cultural values. At a time of economic hardship in Britain and elsewhere, and a concomitant concern that cinema depicted overwhelmingly middle-class values rather than those of the working class, there was a need for a political and cinematic response. Grierson, and later Anstey, were middle class, but possessed left-leaning political and ideological values, and felt uncomfortable at the ignorance of the plight of the working classes on screen. Unemployment, the absence of work, problems of housing and lack of nutritional food were all issues largely ignored by a film industry that, through the 1930s, increasingly looked to Hollywood for entertainment. Peter Stead addresses this point in more detail, suggesting that:

> Hollywood had captured the British market and was very effectively securing financial control of much of British production and distribution, but it had also by 1938 more or less completely won

over British critical opinion. Apart from the out and out adherents of socialist, Soviet and documentary films, the leading critics and moulders of opinion had come to believe that it was the Hollywood feature film that was pointing the way forward. (Stead, 1990)

As Higson (1995) comments, the development of the British documentary movement and the emergence of 'realist films' in the 1930s and 1940s, both in the US and in Europe, signifies an increasing frustration with stage hall performances on screen and a growing desire for distinctiveness within the British film industry. Comedies such as Noel Coward's 'Blithe spirit', adapted for cinema from his West End play, did little to convey contemporary Britain to the vast majority of the audience, with its focus on middle and upper class drawing room exchanges. This overt reliance on the conventions of the stage and its middle-class connotations to inform and develop subject matter for British cinema at this time may have had a negative effect on working-class cinematic audiences' view of British cinema, who turned, in preference, to see Hollywood productions. A further reason, highlighted by Hood (1983), is the actual representation of working-class subjects in cinema. When workers appeared on film, they were frequently the comedy relief, the buffoons, the idiots or the servants.

There were, of course, characters on screen in the 1930s that emerged from working-class backgrounds, including George Formby and Will Hay. But there was also a perception, according to Higson, that British films were being left behind largely because they were less real and less vital (Higson, 1995). Grierson, writing in 1942, suggested that the documentary film movement used cinema because it was 'the most convenient and most exciting' medium available to the documentary protagonists, but its roots also developed within the development of official public relations activity, corporate advertising and propaganda policy in the 1930s (Grierson, 1979). In short, there was a desire for a social and educational cinematic role in Britain that would assist in the forging of a national identity, particularly pertinent in the run-up to the outbreak of the Second World War. Documentary filmmaking, according to Higson (1995), could therefore be equated to public interest, social renewal, something being held in common, shared values, a flow of education, information, and instruction and shared meanings, between the state and the individual.

Grierson highlights this ideological foundation of the British documentary movement:

> The basic force behind [the documentary units] was social not aesthetic.… We were, I confess, sociologists, a little worried about the way the world was going.… The world had become very complex – and civic comprehension difficult. We were conscious of the abstraction of life under the new metropolitan skies. We saw that poverty of community life went hand in hand with the lack of civic comprehension. And of one thing we were pretty sure – that the old stiff-backed educational system was not doing very much to help towards comprehension. Nor particularly was the new myth-making machinery of the star-struck cinema. (cited in Rotha, 1952)

This might be viewed as an attempt to make the invisible, visible, and to constitute, for Higson, some form of 'national community' and, in the words of Grierson again, to put emphasis 'not on the personal life but on the mass life, their continuous attempt to dramatize the relation of a man to his community' (Grierson, 1981a). For Paul Rotha, like John Grierson and Edgar Anstey, the documentary provides the nation with a public and social image in the name of citizenship: 'The Documentary Film, quite simply, aims to bring about an awareness in every person of their place in everyday life and of the responsibilities of good citizenship implied by that membership' (Rotha, 1949).

Higson suggests that this idealism was a deliberate attempt to produce and regulate an official public sphere and an attempt to discipline public – and working – life (Higson, 1995). With this perspective, it is little wonder, perhaps, why documentary films of the 1930s concentrated on the working and living conditions of the working classes.

The documentary movement was encompassed with the establishment of the EMB in 1927 and then the development of a film unit at the GPO from 1933 to 1939 when the outbreak of the Second World War produced a need for a very different kind of information or propaganda film. Both the EMB and the GPO Units drew talent from Oxford and Cambridge and might, as a consequence, be regarded as middle class in practice, but they possessed a socialist outlook (Swann, 1983).

Grierson had been greatly influenced by Robert Flaherty's work and instilled in the documentary movement, from its outset, notions of 'poetic realism' in the making of documentary films (Higson, 1995). Higson argues that it was this quality that was most admired in the films, particularly in the 1940s:

In a sense, poetic realism constitutes the happy balance between the various conflicting and competing ideas and impulses which make up the documentary idea as a whole. It holds all excesses in check; the responsibility of realism blocks off the path to self-indulgent aestheticism or cloying sentimentality, while the poetic sensibility tempers both the objective coldness of the document, and the tendency towards establishing action as the ultimate logic of narrative movement and energy. It attempts, above all, to hold together the irreconcilable discourses of artistic endeavour and public service. (Higson, 1995, p 191)

Grierson, too, noted the artistic or poetic possibilities of documentary: 'realist documentary, with its streets and cities and slums and markets and exchanges and factories, has given itself the job of making poetry where no poet has gone before it' (Grierson, 1981b). Aitken (1990) too notes that documentary films conveyed a visual art of 'a sense of beauty about the ordinary world, the world on your doorstep'. But this poetic element was juxtaposed against realistic elements with their own day-to-day sounds, noises and dialects.

Edgar Anstey, in his papers at the BFI, talks of this realist element in the GPO film *Night Mail,* directed by Harry Watt and Basil Wright in 1936 for the London Midland and Scottish Railway and the GPO, with a narrative prepared by W.H. Auden and music composed by Benjamin Britten:

> The GPO Unit had just acquired its own sound equipment and Grierson brought Cavacanti from France to do research in the use of sound....The actual sound of day to day life were given their true importance, not only to create atmosphere but as a means of evoking what I can only describe as an extra dimension of emotion. (Anstey, 1970)

The quality of sound reproduction or the invented noises that occur in *Night Mail* illustrates the importance of natural sound, and often direct dialogue recording, as an essential part of the documentary experience. One of the best-known examples of the innovative introduction of direct dialogue recording was in one of Anstey's first films, *Housing Problems*, co-directed by Arthur Elton in 1936. This was used to good effect to record the subjects of the films – the people themselves (the tenants of slums) – making their own case for housing improvements. This use of sound was revolutionary, and Anstey remarks:

We narrowed ourselves down in "Housing Problems" to a very, very simple technique, which was open. At the time nobody had done it, and we gave slum dwellers a chance to make their own films. (Anstey, 1970)

Another essential feature, as depicted in *Night Mail*, is the representation of workers, viewed as competent people doing competent and important jobs, even if – at first thoughts – they may appear mundane tasks of little interest to a cinematic audience. In one sequence, an experienced postman from a sorting office is learning the new task of securing pouches to the side-swinging apparatus for mail train collection at the trackside. This scene illustrates to the audience that there is more to this task than may first appear, and further illustrates the infrastructure, training and effort required in posting and delivering a letter. This epitomises the desired effects of the documentary film Grierson was striving for: both educative and informative.

Anstey was one of the pioneers of the British documentary movement and went on to join *March of Time*, a spin-off of the current affairs magazine *Time*. In the postwar period, he became head of BTF.

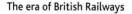

The era of British Railways

THE BTF UNIT

Nationalisation of industry was a central plank of the new Labour government's mandate on election in 1945. The nationalised railways in the form of the BTC, and later British Railways, were to be a principal component in a national transport network. As postwar rationing subsided and people's prosperity increased through the 1950s, so a desire for leisure travel emerged within a new Elizabethan era (the Queen had been crowned in 1953) (Hennessey, 1995).

The government-sponsored Crown Film Unit closed in 1952 under the Conservatives although Grierson, now ensconced in Canada, called on a more systematic approach to documentary filmmaking in Britain and welcomed the establishment of the BTF Unit under Edgar Anstey in 1949 (Enticknap, 2000). For Grierson, the future of the documentary film lay with state-sponsored units like the BTF Unit. Writing in *Sight & Sound* in 1948, he states that:

> We should devote some public money every year to making film poetry about Britain. The only and traditionally English guarantee of this is to put the policy job – I mean the sponsorship – in the hands of two or three imaginatively generous people who have the wit to know what that means. (Grierson, 1948)

Hogenkamp (1976), writing on the development of British film up to the Second World War, remarks that this simple approach formed the parameters for documentary film production in the years immediately after the war, with the appointment of film unit heads in three core industries: Donald Alexander at the National Coal Board, Edgar Anstey at British Transport and Arthur Elton at Shell. As Hogenkamp states: 'Grierson was right.'

In the Anstey Archive at the BFI, there is a copy of an article he wrote for the trade magazine *Film User*, entitled 'British transport films roll for twenty one years'. Within this article, Anstey himself outlines the origins of the BTF Unit:

> In 1949 Jack Brebner and Christian Barman asked me to set up a unit for the British Transport Commission. These two fine public servants were already living in a certain splendid isolation as the survivors of a tradition of public relations which had first flowed in Britain under Stephen Tallents in the early nineteen-thirties. It was of course the same tradition that had encouraged John Grierson to

start the Empire Marketing Board film unit (and by so doing, British Documentary) and had given me the chance in 1931 to begin to learn my craft from him.

The opportunity offered in 1949 was to practice Grierson's creative interpretation of actuality in the area of public transport and to bring it alive on the screen. (Anstey, 1970)

BTC sponsored the BTF Unit to produce three principal types of films:

- films about rail problems and achievements, designed for the general public in cinemas, television or on 16mm;
- traffic promotional films designed to increase revenue by publicising services, routes or areas of the country; and
- staff instructional films on techniques, problems and innovations; these were to be shown to small audiences at staff colleges, training schools, rail cinema coaches, and so on (Reed, 1990).

The promotional or publicity film output is interesting to note here since Anstey himself, writing at the outset of the BTF Unit in 1949, casts doubt on the degree to which a documentary film could be made entertaining, a necessary condition for distribution, financial return and reinvestment:

> Publicity, public relations and instruction are, however, not entertainment – although a measure of entertainment must be present if audience attention is to be held. (cited in the Anstey Archive, BFI)

This clearly strikes to the heart of the issue about whether films sponsored by industry and devoted to depicting transport operations, workers' duties and everyday occurrences would attract sufficient audience interest and a distributor eager to show the films nationally across Britain. Higson notes this point too, by calling into question the legitimacy of the documentary subject represented in film, and the degree to which it is tampered with for the purposes of audience attraction and entertainment (Higson, 1995).

From the objectives set by the BTC for the BTF Unit, there were multiple audiences for the Unit's cinematic output. Charles Potter, a senior figure at the BTF, recalls the reception towards the films across Britain:

> … there were film shows for the staff, their families and friends.
> Screenings were arranged as far apart as Wick, Fort William and
> Penzance. The films chosen for the performance varied according
> to local circumstances…. Despite television, the reactions of
> railwaymen and their families to these screenings of Commission
> films, being shown in Town Halls and other suitable premises all
> over the country, was most impressive. They poured into the halls
> with their wives and families in their hundreds, and there were many
> audiences numbering between 1000 and 2000. (Potter, 1998)

Some of the most popular films of the BTF shown in this format
included: *Terminus* (BAFTA award winner and directed by John
Schlesinger in 1961), *The Travolators, Modernisation, Bridge 114* and
Blue Pullman. Blue Pullman received its premier at the Odeon, Marble
Arch, in 1960, and Reed (1990) notes that this film was shown as
a short feature to coincide with the introduction of the new Blue
Pullman train between London and Manchester, thus providing an
illustration of the traffic promotional film (see the review of this
film later in this chapter). Charles Potter (1998) notes that theatrical
distribution was secured in countries other than the UK, including
the US, Canada, South Africa, Australia and New Zealand, and that
the films recovered in distribution revenue from all sources more than
they cost to produce. Films were distributed through a commercial
company and were sold to cinemas on their entertainment merits,
with the revenue being used to finance further productions.

The travel incentive films were actually travelogues depicting
areas of the country accessible by train or bus, and focused on non-
transport subjects such as country estates, seaside resorts and areas
of landscape beauty, and these were intended for theatrical, non-
theatrical and television audiences. Aware of the publicity potential
available to exploit short duration holidays and day trips, it was
common – according to Potter – for commercial representatives of
the Commission's undertakings to attend the non-theatrical showings:

> … armed with brochures based on the films. At the end of the show,
> questions were asked by the audience about fares, train times, etc and
> it was an excellent opportunity for "our man" [sic] to supply all the
> information required in a friendly atmosphere created by the film
> show.

The instructional film, by contrast, was aimed directly at the
BTC's 725,000 staff in their undertaking of educational courses,

although many were also distributed to specialist audiences such as film societies and transport interest groups. In addition to films on railway safety, modernisation provided a core subject in advising staff on the transition in the railways from steam to diesel to electric operation. The BTC had devised a modernisation plan in 1955 and many films sponsored by the Commission were devoted to these subjects, including electrification, track laying and signal operation (BTC, 1955). One of these, *The Third Sam*, narrated by the actor Stanley Holloway, received a BAFTA.

Non-theatrical distribution occurred via the posting of prints to BTF-approved projectionists or through the use of 100 mobile projectors that had been distributed throughout the British Railways network. The BTF Unit also possessed two cinema coaches that were fitted with 16mm sound projectors and, being mobile, could travel around the railway network to provide staff instruction to a maximum audience of 58. These coaches could also be coupled to special excursions and conference trains. Finally, since the BTC also

Trams of the modern era: Metrolink at Manchester's St Peter's Square

owned hotels and ships in addition to stations, films were sometimes shown on especially installed screens to entertain passengers in waiting rooms or lobbies.

The Commission undertook assessment of the distribution of films twice a year. The figures reveal that an aggregate audience of over 200,000 people was achieved each month in British cinemas in the 1950s and 1960s, and over 1.5 million people saw BTF productions in non-theatrical settings during each of the six months between September and February. Potter (1998) estimates that non-theatrical distribution alone eventually yielded a public audience, per title, of over three million, at a cost of a halfpenny per head.

The attraction and entertainment value of BTF theatrical circuit films did not always materialise, however. John Legard (former chief editor of the BTF Unit) recalls one film made by BTF that was not well received by a cinema audience. *Train Time* (1952) had been touring with *The Gift Horse*, the latter film starring Trevor Howard, Donald Sinden and Sid James, a wartime naval drama based on aid given by the US to help Britain fight the Second World War:

> Before the audience got to the main "feature" they had to sit through thirty minutes of "propaganda" or information on the freight and passenger services provided by the British Transport Commission. This film featured the device of people speaking for themselves as well as an actor playing a role. "Train Time" was given a slow hand clap by an audience who had come to see a British "entertainment" film with a group of actors playing Officers and Men stereotypes, as opposed to the "real" people represented running a complex railway industry…. A lesson was drawn from this experience and films in future were more entertaining. (Legard, interview with Paul Smith, undated)

Despite this blip, Potter (1998) argues that Anstey saw the success of the films as being derived from depiction of the workers themselves and for a desire to take pride in their duties, epitomising the national community sentiment highlighted by Grierson in the 1930s. Writing in 1960, he states:

> There is perhaps even more evidence of sound film investment in the reactions of audiences of railwaymen and their families to screenings of the Commission's films now being given in Town Halls and other suitable premises all over the country. Audiences of 1,400 in Darlington, 1,900 in Newcastle, 1,600 in a 1,500 capacity hall

in Leeds and 800 filling the Hornsey Town Hall. They have found films like "Report On Modernisation" (1959) contributing much to the restoration of morale, morale which sometimes seems to have become an Aunt Sally for anyone with access to press, radio or television and a supply of personal or political brickbats. (cited in the Anstey Archive, BFI)

Even by the early 1960s, television and other forms of home entertainment remained comparatively rare and black and white, so this may also explain the 'success'. Quality and cinematography were facets of the BTF output that also made them appealing to audiences, according to John Legard (Legard, 1998). Each film was shot on 16mm Kodachrome film and then enlarged to 35mm by Technicolor. David Watkin, who originated in the BTF Unit as a camera assistant and cameraman before going on to work on major Hollywood productions as a cinematographer, suggests in his autobiography that Anstey was walking a tightrope between sponsors, who wished to portray the coming of the new, and the man himself, who wanted to record something that was passing into history artistically (Watkin, 1998).

BTF UNIT FILMS

The titles of the BTF films reveal the three types of film output requested of the Unit by the BTC and, later, British Railways, British Road Services, London Transport and the Inland Waterways Board. By way of illustration, *Channel Islands* may represent the travelogue film, *People in Railways* is an example of the transport workforce and informational film, and *Pressure Heating and Ventilation* is an operation film. It should be noted that some films do cross over this typology. It seems that certain points must have been considered by the BTF Unit in choosing subjects for films, including the increasing propensity of the predominantly urban British public to think of leisure and holidays and the need for public transport to move people to resorts and other places of leisure. Furthermore, as Higson notes, cinematic audience figures during the 1950s were high (Higson, 1986).

It is clearly beyond this examination to consider a large number of the BTF's cinematic output, how they were selected and how they were received. Various industry catalogues were produced through the 1950s to 1970s to illustrate available titles, new releases and details of how to obtain copies of the films for hire. In their recollections, BTF staff note the ease with which the films were made on location. Edward Scott, an assistant director, notes the cooperation of transport staff to the film crews in making these short films (Scott, 1998), and David Lochner, a producer of some of the later films, talks of the accomplishment of the film crews operating around and not disturbing the transport operations in practice (Lochner, 1998).

It would be appropriate here to review a small number by way of illustration of the BTF Unit's output. The three chosen films are representative of the main types of film output. They are: *All That Mighty Heart* (1962), *Blue Pullman* (1960) and *A Future in Rail* (1957). Following a review of the subjects in each film, assessments are provided of their pitch and contribution.

All That Mighty Heart

All That Mighty Heart, directed by R.K. Neilson–Baxter, photographed by David Watkin and edited by John Legard, is a colour film made in 1962 for London Transport. The 25-minute film is effectively a portrait of a summer day in the life of London Transport and Londoners. It sits both as a promotional film for London Transport and as a travelogue for London, and depicts both the public's use of transport and London Transport workers.

The film opens with a panoramic shot of London at dawn, with the dome of St Paul's in the distance and a voiceover reciting lines from a Wordsworth poem (from where the *All That Mighty Heart* title is taken). We hear the sounds of a city awakening: riverboat horns, milk floats clattering along roads, distant traffic. As the chimes of Big Ben strike 6.00am, we are subjected to a montage of shots showing London awakening, including London Transport workers arriving both at Stockwell bus depot and Upminster tube depot, streetlights going out, and aerial views of deserted Trafalgar Square and Bank. The gates of an underground station noisily wrench open and workers start saying "Good Morning" to each other in friendly spirits. There is little dialogue in the film other than captured sounds of the city awakening, a mix of natural and invented sounds. Newly introduced Routemaster buses start to depart from Stockwell garage, the signalman sets the points for a tube train to depart from Upminster depot, road sweepers march in formation along a

Icon of London and an advertising
agency's dream: the Routemaster bus

highway to their destinations and controllers at London Transport stations change shifts.

At this point, the subject matter of the film moves away from the workers to the public, and this marks the point of entry for the sound of morning radio broadcasting, and specifically, Radio 4. We see a middle-aged couple arising from bed, the man lighting a cigarette and spluttering and wheezing in the process. The radio commentary talks about the prospect of fine sunny weather. A younger married woman bids her husband farewell as he departs for work. There then follows a montage of shots of people embarking on different modes of transport for the commute to work, both at stations and stops and on board tube trains and buses. All this occurs without any form of commentary other than the radio, where the broadcaster reflects on minor stories from the newspapers of how people have been spending their weekends, ending it with the rhetorical comment: "Who says we don't know how to use our leisure?"

The film continues to show the public using tubes and trains, interspersed with shots of bus-filled Trafalgar Square, Regent Street and Piccadilly Circus. We see housewives waiting for a department store's doors to open at 9.00am while the radio plays Eric Coates themes, music which might be regarded as symbolising postwar London. There is also a hint at continuity and normality about the London life shown despite the confusion, the crowds and hectic urban scene. On a cut back to a London Transport controllers' office, one of the controllers remarks to another, "Well, that's another day started. I'd better go and brew up." In the meantime, domestic life is shown to continue with housewives washing, vacuuming and embarking on shopping trips, interspersed with shots of buses and tubes being washed, vacuumed and cleaned.

We follow one suburban housewife's journey from her new modern house, taking the bus from a newly built car-less tree-lined new avenue to the shopping precinct in the middle of Stevenage new town. The sun is shining; children are playing in the town square's fountain; dogs are lying peacefully. She enters a supermarket, still a relatively new concept even by 1962, where she sees another woman: "Hello Mrs Mason, what are you doing here?" The lady replies, "Oh I often come over here to do my shopping these days." How little is needed to focus the audience's attention on convenience and modernity, during Harold Macmillan's era of 'You have never had it so good'. We then cut back to central London to show buses continuing to dominate the urban landscape of well-known London locations such as Tower Bridge, Hyde Park and Trafalgar Square, all accompanied by Coates' music.

To emphasise the leisure potential available, the film then turns to sporting and leisure pursuits once again, by utilising BBC radio commentary of actual events to accompany film of tennis at Wimbledon, test cricket at the Oval, horse racing at Epsom, the

Entrance to Bank underground station; alcohol consumption is banned on trains

regatta at Henley, motor racing, together with a family's visit to London zoo. All these are juxtaposed against the public queuing for buses and being transported easily and quickly by London Transport. As the buses take the public home, the sound returns to a radio news broadcast discussing the continued work on building the Victoria underground line. The radio commentary refers succinctly to the 20 miles of tunnelling being constructed, the 12 new stations, the opening up of the north east of London to the tube network, and the five-year construction timetable. This is accompanied by shots of the line's construction itself below ground.

The film then enters the final phase of its narrative, by concentrating on the evening economy. The West End at night is depicted in all its colourful glory, from aboard the upper deck of a bus with the public amazed at the sites and neon lit advertisements and theatres. The public is shown entering theatres, restaurants and cinemas, attending a performance of 'That Was The Week That Was' and watching chefs make pizza in the large spectacle-lit windows of a West End Italian restaurant. As the chimes of Big Ben return to strike midnight, and theatre lights go off, last buses and tube trains depart, and tube stations gates close, we return to an aerial shot of the city with another recital of lines written by Thomas Hood.

The film is not that unique for its lavish cinematography or directing, but it does provide a fascinating picture of London in the early 1960s and can represent a number of BTF films that look at urban life and movement during a period of change. Like other

Symbol for London and the metro system: the roundel sign

BTF productions, it was the recipient of an award, receiving Third Prize for Best Short at the 1964 London Film Festival.

Blue Pullman

Blue Pullman was photographed by David Watkin and written and directed by James Ritchie in 1960. Representative of a rail promotional film and one depicting railway workers, the 25-minute feature was intended to promote the introduction of a new train service: the diesel-hauled luxury Midland Pullman service between Manchester and London. The six car trains were more commonly known as 'Blue Pullmans' because of their distinctive colouring scheme. One problem that may have been encountered by the film crew when attempting to promote new facilities or services was the need to show the train in operation but to complete filming prior to its first introduction. James Ritchie seems to have provided the solution to the problem by filming the train under test and being prepared for its inaugural journey. This also enabled the distinctive features of the train to be highlighted cinematically.

The opening shots of the film are very distinctive and are accompanied by especially composed music by Clifton Parker that possesses a hint of the sinister or curious. We are aboard a moving train and the camera pans down, from a cream-coloured ceiling to seat height, to reveal a deserted and largely unfamiliar carriage: open plan with tables and seats facing each other. At the time, this type of internal carriage design was virtually unheard of on British railways. The camera tilts further to reveal a piece of recording equipment on the floor. Someone exits a toilet and slams the door behind him, upon which is a handwritten notice stating 'Darkroom – Keep Out'. The ladies lavatory door is wedged open to reveal a further piece of recording equipment. A pair of spectacles rest upside down on a ledger, and wires hangs down from the ceiling all along the carriage. A pair of headphones rests on a seat and, on a nearby table, sits a stopwatch. As the train enters a tunnel, we briefly witness two men in the window's dark reflection, unwrapping a long steel component. The film cuts to a shot of the tracks from the front of the train and to the driver, a pinstripe suit-wearing gentleman beneath a bowler hat. Finally, the camera is positioned in the inspection pit of a train depot to reveal the train entering and travelling over it. The sinister music dies away and we finally witness, from outside, the closing of the depot doors once the train has stopped inside. What on earth can it all mean?

The lack of dialogue continues and the only sound is that of the diesel engines themselves, occasionally toned down to reveal "Hellos" and "How's it all going?", dubbed dialogue spoken between the portrayed railwaymen. Finally, the train is revealed, with the film capturing the printing of large colourful posters announcing 'The Midland Pullman', a press release talking about the introduction of a new 95mph luxury train and an *a la carte* menu and wine list.

Returning to onboard the train once again, the carriages are now full of people, but all are railway employees, either testing equipment or finding their way around. The train is about to depart the depot for its inaugural journey: the train destination board rolls down the list of Pullman services until it reaches the 'Midland Pullman' board, a useful way to highlight the fact that new Pullman services are also being introduced on many other routes . We accompany the chief steward and two apprentices as they are introduced to the onboard features of the train by, we must assume, a designer: table lights are switched on and off, conductor call buttons next to seats are tested, seat reclining and adjustment checked, window blinds are adjusted,

Poster for the introduction of the Blue Pullman

The New **MIDLAND PULLMAN**

First Class de luxe travel — Supplementary fares

8.50 am	Manchester Central ↑	9.21 pm	Mondays to Fridays from 4th July	12.45 pm	St. Pancras	↑ 4.00 pm
9.04 am	Cheadle Heath	9.07 pm			Leicester	
12.03 pm ↓	St. Pancras	6.10 pm		2.10 pm ↓	London Road	2.33 pm

The last word in rail comfort. Limited accommodation, book in advance

emergency cords checked and air conditioning units tested in each carriage. The team pass through the kitchen and dining car; the chef is unpacking the kitchen equipment, checking the hot water boiler, storing cases of wine and polishing glasses. Elsewhere on the train, drivers scrutinise timetables and route maps, receiving a brief pause and friendly smile from the team as they pass through. There is a montage of shots showing tea being served with heavy reference to social class: to the stewards with their mugs, to the station masters in bone china cups and to the driver pouring himself one from a flask. The whole emphasis suggests everyone pulling together, worker harmony and pride, whatever one's position.

The day has arrived. At Manchester Central station, the stationmaster polishes his top hat in expectation as he greets the first passengers. Porters and stewards show the predominantly business passengers to their seats individually, and are welcomed onboard via an announcement in each carriage, informing them (and reminding the audience?): "This train is fully air-conditioned. If the temperature is not to your liking, please inform your steward." One might even believe that the only appropriate word not used to describe the new train is 'deluxe'.

After the train departs, the fayre is displayed. Complimentary drinks are served and breakfast prepared. Silver service provides passengers with English breakfasts, kippers, boiled eggs and toast. Later in the journey, we witness salmon and lobster being prepared by the chef, wine and large brandies being served, with tracking shots along the carriage of the passengers reading, relaxing, drinking and chatting to their neighbours. Meanwhile, the train ploughs on through the English countryside at high speed, the film reaching its climax with aerial shots of the train taken from a helicopter. Finally, the train arrives at London St Pancras station, on time (of course), and is greeted by the stationmaster in his top hot as the passengers disembark.

Blue Pullman is one of BTF's most widely recognised and popular films, containing lavish photography, skilful editing and a memorable music score. This was considered the height of luxury and modern train travel in the 1960s and it makes one realise today just how much times have changed since. The film was shown in national cinemas but also at film festivals in 1961, and was the recipient of the Gold Plaque at the Rome International Film Festival, Certificates of Merit at the Vancouver and Manhattan Film Festivals and a Gold Medal and Silver Cup at the Genoa International Film Festival in 1965.

A Future in Rail

This film is a mere eight minutes in length and was compiled and edited by John Legard from existing footage held at the BTF Unit from its archive of the previous eight years and from the archive of the privatised rail companies prior to 1948. It is a very different genre compared to the two films discussed above in the sense that it is a black and white feature, is intended to highlight railway operation first and foremost and has a continuous voiceover narrative. The latter is spoken by an actor, purporting to be a railwayman who was, originally, not convinced to take a job in the railway industry but who now has 10 years' experience behind him and who is encouraging the audience – all supposedly male – to enter employment in the railway industry too.

The film depicts a range of railway operations, from signalbox operation, to track laying, to engine driving, to goods haulage, to crane driving. As each activity is presented, contextualised by shots of the modernisation of the railways – from steam, to diesel, to electric – the narration talks warmly of the changed environment of

The idea of a luxury train travelling on standard rail routes in Britain has all but disappeared, thanks to privatisation

railway employment. At the outset the narrator states: "A new word has come into the railways and with it a lot of exciting changes. The word is modernisation." The film contrasts the old style of working with the modern world – hand lever signals and modern power boxes, goods handling and 'palletisation' and 'conveyorisation', groups of men manually laying track and mechanised cranes lifting track into place, drivers ensconced in warm cabs of diesel trains with adjustable seats juxtaposed against the grime, sweat and cold of working as a steam engine driver and fireman. The film, a blatant piece of employment promotion in an age of change, appears almost desperate to convince the audience that times really have changed for the better. As the voiceover makes clear: "If you like working as a member of a closely coordinated team, you can get a lot of satisfaction out of this job, still more if you're the gaffer and have to organise it all. Out in the open, what's more! Just look at that twin-jib crane! Fancy the job of handling that?" It is easy, in watching this film, to forget that it is not intended to be humorous.

One final quote is worth highlighting. The narrator suggests that there will soon by a rush for railway jobs and the audience had better act quickly before it's too late: "This is only the beginning of modernisation. And the day isn't far off when there'll be quite a few wishing they joined in when they had the chance." The script was written by Paul Le Saux, who wrote many other scripts for the BTF

New Street station, Birmingham, after electrification of the line; even the IRA failed in its attempt to blow up the brutalist signal box in the 1970s

in the 1950s and 1960s. It emphasises the forward-thinking aspect of transportation in the 1950s and 1960s, even if this particular example remains problematic. Yet it is also of its time and was produced, no doubt, in response to a request by the BTF Unit's sponsor, the BTC. In the late 1950s, Reed (1990) describes, the government was investing £391 million in the then ailing and loss-making railway industry. It comes as little surprise that the potential development of this investment should be promoted via the BTF Unit to both public and staff via the medium of film. It is problematic in the sense that, in creating a sense of realism by employing a railwayman to talk up his experiences of railway working, the film falls into the trap of parody, with the narrator – actor – impersonating not only a working-class accent but a working-class accent from the North of England. In attempting to reach a working-class public, and simultaneously represent working-class endeavours, the film appears a little patronising, and also moves away from Edgar Anstey's assertion from his 1930s' experience that part of the success of documentary film was having working-class people speak for themselves. To all intents and purposes, it is working class only in the sense that it portrays the workingman's duties on film; other than that, it portrays all the hallmarks of a middle-class interpretation. It is difficult to suggest that this film is of entertainment value, even if it performs an educative and informative role.

CONCLUSIONS

There can be little doubt that the output of the BTF Unit did provide a significant contribution to the British film industry in the period 1949-82 and also captured and represented social and economic change and modernisation within Britain. Reference to the number of senior awards and accolades given to the Unit in these years indicates high quality films, and also, as short features and documentaries, they provided interesting, informative and at times entertaining features. Between 1955 and the penultimate year before the Unit's dispersal in 1982, BTF had won 185 awards including the Hollywood Oscar for *Wild Wings*, directed by John Taylor in 1966, for best live action short subject.

The Unit also provided a useful training programme for aspiring filmmaking talent. Edgar Anstey combined the tensions of delivering to a sponsoring body while at the same time making educative and informative films in the spirit of John Grierson.

The principal function of the Unit was to make films that would encourage travel by public transport and to inform the public of the technical, organisational and operational efforts needed to provide public services. Whether the Unit succeeded in encouraging further public transport usage is a moot point, perhaps because in the 1940s and 1950s it must have been difficult to foresee the rise of motor car usage and ownership in the 1960s and beyond. There was also an associated turning away by the public from public transport and increasing financial worries for a publicly subsidised transport system, particularly when the BTC modernisation plan was itself replaced by the Beeching plan that proposed and indeed implemented the drastic reduction of services and direct withdrawal of railway routes (British Railways Board, 1963).

The theatre audience numbers may not have been successful either, but perhaps this had as much to do with the fortunes of short films in the 1960s and 1970s as the subject matter on offer, most of

Awaiting the all-clear for a race to the north: 'York Minster' at King's Cross

which was possibly unappealing to cinema audiences. Nevertheless, many of the films do display a poetic realism and an ability to display working-class characters undertaking routine but important jobs, even if the narration that accompanied the films often appeared patronising. At least working conditions made it to the screen. The realism aspect is important in judging the success of the films. These had started in 1950 although it is interesting to note Lindsay Anderson's comment made in 1960 that:

> The number of British films that have ever made a genuine try at a story in a popular milieu, with working class characters all through, can be counted on one hand. This visual rejection of three-quarters of the population of this country represents more than a ridiculous impoverishment of the cinema. (quoted in Lowenstein, 2000, p 226)

Although Anderson may well have been correct about narrative features, it does suggest that he was overlooking the documentary movement generally in Britain, and certainly the BTF features do provide exactly the sort of elements he was searching for, albeit in a non-narrative form.

The films did provide Britain with a public and social image in the name of citizenship and modernity, and they still attract a great deal of attention. These was a screening of some of the BTF films at the National Film Theatre in 1999 and throughout the 1980s and 1990s British Channel 4 television screened 60 or so of the films as 'fillers' during their daytime schedules. Since 2000, the BFI has been releasing video and DVD compilations of the best films: nine boxed sets have been released to date.

Integral to London's image: the red bus and classical architecture

FIVE

"Look at all those chimneys. That's money." Urban space and social realism

INTRODUCTION

As discussed in Chapter One, urbanisation and industrialisation had changed the form and scale of British towns and cities. The urban planning movement had been introduced to manage the externalities of rapid urbanisation but by the time that liberal and socialist governments had put the initial elements of urban planning in place, the social and environmental damage had already been done. New legislation and new modern designs to housing and industrial activity benefited new developments; a significant proportion of poor or sub-standard 19th-century industrial legacy remained in place across Britain even by the 1950s and 1960s, and were largely untouched by urban planning and the modernist movement.

Debates in the social sciences, especially Urban Studies and Cultural Geography, have focused on spatialisation. Spatial analyses of a variety of different forms of culture and landscapes have assisted in our understanding of the concept of space within particular societies and geographies. Cinema and film have been used increasingly as one aspect of this analysis. With this chapter, an examination is provided of the British social realism films of the late 1950s and 1960s to demonstrate not the impact and benefits of urban planning and modernity, but rather the types of places left behind. There was a rash of films released in Britain from the late 1950s onwards that focused on social realistic domestic situations but which utilised the post-industrial urban landscape as a backcloth or setting. Films such as *Room at the Top* and *A Taste of Honey* were considered innovative when released, for their revelation of the British working class at a time when the working classes had been largely excluded from cinematic depictions, and their depiction of community, urban landscapes and an attachment to place. Comparison is drawn with British films from the immediate postwar area, and the argument put forward is that there are both continuities and differences between the uses of urban place in the narrative as locations for action that have been depicted in cinema for decades. A deeper reading of cinematic representations may not only assist in our reading of the urban, but can also assist in how observers and professionals might learn and understand how particular people and communities possess attachments to particular urban landscapes, even if they have not been created by an urban planning process.

The British social realism films of the late 1950s and 1960s were defined in opposition to the middle-class comedies and the somewhat backward-looking war films of the immediate postwar period. The films revealed a great deal about the working class at a time when the working classes had been largely excluded from narrative cinematic depictions, but they also revealed a great deal in relation to community, landscape and an attachment to place. Films such as *Room at the Top, Look Back in Anger, A Kind of Loving, A Taste of Honey, Saturday Night and Sunday Morning, This Sporting Life* and *Billy Liar* focused on what may be thought of as the 'real' in society. As Hill remarks, these films derive from 'a variety of cultural and political assumptions about the workings of society and the role within society that cinema should play' (Hill, 1986, p 177). Lowenstein (2000) argues that the films were welcomed by audiences and reviewers at the time because they marked a change in direction for British cinema and focused on life as it was being experienced at the time by large sections of society, often focusing on sensitive or controversial issues.

By contrast, the British narrative films of the 1945-55 period tended to focus on middle-class subjects, whimsical comedies set within a pre-defined institutional, political and cultural context that was fairly static. Sir Michael Balcon, Ealing Studios' producer, had set out to make films that projected Britain and the British people, and Charles Barr (1993) has suggested that Ealing Studios films imagined the nation as a relatively centred, stable and consensual community. As was mentioned briefly in Chapter Two, films such as *Passport to Pimlico*, *Whisky Galore*, *The Titfield Thunderbolt*, *The Man in the White Suit* and *Hobson's Choice* all depict a class–ridden community where the narrative takes place within the established class structure, and where landscape is portrayed as a background and less important feature other than to provide context. The Ealing comedies often depict a community attempting to break free from the nation or from control, or are portrayed geographically as being at the periphery (defined in various ways) of Britain.

This chapter attempts to compare and contrast urban landscape and place within British films of the 1955-65 period with those of the previous 10 years. The aim is to assess, in the spirit of Higson (1984, 2000), how and to what extent there are continuities and differences between the use of urban place in the narrative as locations for action. The key films selected for analysis are drawn from the above titles. The argument put forward is that what might be termed the traditional approach of commentators towards social realism films of the late 1950s and 1960s is misleading. Social realism films offer a unique sense of urban place as an essential component of narrative and develop a genre that breaks new ground in contrast to British

Legacy of the industrial age: Lancashire Cotton Mills

film output of the 1940s and 1950s, and we can learn much from how modernity, and societies struggling to cope with modernity, are depicted. But there are also many similarities with the British films of the earlier period that suggests that the genre requires sensitivity in any analysis. This also requires a reconsideration of the contribution of the films of the period 1945-55 to interpretations of landscape, place and urban change.

GEOGRAPHIES OF URBAN CINEMATIC LANDSCAPES

Nowell-Smith (2001) has suggested that the increasing role of film studios and production companies in the early 20th century made a casualty of the built environment in cinema. The retreat into the studio marked the entry of the artificial into filmmaking – the use of artificial snow within supposedly outside studio shots and the cinematic highway backdrop of lovers riding along in a car. And although outside shots and the development of film sets enabled a degree of authenticity in the representation of places, it did not mask the fact that these cinematic geographies were completely manufactured. In some cases, this was intentional from the outset, such as in Fritz Lang's *Metropolis* of 1927 that created an imagined dystopian city. In other cases, built environments were recreated for film sets but often appeared false in comparison to the real, such as in Powell and Pressburger's *Black Narcissus* of 1947.

The use of urban landscapes for the setting of films takes varied forms, and Nowell-Smith (2001) has identified two typologies of cinematic urban landscapes. These comprise: first, studio urban landscapes, possibly employing special effects and popular with film noirs, that serve to represent everything that is dark and dangerous about city living (Lang's *Metropolis* of 1927 and Ridley Scott's *Blade Runner* of 1982); and second, location urban landscapes, popular in Britain in the 1940s, 1950s and 1960s, where places are recognisable either by setting and/or by name (the Boutling Brothers' *Brighton Rock* of 1947 and Tony Richardson's *A Taste of Honey* of 1961, both of which represent quite clearly Brighton on the South England coast and Salford, Manchester, respectively). This typology is a little simplistic, however, since one can additionally think of the use of specific places to falsely represent other geographies (the use of Snowdonia, North Wales, to represent the Khyber Pass in *Carry On Up the Khyber*, directed by Peter Rogers, 1967), and the use of specific places to represent more anonymous urban industrial or post-industrial landscapes that are symbiotic of wider socio-political issues (see, for example, *Room at the Top*, directed by Jack Clayton, 1959, and Mike Leigh's use of London as the setting for *Naked*, 1993). Films occupying the space of the latter category – anonymous industrial and post-industrial landscapes – form the principal subject matter of this chapter.

Set amidst a rapidly changing modern urban environment, and usually seen as representing social realism and some sort of urban wasteland (Hill, 1986), Mason (2001) has suggested that films set on locations within these industrial urban spaces are noted for their sparse anonymity, the evidence of capital, busy thoroughfares, and familiar architectural landmarks. In a British context especially in the early 1960s, the depictions display a post-industrial legacy of rooftops of terraced housing, cobbled streets, children playing in the street, factory chimneys and wet paving stones. Mason (2001), after Hill (1986), describes this particular strand of narrative as 'British social realism' or the British new wave, since they possess structural similarities, and casual links between economics, environment and social behaviour. Hill (1986, p 54) asserts that:

> … the ideas and attitudes expressed by the social problem film and the films of the British "new-wave" do not derive simply from the focus of their subject matter but also from the deployment of certain types of conventions (in accordance with what an audience "accustomed" to the cinema expects) which, then, inevitably structure and constrain the way in which that subject-matter can be presented in the first place.

Mason (2001) contends that the urban landscapes form part of the narrative text to these films since they serve to represent and promote a discourse on particular social conditions of urban existence that appear to be unified. This (selective) construction of the city in turn leads to discourses concerning the lives and portrayal of personal identities and interpersonal communication between family, friends, work colleagues and fellow urban habitants, and the social relations between them. As Mason (2001, p 245) states:

> Through the selective use of locational and temporal zones in the film, emphasis is placed on the isolation and alienation of characters central to the narrative and, through this, typical themes concerning community and economics that may form a generic base for social realist narratives are given a particular postmodern inflection.

Greater Manchester

Higson (2000) and Mason (2001) raise two issues for attention within this debate. The first concerns the use of locations to represent transitional zones for the characters, between the public area and the private area, and what actions and language may be appropriate for one but not the other. The other concerns the loyalties of the central character to particular communities, especially if they are undergoing modernisation and change. Associated with the latter, characters displaying this sense of loyalty within films frequently employ class distinction, social status concerns and relative economic prosperity (or the lack of it) to illustrate graphically the inherent tensions that may exist – possibly within themselves – about their physical, economic or geographical positions. Higson (2000) suggests that such features within the British social realism cinema characterise a shift in representation in the last half of the 20th century in British cinema generally, between images of homogeneity to images of heterogeneity. What are often termed the 'kitchen sink' dramas of the late 1950s and early 1960s are to be seen, for Higson, as the response to inevitable change and the emergence of new socio-cultural and sub-cultural communities organised around ethnic challenges or youth styles and a response to changing local circumstances. These are themes that would eventually be carried through into soap operas on television in the latter half of the 20th century, and it is little surprise to learn that the first of these in Britain, *Coronation Street*, emerged in Greater Manchester in 1960 at exactly this time.

THE IMPORTANCE OF PLACE IN THE SOCIAL REALISM CINEMA

Room at the Top (directed by Jack Clayton, 1959) was one of the films that launched the British social realism period in British cinema. Following the life of Joe Lampton on his arrival in a new job in the treasurer's department at the town hall of a northern industrial town in the immediate postwar era, the film depicts a character that is ambitious for success both in his career and in his love life. Having escaped from his former community of Dufton to Warnley, Joe is enthused by the new opportunities available to him and tells his work colleague, "It's so different here. I'm going to get it all." He is disadvantaged, however, by his class background and inability to enter into the social ranks he so obviously covets. He views the backdrop landscape of factories and engineering works as signs of success. Viewed from the top of a hill where a greyhound track is located, he says, "Look at all those chimneys. That's money. Beautiful, beautiful brass, belching out every minute of the day and night." The aerial shot from the hill over the town is telling. It provides us with an image of the urban landscape, its commercial activity, its perceived class structure, and, when associated with Joe's ambitions, reveals success in the eye of someone who has just

Prince's Wharf, River Avon

arrived in a changing and developing city for the first time. The community he has left behind could not be more different in many ways: the bombed-out shell of his house where his parents had been killed in the war, the desolate and still devastated urban environment, the meagre and ambitious-less lives of his uncle and aunt.

Later in the film, Joe drives Alice, a culturally aware married French woman working within an amateur dramatics company, to Sparrow Hill, overlooking the town. This scene represents an escape for Alice and her loveless marriage but it also signifies a different representation for Joe – one of possibilities. Against the backdrop of industrial chimneys and the sound of wagons being shunted in the railway yard and children playing nearby but out of sight, they embark on a relationship that will ultimately end in turmoil. Several scenes later, Joe is viewed with his friend and work colleague, waiting for a bus on a hill overlooking the town with the same urban industrial backdrop.

When the film was released in 1959, critics were delighted by its representation of urban and northern industrial landscapes and its fearless approach for dealing with not talked about issues such as adultery, sex, pregnancy and class. Leonard Mosley, writing a review in *The Daily Express*, stated:

> *Room at the Top* was the real eye-opener for me – the real proof that something had happened in the cinema. For here was a British film which, at long last, got its teeth into those subjects which have always been part and parcel of our lives, but have hitherto been taboo subjects on the prissy British screen…. It is savagely frank and brutally truthful. (quoted in Lowenstein, 2000, p 224)

Critics hailed the film for its focus on working-class characters from the North of England. For Hill (1986), this represented a debt to the documentary style of the Free Cinema of the 1930s and its depictions of English working-class life. Quigley also commented at the time, 'At last, at long last, a British film that talks about life here today … slap in the middle of the dissolving and reforming social patterns of our time and place' (quoted in Hill, 1986, p 136). With the onset of the 'angry young men' of the late 1950s, such as John Osborne, this new subject matter appeared to reflect wider changes in the social fabric of the country.

For Hill (2000), too, the social realism films such as *Room at the Top* were defined in opposition to the middle-class comedies and pre-war perspectives films of the period. Hill contends that the focus on the real was not necessarily deliberate; rather, it was the product of a variety of cultural and political assumptions about the workings of society and the role within society that cinema should play. The working class were not portrayed simply as the working class but as the working class within a distinctive period of social and economic change in Britain.

Echoing the work of Castells (1989) on places in the face of globalisation, Hill (2000, p 250) suggests that the new realism period in cinema of the 1956-63 period reveals 'an anxiety about the demise of the "traditional" working class, associated with work, community and an attachment to place, in the face of consumerism, mass culture and suburbanisation…'. In his earlier work, Hill (1986) argues that it is place, rather than action, that assumes importance within the narrative. Rather than place providing a setting for narratively significant action, it is insignificant action that provides the pretext for visual display of place.

The next section considers briefly two films from the social realism period for further analysis. These are *A Taste of Honey* (directed by Tony Richardson, 1961) and *A Kind of Loving* (directed by John Schlesinger, 1962).

Salford today, a very different depiction to *A Taste of Honey*, 1961

A Taste of Honey

Tony Richardson's decision to film Shelagh Delaney's script was his first venture into the northern industrial landscape and was shot on location in Salford, Manchester. The film portrays Jo, the teenage schoolgirl of an unmarried mother, eager to escape the drudgery of her domestic situation and of her urban life. The film weaves a relatively simplistic story around Jo's relationship to her mother, Helen, her mother's boyfriend, her casual meeting and relationship with Jimmy, the ship's cook who was black, and with Geoffrey, the young gay man that eventually, she relies on in having to deal with her pregnancy and who becomes her surrogate 'mother'. Good accounts of the film's subject have been written by Higson (1984) and Lovell (1990), and so this section restricts discussion to the representation of place in the film.

The film constantly depicts northern urban landscapes, with rooftop panoramas, factory chimneys, terraced housing and cobbled streets. Children are seen playing around the streets or in back alleys, and Jo and her mother are viewed ascending and descending long flights of steps between terraced houses across various hills of the town, representing their search for a new utopia and places to live. In its representation of a distinct urban and regional geography, there are similarities here to *Room at the Top*. Jo walks back along the side of the polluted canal from school against the backdrop of a post-industrial landscape of mills, chimneys, ships and gasometers. When she meets and confides in Geoffrey about her pregnancy, the location is in a park on a hill overlooking the town, an unromantic setting for the romantic moment in the film when Geoffrey asks Jo to marry him. The location and the subject matter reveal flights of fancy, a temporary escape out and above the town into make believe. The parkland setting mirrors *Room at the Top* – for both Jo and Helen, the park is an escape from urban life and its social problems; for Geoffrey and Jo, the setting is one of opportunism and reflection simultaneously.

The day trip away to Blackpool emphasises the escapism for Helen, Jo and Helen's boyfriend, Peter, away from the urban landscape; the ride in Peter's new car, the excursion to the seaside with fairground rides, the use of magic mirrors to reflect their lives and the visit to Peter's new bungalow which, as Helen points out in awe in contrast to Salford housing, is "A bungalow with bay windows and crazy-paving!"

These structures created a particular landscape character in northern cities

Lovell (1990) suggests that the urban landscape setting of *A Taste of Honey* draws attention to itself simply because it warrants the viewer to pay attention to the pictorial beauty of the setting. For this reason, the film's action is slowed down by the topography; the townscapes undergoing transition from industrial to post-industrial sites, the modern movement in full swing, become sites of personal expression as well as providing a sense of realism to the narrative. This is reflected in *The Guardian*'s review on the film's release in 1961: '[*A Taste of Honey*] is memorable ... for the air of naturalness with which the words have, so to speak, been taken out of a small stage set and put into the large, drab, yet picturesque hurly-burly of a Northern industrial town' (quoted in Higson, 1984, p 9).

A Kind of Loving

A Kind of Loving was directed by John Schlesigner and released in 1962. With audiences having already been able to view *Room at the Top*, *Look Back in Anger*, *Saturday Night and Sunday Morning* and *A Taste of Honey* by the time of the release of *A Kind of Loving*, this particular genre of social realism films may have been starting to be established at this time. The film follows the fortunes of Vic, a draughtsman employed at the local factory, and his lust after Ingrid, a secretary at the same establishment. Ingrid lives with her mother who clearly disapproves of the relationship. When Ingrid becomes pregnant, Vic marries her but after the marriage Vic realises that he does not love her. Ingrid comes from a slightly different social background to Vic; she lives in a suburban development on a hill overlooking the industrial landscape of factories and terraced streets, the latter the home of Vic. When Vic and Ingrid are 'courting', Vic is shown making the long walk down the stone steps to the older part of the town, with panoramic shots reminiscent of both *Room at the Top* and *A Taste of Honey*. He meets her in the Victorian park on the hill overlooking the town, with a backdrop of a railway viaduct, shunting goods trains and textile mills. For this couple, this marks escapism, but unlike *Room at the Top* and *A Taste of Honey*, the escapism for Vic eventually becomes one of escapism from a loveless marriage. He talks of going abroad and of not being able to stand the sight of her at times.

The area is changing, and so too are the people. Vic's father visits his daughter and brother-in-law in a new flat, and from her window remarks: "It's changed a bit since the last time I was around here. Look, that's where the Coach and Horses stood." The flats mark a new era and optimism for the family and yet, at the same time, the family cannot help but be reminded of their spatial situation – at the end of the new flat block lies an enormous industrial chimney.

A Kind of Loving is similar to *A Taste of Honey* and *Room at the Top* for its portrayal of working-class people's supposed enthusiasm for casual sexual encounters and ambition for change; the lead characters are disappointed by their minor escapism opportunities within the narrative and once they achieve their escapism, they come back down to earth with a very solid bump in the same town, within the same sort of employment, and within the same class and social structure. The geography of place is important for it acts as a context for the narrative but also sets parameters for the characters' lives and their (in)ability to leave their places. The next section goes on to discuss aspects of this geographical context within these narratives in more detail.

St George's Hall, Bradford; Victorian buildings such as these were emblematic of a bygone era that alienated the younger characters in many of the 'kitchen sink' dramas

A NEW ERA? WORKING-CLASS CHARACTERS AND INDUSTRIAL LANDSCAPES IN CINEMA

Higson (1984) pays particular attention to what he terms 'That long shot of our town from that hill', a symbiotic shot from the top of a town or city over the rooftops of terraced housing and usually depicting church spires and factory chimneys. The 'long shot' is organised as pure spectacle, and situates the viewer in a high vantage point. The shot works, argues Higson (1984), because it is organised around the twin poles of presence/absence, and 'around the paradox of the sure and centrally embracing view and the overwhelming vulnerability of the subject' (1984, p 19). The long shot is used to particular effect in *A Taste of Honey*, but it was also used within *Room at the Top*, as noted above. Within *This Sporting Life* (directed by Lindsay Anderson, 1963), it is used to depict Richard Harris's character's window and view from a boarding house in the backstreets of an industrial town. Higson marks out the importance of the long shot in the 'kitchen sink' dramas of this time, not just to display the spatial setting of the film and narrative, but also to situate the characters and their lives into a particular sense of place.

For Higson (1984), and Lovell (1990), such situationalism heralded a new genre in British cinema in the late 1950s and early 1960s that had a marked impact on film and television after this time; the British soap opera, *Coronation Street*, for example, utilised the 'long shot' in its opening titles sequence on broadcast in 1960, and it is still used in parts to this day. Furthermore, the depiction of northern industrial landscapes and working-class people, as Anderson pointed out in Lowenstein (2000), marked the reduced importance and status awarded to London and southern-centric British characters in film and television. But to what extent did the portrayal of the northern landscape and northern people in films after 1959, a concentration on moves toward a modern city, mark a complete change for British cinema? The next section goes on to discuss British cinema in the 1940s and 1950s with reference to two films, *The Man in the White Suit* (directed by Alexander Mackendrick, 1951) and *Hobson's Choice* (directed by David Lean, 1954).

The Man in the White Suit

As one of Ealing Studios' most successful comedies, *The Man in the White Suit* is set within a Lancashire mill town and focuses on Alec Guinness's flawed scientist character and his attempts to develop a textile that does not get dirty or wear out. The story has been analysed comprehensively by Barr (1993) and it is not necessary to repeat the narrative here. The reason why this film has been chosen to be assessed here is because of its similar northern industrial location and the importance attached to urban landscapes as a context for the narrative.

The opening shot of the film encapsulates the location immediately: industrial and railway landscapes and a northern city location. From the outset Mackendrick utilises documentary-style shots and voiceovers to place the narrative within a working-class frame. On this latter regard, there are close similarities here to the opening shots of *Saturday Night and Sunday Morning* and of the British documentary movement films from wartime, of government public information films portraying industrial output as part of the 'war effort'. The camera captures Guinness's character walking towards the mill, along terraced houses and cobbled streets and beneath railway viaducts, where children are playing in the streets and alleyways.

The world's first industrial suburb: Ancoats, next to Rochdale Canal

Again there are parallels here with the social realism films of the latter 1950s and early 1960s. Guinness's character gets himself into trouble with the mill owners and his visit to one of their houses, situated overlooking the town and industrial output, is reminiscent of what follows later in the decade in the 'kitchen sink' dramas. The mill owner's house is located in a prominent position on a hill near the town and is almost identical to shots used later in *Room at the Top*. As Joe Lampton would have remarked in the latter film, "Look at all those chimneys. That's money." In fact, although the cinematic landscape is meant to portray money and class distinctions between workers and capitalists, Alec Guinness's character is quite unlike Joe Lampton. Lampton has ambition and this is one of the factors that led to his move to the city from an outlying community – that is, intra-urban migration. Guinness's character, on the other hand, is constrained by the urban environment, and within *The Man in the White Suit*, when Guinness and Joan Greenwood are walking on top of a hill, the former states, "I hate this town, this mill, everything. I want to see the world beyond this little town", a line that could have been stated – and was in subtle variation – by Vic in *A Kind of Loving*.

We see here, therefore, clear parallels between the northern industrial urban setting for *The Man in the White Suit* and the 'kitchen sink' dramas developed 10 years later, but we are also able to identify similar problems of lead characters wanting to escape their urban settings or their urban lives. In cinematic terms, there are also parallels between setting characters high up on hills overlooking the town and walking or running along wet cobbled terraced streets, with the sound of children playing and steam trains shunting in the goods yard.

Hobson's Choice

Hobson's Choice was directed by David Lean in 1954 and is set within the industrial urban location of Salford, Manchester. Again, here, *Hobson's Choice* is another film set within Lancashire in northern England. The film follows the story of a cantankerous businessman and shoemaker, Hobson, played by Charles Laughton, living with his three unmarried daughters, their duties toward their father and their longing to escape his clutches and domestic constraints for lives of their own. The eldest of the daughters, Maggie, takes the initiative herself, sets up business with Will Mossop, one of the

A former textile mill, Rochdale, now put to
community use

shoemakers at Hobson's, marries him, and gradually takes business away from her father as the latter's social life starts to unravel following his daughters' move from home.

The film opens characteristically with shots of the urban fabric: it is raining heavily, the cobbled streets are deserted, the rooftops of terraced houses and shops shine and the camera focuses on the shoemaker's sign of Hobson's shop as it swings noisily in the high winds and rain. *Hobson's Choice* is set within Edwardian times and is therefore quite distinct in its historic setting than either *The Man in the White Suit* or the 'kitchen sink' dramas of the late 1950s and early 1960s. Nevertheless, the similarities between the importance of urban setting and even social livelihoods between *Hobson's Choice* and these other films are noteworthy. There are the walks along the cobbled streets and terraced housing, the groups of gossiping women, children playing in back alleys and a Salvation Army band marching down the middle of the road.

In one part of the film, Maggie meets Will in Peel Park, situated on a hill above the town with views overlooking the mill chimneys and terraced housing. The pair have escaped the shoe shop and their strictly separate social and professional lives, and Maggie's father's watchful eye. They can now relax, notwithstanding the fact that Maggie wants to make a statement about her intentions to other people in the park, including her two sisters and their courtiers, and sit down on the banks of the canal, opposite a factory, mill and a polluted waterway. Similar to the settings in *Saturday Night and Sunday Morning*, *A Kind of Loving*, *A Taste of Honey* and other social realism films, the river or canal bank usually forms the distinctly unromantic backcloth for a romantic setting between the lead characters. A similar effect is used when Maggie propositions Will to kiss her in an archway leading to a culverted alleyway within terraced housing. With parallels to some of the male characters in the later social realism films, particularly Joe Lampton in *Room at the Top*, Will Mossop says in reference to the urban living conditions he had been experiencing, "This is a stinking little pond and I'm getting out of it!" On Will and Maggie's wedding day, the setting is a wet churchyard full of slightly toppled gravestones and tombs, high on a hill overlooking the industrial town. Could it be the same churchyard utilised to similar effect by Tony Richardson in *A Taste of Honey* where Jo and Geoffrey talk about her pregnancy?

David Lean appears to be one of the first directors to utilise both the canal scene and the 'long shot' over the town from the hill, and possibly set in motion thoughts of how the most unglamorous

Shipyard walls

urban landscape could be useful in forming a frame to social change and human desires.

BRITISH SOCIAL REALISM AND THE 1940s AND 1950s COMPARED

Higson (2000) contrasts the social realism films with the British films of the late 1940s onwards. Sir Michael Balcon, the producer of Ealing Studios, had set about during the Second World War to make films at Ealing that projected Britain and the British image (Barr, 1993). Barr has argued that Ealing Studios films imagined the nation as a community, and a relatively centred, stable and consensual community. For Higson (2000), these films represent a vision of the plural, complex, heterogeneous and hybrid nation, and a sense of multiple British identities. Interestingly, he marks out some of the Ealing films of the immediate postwar era for specific attention, and specifically contrasts these with some of the social realism films. His intention here is not to identify similar use of landscapes and geography as the essential backcloth to the narrative, but rather to signify another element that runs through both sets of films: 'liminal spaces'. For Higson (2000), liminal spaces are represented in film in the late 1940s and early 1960s. They are the spaces at the margins of the nation, and are particularly effective in films in order for the audience to grasp the true meaning of the nation itself. He contrasts both *Passport to Pimlico* (directed by Henry Cornelius, 1949) and *Whisky Galore* (directed by Alexander Mackendrick, 1949) with *Saturday Night and Sunday Morning* (directed by Karel Reisz, 1960) and *Billy Liar* (directed by John Schlesigner, 1963). The liminal space in each film is quite marked and the use of the word 'margin' is not meant in a geographically peripheral sense alone, but variedly, in relation to the isolation of the characters and space in combination from either elsewhere or other communities of people.

For *Passport to Pimlico*, for example, this reflects the isolation of the people of Pimlico from Britain by Whitehall officials when it is discovered that part of their community is Burgundia, foreign soil, within which British laws cannot apply. For *Billy Liar*, the liminal space concerns the fictional state of Ambrosia, created within Billy's dreams, where he rules and governs, separate from the tedious daily existence he finds himself within. Both sets of films reflect alienation from the metropolitan centre of Britain. But this contrast by Higson

(2000), although valuable, is far more complex than his comparisons suggest and, I would argue, reflects only some of the issues that warrant comparative attention.

CONCLUSIONS

A theme of this chapter has been that the traditional approach of commentators towards social realism films of the late 1950s and 1960s specific to landscape and setting has been misleading. Social realism films have offered a unique sense of place as an essential component of the narrative and did develop a new genre in contrast to British film output of the 1940s and 1950s. But there are also many similarities with some of the British films of the earlier period 1945-55, particularly with regard to use and interpretations of landscape and place, and alienation of the characters to their changing environments.

Directors prior to 1955 were distinctly aware of space, how to treat and use space within the narrative, and how to embellish narratives by providing distinct locations to shape human stories. 'The long shot of our town from that hill', identified by Higson (1984) as being a distinctive element within the new genre of social realism films of the latter 1950s and early 1960s, was apparent earlier in British films, particularly those set in northern England. These films also, in contrast to Lindsay Anderson's opinion, also utilised northern working-class characters, and are in marked contrast to much of British film output at this time. So why have commentators decided to overlook these earlier films in relation to landscape, place and change as an element of cinema narrative?

One possible reason for this oversight, intentional or deliberate, is that the earlier period films were comedies. For this reason, their comedy context may be one of the reasons why their underlying social realism narratives (and concomitant landscapes) have been played down. If *The Man in the White Suit* and *Hobson's Choice* had not been comedies, for example, perhaps their significant contribution to our understanding of the changing northern industrial and urbanised landscape for social realism narratives may have been acknowledged. Both films, after all, depict some serious social issues: employee repression and harassment, class structure and relationships and community and political tensions for *The Man in the White Suit*; domestic strife and violence, alcoholism and class structures for *Hobson's Choice*. Their status as comedies should not overwhelm the narrative and landscape elements to the films and the importance that these would have formed in setting patterns for later British films. Commentators' assertions that the use of a northern urban landscape forms an essential element to the emergence of a new social realism genre in the latter 1950s is, as a consequence, overstated. This period may have marked a watershed in socioeconomic and political terms for Britain, and this undoubtedly influenced the way filmmakers started to shoot films, but the use of landscape and realism in film narrative had already been proven.

The Albert Dock, Liverpool

SIX

"It's like living in heaven up here!"

Liverpool's skyline, from the 1970s and 2000s

Alexandra Road Estate, Camden, 1972–78

The Barbican, a complex of over 2,000 apartments across 35 acres

Trellick Tower, North Kensington, Erno Goldfinger's 31-storey tower of 1972; each bridge is modelled on the dimensions of a railway carriage

The Brunswick Centre, Bloomsbury; mixed use development from the mid-1960s

The Heygate Estate, Walworth, from 1974; soon to be demolished

Hall Ings, Bradford, comprehensive development from the 1960s and home to some not-so-grand architecture

London Wall; the original Roman-defined defence line survived for over 1,600 years; this road was developed after 1957

Hove seafront where the modern encroaches on the Georgian and Victorian

Institute of Education, Woburn Square, to a design by Sir Denys Lasdun

Newcastle's skyline changed in the 1960s under the city leadership of Thomas Daniel Smith

St Alphage House, Moorgate, neatly built around the bombed out remains of St Alphage Church

Colston Tower, Bristol, 1973, subject of recent refurbishment

Turnpike House, Clerkenwell; local authority housing and the subject of Saint Etienne's 'Tales from Turnpike House' album from 2005

SEVEN

"The planners did their best." Utilising irony and prose to protect the past

INTRODUCTION

The introduction of film and early television in Britain enabled the arts, factual material and expert opinion to be communicated to a wider audience (Attenborough, 2002). This was particularly true of town planning, which was in its ascendancy during the 1940s and 1950s, and was playing a prominent role in coordinating physical restructuring, rebuilding or planning new cities, and helping to create better societies (Aldridge, 1979; Hardy, 1991). At a time when planning in the UK possessed very little by way of formal public consultation processes to enable the public to either receive detailed information or express opinion about the form of change occurring (Ward, 2002), the media and film played a vital role in communicating plans and visions to a wider audience (Gold and Ward, 1997). Broadcasters found these serious (possibly even dull) subject matters difficult to convey and to transmit to a mass audience, and various approaches and innovative programming were attempted between the 1930s and 1970s (Wyver, 1989; Walker, 1993). One artist who played a pivotal role in developing television arts documentaries and who possessed knowledge and strong opinions on planning and development was John Betjeman (1906–84), later to become Poet Laureate.

Betjeman did not possess formal qualifications in architecture, planning or the arts, but his work as an associated editor of the

Architectural Review had enabled him to gain some experience on the subject, and he had been a regular performer on arts broadcasts on the radio (Lycett Green, 1997). From the number of radio and film broadcast commissions he undertook, he appears to have relished the opportunity to utilise the new medium of television to educate and entertain the public. But Betjeman also adopted a unique approach to television filmmaking that involved a collaborative, hands-on approach with film crews and film production. In communicating the processes of physical change in cities and the countryside to a mass audience, Betjeman was assisting in performing an educative and informative role but, additionally, took the opportunity to provide his own personal critiques on the form of reconstruction and planning that was occurring.

Betjeman utilised the new medium of television to campaign for subjects that interested him personally: Georgian and Victorian architecture, old railway stations and the last vestiges of Edwardian Britain. As a skilful player of television and someone who was totally at ease in front of the camera, Betjeman turned many of his television broadcasts into propaganda statements against those issues he perceived as threatening Britain and against those in charge of restructuring the state (Tewdwr-Jones, 1999, 2005). He used film to juxtapose the official expertise from the planners and government, a particular filmic style of the period, with his own perspectives that he genuinely believed to be the 'voice of the people' (Lycett Green, 1997).

This chapter considers the films of John Betjeman, his contribution to planning and filming on early British television and, in so doing, presents the argument that he may be seen to constitute an alternative planning expert during the modernist project. More particularly, we need to assess broadly the importance of broadcasting in bringing development, modernism and conservation issues to a wider audience at a time when the public had very little opportunity to be involved in development decisions. The subject is also of direct relevance and interest for an academic audience, in reassessing the history of planning between the 1930s and 1970s, not only through historical archives, but also via film, through the eyes and words of those attempting to depict the changing landscape to the public through celluloid. We also need to understand the desire and attraction of televising development, physical change and 20th-century architectural issues for a television audience. It may be the case that to many people, the representations of change to towns and cities through the medium of television, provided through the films of John Betjeman especially, was a source of interest and, possibly, an attraction in itself.

Following a brief review of the development of town planning in the 20th century and the history of film relating to planning and development, attention is focused on the modernity project, its components and attributes. The chapter focuses on the role of John Betjeman who was, admittedly, just one of a number of commentators providing personal perspectives on assessing physical change in Britain. Betjeman's life and work is discussed briefly, together with an assessment of his broadcasting work, the influences on his work and the people he associated with. Attention is then paid to two of his television series as brief case studies: Jonathan Stedall's *Wales and the West*, a series of 12 programmes Betjeman made for Television Wales and the West (TWW) in 1962-63, and three programmes he made for Edward Mirzoeff's *Bird's-Eye View* series for the BBC in 1969-71. A final concluding section draws together the work and attempts to assess Betjeman's contribution to arts filmmaking in Britain.

THE DEVELOPMENT OF 20TH-CENTURY TOWN PLANNING

In the 1920s and 1930s, the proactive role for urban planning – creating better places for people in the interests of better housing, improved public health, better housing standards – was shadowed by a reactive role intended to control, stop or regulate development interests in the name of the preservation of agricultural land; Stephen Crow describes this ascendancy of development control as 'the child that grew up in the cold' in the history of the profession (Crow, 1996). Planning from the 1930s had to henceforth undertake both roles simultaneously: to plan ahead and to limit development and to create plans embodying vision while being pragmatic.

In the late 1920s and 1930s, rising stars of the British literati such as John Betjeman, Dylan Thomas, George Orwell, and J.B. Priestley, had independently expressed concern about, inter alia, sprawl, community, continued building in the countryside and modernist architecture. Clough Williams-Ellis's book, *England and the octopus*, had been published in 1928 with an epilogue by Patrick Abercrombie, calling for more civilised, ordered, forms of planning (Williams-Ellis, 1928). The octopus in the book's title symbolically represented urban sprawl, with the tentacles of ribbon development spreading out haphazardly from the large towns and cities, encroaching on

The old town, Bath

the surrounding tranquil countryside. It was the forerunner of the sentiments of the CPRE that Williams-Ellis, Abercrombie and Betjeman helped found – a desire and recognition for planning but planning that contained urban areas rather than expanded them.

We may regard these reactions not only in the context of the undesirability of urban expansion (Elson, 1986), but also in terms of the perceived threat to social order and cultural conditions associated with traditional ways of life in the countryside (Mingay, 1991; Humphries and Hopwood, 2000). Britain's cities were undergoing rapid physical change in the 1930s, thanks to the changing economic base, the decline of heavy industry and the growth of the service sector, and – within some larger urban areas – through the rise of car ownership and the desire to accommodate the car through road building. The countryside, by contrast, was largely untouched, even if British agriculture was already in decline and rural areas had witnessed large-scale migration from the rural to the urban. It appears as though the fight to protect the old order rested on a campaign by the British literati to protect rural areas from 'foreign' architecture (of new developments such as petrol stations in vernacular form) and the societal structure breakdowns that urbanisation was perceived to bring to areas. It was a reconstruction of the countryside as a rural idyll that also symbolised much more than local vernaculars, since the 'threatened rural' was 'a new vision of the nation as England, which was itself reduced to a particular vision of the South Country' (Higson, 1997, p 274). The threat to the country, to a particular way of life, was from urbanisation, a process that was perceived to destroy the virtues and values of the countryside, described by Richards (1997, p 102) as 'freedom, stability, tradition, peacefulness and spirituality'.

The impact of the Second World War on the economy of the country and the need to rebuild towns and cities in the aftermath of war devastation necessitated a new central role for planning in coordinating change, improving economic growth and organising space (HM Government, 1940, 1942a, 1942b). Between 1939 and 1945, Britain had lost 264,433 members of the armed forces, 30,248 merchant navy seamen and 60,595 civilians (Gilbert, 1990). A quarter of Britain's wealth had been used on the war effort, and the country became reliant on US Lend-Lease. One third of the total housing stock had been damaged or destroyed by enemy action, and other buildings such as factories, schools and hospitals, had also been targeted (Childs, 2001). Many of Britain's cities had been blitzed and large parts of Coventry, Swansea, Bristol and the City of London, to name but four, were reduced to rubble. Britain's public voted the wartime Prime Minister Winston Churchill out of office at the 1945 General Election and a new socialist Labour government, led by Clement Attlee, was elected and charged with the task of reconstruction. In 1947, a modern planning system was created with the introduction of the Town and Country Planning Act, building on the centralising planning legislation (creating a ministry and office of minister for town planning) passed during the war years. The rebuilding of urban areas after 1945 and through to the early 1970s, during the modernist era, was planning at its height (Ward, 1994). Planning, as a component of the welfare state in the UK, was recognised as a primary element of the state's duty to command and control within a country that was set in austerity, but was optimistic, longed for better conditions and looked forward (Bullock, 2002). But social and economic circumstances were changing rapidly.

During the 1950s and early 1960s, significant increases in population, greater mobility, higher levels of car ownership and greater traffic movement, and economic rejuvenation had given the country new prosperity (Sked, 1979). Planning was criticised for its over-optimism and its inability to update plans quickly, perhaps partly because the visions were not realised in the way people had imagined (Gold, 1997; Docter, 2000), and also because economic and social prosperity beyond expectations had been achieved *despite* a political commitment and reliance on planning and state control (Hopkins, 1964, Geraghty, 2000).

MODERNITY, EXPERTS AND THE USE OF FILM

Berman (1982) suggests that modernity may be considered from two perspectives: as a project that develops over time and influences and explains the development of modern society; and as an experience of living within, and sometimes against, the modernisation project. Jervis also defines modernity as 'the experience of the world constantly changing, constantly engendering a past out of the death of the here and now, and constantly reproducing "here and now" as the present, the contemporary, the fashionable' (Jervis, 1998, p 6). But he also states that the project of modernity is also associated with an orientation and rational control of the environment, to understand it but also to transform it. Time and space are separated, and there is an emphasis on technology, the industrialisation of production, demographic upheavals, rapid urban growth and mass communications.

Giddens (1990, p 27) refers to these processes as the development of social relations that are not location specific and of 'disembedding mechanisms' that lift out social relations to give rise to new mechanisms across large time–space distances; one of these mechanisms, and a feature of modernity, is the rise of experts and technical and professional expertise. For Giddens, a mark of modernity is the way in which knowledge is continually gathered, examined and reformed in the light of new evidence; this allows for rational control but also suggests continual change or upheaval (Giddens, 1990, p 53). The nation state is pre-eminent in controlling and supporting citizens through bureaucratic arrangements, and relies on and trusts technical and professional knowledge and the experts that propagate the knowledge (Clarke, 1997).

But enthusiasm for modernity is often double-edged: Britain in the period 1945-51 celebrated new architecture, improved housing conditions, faster transport and economic growth (Hennessey, 1994), but was also agitated by the onset of change and the effect this would have on traditional ways of life, a particular feature of modernity and society (O'Shea, 1996). Berman sums up these dual feelings well, suggesting that it is possible 'to make oneself somehow at home in the maelstrom' (Berman, 1982, p 344), and 'to relish that the process of modernization, even as it exploits and torments us, brings our energies and imaginations too life, drives us to grasp and confront the world that modernization makes, and to strive to make it our own' (p 348). For others, anxiety about the modern world leads to 'the desire to preserve and retain' (Light, 1991, p 145) that has its focus in a concern with the past, described by Wright (1985, p 70) as 'the backward glance which is taken from the edge of a vividly imagined abyss'.

In the postwar period, this attitude was prevalent in Britain. It was as much a concern about the onset of war and its aftermath as a concern about how new development was sweeping the old away. It was also a symptom of concern about the ascendancy of experts and professionals who, people were constantly reminded, 'knew best'. This was a modernisation project where professionals and scientists reordered society according to their own dynamic expertise, and politicians and members of the public 'dare no longer disagree' (Hopkins, 1964, p 375). For Geraghty (2000, p 29), the expert in this sense was 'an imaginary figure who combines almost magical powers in science and technology with a bureaucratic emphasis on planning and detail'. When this argument is placed within the planning history literature, the names of key figures as champions of planning during this era of reconstruction become apparent immediately (for example, Raymond Unwin, Patrick Abercrombie, Frederick Osborn and William Holford).

Today, in an era of television where the highest audience ratings are game shows, soap operas and light entertainment, we may be forgiven for wondering about the appeal of planning and development subject matter as entertaining topics for peak time television viewing. However, during the modernist era in the UK between the 1930s and 1970s, and also perhaps because of the early days of broadcasting when topics for films were not as sophisticated as they are today, there was an excitement apparent on the part of the public who possessed a desire to witness the process of change in a new technologically advanced way. Television provided a useful medium to represent the rapid period of change, socially, politically and architecturally, and – simultaneously – reflect the concern of the British people (Burns, 1986). But television was not the only medium concerned with this ongoing process of change. Cinematic film also focused on changing societal and economic conditions. Charlie Chaplin's *Modern Times* of 1936 – although a comedy – depicted industralisation, Fordism and the effects of economic depression in the US in the 1930s; the output of Ealing Studios between the 1930s and the 1950s had also depicted changing community in Britain, a deliberate policy on the part of its producer, Sir Michael Balcon (Barr, 1993); while the 'kitchen sink' neo-realism films of the late 1950s and early 1960s attempted to provide a more social realistic dimension to film output, depicting working-class characters, social problem narratives and industrial landscapes (Higson, 1984; see also Chapter Five).

The depiction of change to the landscape started to be viewed as a subject for film and television. As discussed in Chapter Four, from the early 1930s, the documentary film movement – founded by John Grierson (Aitken, 1990) – had started to make realist public information films centred on working-class urban conditions (Garside, 1988), and these included *Housing Problems* (1935), *The Smoke Menace* (1937) and *Housing Progress* (1938). This trend continued in the war years with features looking at planning and reconstruction such as *The City* (directed by Alberto Cavalcanti in 1939), *New Towns for Old* of 1942 and *Proud City* of 1946 (Gold and Ward, 1994). Many of these features were commissioned by official agencies, such as the GPO, the Ministry of Information and the Oil and Gas Company. Most of these films are authoritative in style, with factual information, commentaries provided and lectures to camera by experts and officials.

The demise of the British documentary movement coincided with the closure of the Crown Film Unit in the early 1950s, but this did not mean the complete withdrawal of neo-realist cinematic features, since its legacy influenced the realist directors of the 1950s and 1960 in narrative forms and continued in other genres, such as short documentary features of the BTF Unit until the 1970s. Another impact the tradition may have had was in the depiction of the expert and professional talking to the audience and explaining the intricacies of – often – quite dull technical issues. Professor Sir Patrick Abercrombie's prominent role in several of the documentary films in the 1940s (*Proud City*, for example) certainly extended the image of the planner to the public, who was frequently portrayed as a visionary or scientist with a plan to make things better. There is no greater illustration of this than Abercrombie's starring role in Jill Craigie's *The Way We Live* of 1946, an 80-minute feature length, Rank-distributed film about the planning and reconstruction of Plymouth (see Enticknap, 2001; While, 2006). At the start of the film, to images of a gentleman walking amidst Plymouth's few remaining historic buildings, the narrator informs the audience that: "The heroes or villains [of this film], according to your point of view, are two men with a plan: James Paton Watson, the City Engineer, and Professor Patrick Abercrombie. What they have to say is something of a challenge to the way we live." And later in the film, as if to emphasise the mystique surrounding the original thinking of the professional expert, the narrator states: "No one knew what the professor was up to."

Abercrombie's work in the reconstruction of Plymouth and other cities sits alongside Gibson's work on rebuilding Coventry and Sharp's plan for Exeter (While and Tait, 2009). These accounts and depiction of the rational man of science, the expert, have been commented on by Gold and Ward (1997), who suggest that the portrayal of a central hero – 'a planning wizard' – in films related to a desire to make features about planning, development and reconstruction entertaining, informative and forward-looking within a film genre. It was not so much stories about how planners and architects engaged with members of the public in rebuilding towns, but rather about the way planners were transforming landscapes to provide new rational visions of the future, and this relates directly to the modernist arguments of Hopkins quoted earlier. Within the 1950s, this portrayal of the planner as expert had moved on, relegated to second place behind the central messages of building and renewal. But this is in stark contrast to many of the outputs of the British documentary movement in the 1930s that had adopted a realist approach by allowing members of the public to talk directly about their experiences to camera. Nevertheless, the depiction of planners as rational professional experts had already been lodged within the mindsets of audiences by the late 1940s, thanks to the wartime films of the Ministry of Information. Raising the planner to the status of visionary genius on film would always be a hostage to fortune, and possibly lead to serious consequences when modernism started to be questioned more prominently in the latter half of the 20th century. It was even more risqué for film (and therefore audiences) to focus on the planner alone, since, during these formative years, the public placed a reliance on and injected an element of trust into these prominent individuals in the absence of alternative forms of formal public participation within development planning.

SETTING THE SCENE: JOHN BETJEMAN, LANDSCAPE AND HIS FILM INTEREST

John Betjeman was born near Highgate, London. He was educated at Marlborough College and Oxford, but failed to complete his degree. He then taught at various preparatory schools before joining the staff of the *Architectural Review* in 1929. His first book of poems, *Mount Zion*, was published privately (Betjeman, 1931a), while his second book, *Ghastly good taste*, was an architectural commentary (Betjeman, 1933). He was an impassioned defender of Georgian, Victorian and Edwardian architecture at a time when they were unfashionable, doing much to turn opinion in their favour. His numerous works on English architecture include major contributions to the Shell Guide series on the counties of England.

Betjeman's poetry also celebrated architecture, but concentrated mainly on middle-class social life in the metropolitan suburbs and Home Counties. During the 1930s and 1940s, he wrote a considerable quantity of poetry and architectural journalism. After the Second World War, Betjeman returned to his role as poet and architectural critic, and by the 1950s, he was a well-known figure, campaigning for threatened buildings and making frequent appearances on BBC radio and television. His architectural works included *First and last loves* (1952), *The English town in the last hundred years* (1956) and

Brighton and Hove, 'the best looking seaside resort'

English churches (1964, with Basil Clarke). His *Collected poems* (1958) was a bestseller, as was the autobiographical verse cycle, *Summoned by bells* (1960). His poetry collections included *High and low* (1966), *A nip in the air* (1974), *Church poems* (1981) and *Uncollected poems* (1982). He was knighted in 1969 and, after the death of Cecil Day Lewis in 1972, became Poet Laureate.

Betjeman was no stranger to broadcasting by the advent of arts-themed television in the 1950s and 1960s. He commenced a long-lasting relationship with the BBC in 1932. He had been appointed assistant editor of the *Architectural Review* in 1929, and his role in the *Review* involved penning short articles on English architecture, usually in a candid fashion, and even in these early years it was clear that he had strong views on the form and shape of the landscape of Britain that would carry through in his own writings and broadcasts throughout his life. In December 1931, for example, he published an article in the *Architectural Review* entitled 'The death of modernism' that describes the loss of the countryside to rapid industrialisation and the absence of a coherent style of architecture suitable for the times: 'We have prepared and planned the world beyond recognition, and can hardly be blamed for not turning out attention to the rubbish heap' (Betjeman, 1931b).

In 1932, in a speech to the Incorporated Institute of British Decorators, when aged just 25, he remarked further on modernism, suggesting that the future architecture:

> ... would not consist of the varying indigenous styles of a county or a country, but of one style for a continent. The increase of transport, the spread of knowledge, the universality of many materials would cause much of Europe to have the same style. We are being leveled down.... (cited in *The Times*, 22 July 1932)

While employed by the *Review*, in 1934 he also became a film critic for the *Evening Standard*, reviewing over 500 films for the newspaper, although his daughter Candida Lycett Green notes in her compilation of his work that from reading his reviews, it is noticeable that he became bored with simply writing about films and film stars and would write instead about architectural jaunts to a cinema miles out in the London suburbs:

> To alleviate the monotony of studio gossip, first nights and viewing rushes, he started going to see new or celebrated cinemas outside central London in such places as Streatham, Hammersmith, Kilburn, Stepney, Acton, Ealing, Northfields, Edgware, Tooting, and Wood Green, and made observations on the districts in which cinemas did their business. (Lycett Green, 1997, p 5)

He also had a lifelong friendship with the documentary filmmaker, Arthur Elton, from his days at Marlborough, who was, during the 1940s, heading the Ministry of Labour's film documentaries; one of Elton's noted outputs had been *Housing Problems* in 1935, co-produced with Edgar Anstey (see Chapter Four). This friendship may have influenced not only Betjeman's attitude towards films, but may also have shaped his approach to broadcasts and arts documentaries on both radio and television from the 1950s, according to Lycett Green. As Lycett Green notes, 'The revelation of ordinary Britain in short black and white films excited JB the most and these were to influence him and help him when he later began his television career' (Lycett Green, 1997, p 5). In a piece for the *Evening Standard* published on 13 May 1935, his film reviewing writings were already reflecting this interest and the work of the documentary movement in Britain, led by Elton, Anstey and Grierson:

> It occurred to Mr John Grierson, as it has often occurred to me, and even more frequently, I expect, to you, that there is nothing more irritating than the sickening commentaries provided for short films.... The photographs are so good and the scenery they depict is so interesting that it is a pity our enjoyment should be ruined listening to futile jokes and obvious comments. (Betjeman, 1935a)

Betjeman was threatened with the sack for refusing to review Hollywood films and, in a final review piece for the *Evening Standard* on 20 August 1935, he resigned from his post publicly, citing the onset of Hollywood influence on British films as the reason he was unable to continue to review general films for the readers:

> The last great awakening came with *BBC – The Voice of Britain*, John Grierson's documentary film now showing at the Carlton. Here is a film which makes you think and which really is the good old "art" that I was looking for in my early days. I do not think this sort of film, nor indeed the thrilling sort of news-film promised in "The March of Time" series, will supersede the fictional films with stars in them. But they will become vastly more important. (Betjeman, 1935b)

BETJEMAN'S BROADCASTING CAREER

Betjeman's attitude towards the changing face of Britain intensified in the middle of the 20th century, as major redevelopment occurred in parts of London, such as Grosvenor and Berkeley Squares, and in Brighton and Bath, and through the gradual erosion of rural England. A boom in the building of arterial roads and bypasses, of ribbon development, suburbia and housing development, the onset of increased motor car usage and urban renewal programmes clearing away older properties in favour of new and wider road schemes, all occurred more intensively from the 1930s. Betjeman was a key figure in the establishment of the Georgian Group, intending to conserve Georgian buildings and fight plans for redevelopment, and in CPRE. By 1935, Betjeman's foot was firmly in the door of the BBC, after which time he began to work for them in earnest. As Lycett Green recalls, 'He saw the Home Service as a brilliant soapbox from which to expound his views on the despoliation of Britain and the need for careful planning. His scripts were often so libelous that they ended by being heavily cut by his producers' (Lycett Green, 1997, p 73).

Among his series of radio broadcasts were scripts on 'Town tours', 'Seaviews' and 'Built to last'. One radio broadcast, from the Home Service on 8 May 1937, reflects his soapbox approach:

> People who do not live in Swindon consider it a blot on the earth.... Now it flounders like a helpless octopus, spreading its horrid tentacles into quiet untroubled places, waiting no doubt til one long and loathsome tentacle shall twine with that of the vile octopus London and Bristol will stretch out a tentacle to meet it from the West. (Betjeman, 1937)

Meanwhile, a broadcast entitled 'The country town' from 27 June 1939 also provided a lengthy rant on 'progressive development', his loathing for local government and public officials, and a concern that new building design did not match the local vernacular (Betjeman, 1939a). His poetry of this time also contained similar topics, with subjects such as public officials, modernism and development all

Betjeman was called on frequently in Victorian 'save' campaigns: Cromer Pier, Norfolk

ridiculed in 'The town clerk's views', 'Inexpensive progress', 'The planster's vision' and – famously – 'Slough' (Betjeman, 1979).

In 'The town clerk's views', he outpours his frustration with town planning and the concomitant growth of bureaucracy:

> In a few years this country will be looking
> As uniform and tasty as its cooking.
> Hamlets which fall to pass the planners' test
> Will be demolished. We'll build the rest
> To look like Welwyn mixed with Middle West.
> All fields we'll turn to sports grounds, lit at night
> From concrete standards by fluorescent light:
> And all over the land, instead of trees,
> Clean poles and wire will whisper in the breeze.

In the later poem, 'Inexpensive progress', he revisits the debate by criticising the way the country was moving in the 1960s and 1970s, but seems to channel his anger against town planners specifically:

> Let no provincial High Street
> Which might be your or my street
> Look as it used to do,
> But let the chain stores place here
> Their miles of black glass facia
> And traffic thunder through.
>
> And if there is some scenery,
> Some unpretentious greenery,
> Surviving anywhere,
> It does not need protecting
> For soon we'll be erecting
> A Power Station there.
>
> When all our roads are lighted
> By concrete monsters sited
> Like gallows overhead,
> Bathed in the yellow vomit
> Each monster belches from it,
> We'll know that we are dead.

In 1939, in a pamphlet entitled 'Antiquarian prejudice', Betjeman criticises the experts who possessed 'that wonderful gift of turning life to death, of interest to ashes':

> Perhaps long ago the expert really did like acquaints, but now he only likes knowing about first proofs, raw state, etc, etc. His word for 'beautiful" has become "interesting". (Betjeman, 1939b)

In the Second World War, the BBC utilised Betjeman's broadcasts as part of the war effort domestically, and required him to pen homely subjects to keep spirits up. In 1943, he was also appointed to the Ministry of Information Films Division, assisting in making documentaries about Britain's war effort, and was responsible for commissioning a series of films under the title *The Pattern of Britain*. Worried about the scale and nature of rebuilding required in British cities following the Blitz, Betjeman continued to discuss issues relating to architecture, planning and rural preservation directly within his radio broadcasts as a way of raising public awareness, and for influencing those in government. Associated with this broadcast output, Betjeman continued to publish reviews, short articles, poems and periodical columns on similar themes, and these included *The Spectator, The Daily Herald, Punch* and *The Times Literary Supplement*. Having become accustomed to the challenges of broadcasting, and since he always provided entertaining, sometimes controversial prose, on filmic subjects cherished by audiences, he appears to have adapted to television with ease.

By the mid-1950s, Betjeman had become a popular and well-known public figure, appearing on 'The Brains Trust' on radio and in conversation pieces on camera with the likes of Gilbert Harding, Hugh Casson and Kenneth Clark for the BBC. His daughter, Candida Lycett Green, reports that he relished television appearances: 'Despite the fact that many of his peers, even Evelyn Waugh, thought that if you went on television it meant you couldn't have any real integrity, JB appeared more and more' (Lycett Green, 1997, p 101). He was commissioned in 1955 to provide the commentary for 26 short films for Shell entitled *Discovering Britain*, and in 1960-68 made 26 short films for the BBC entitled *ABC of Churches*. He also made three films for the BTF Unit: *John Betjeman Goes By Train* (1962), *A 100 Years Underground* (1964) and *Railways Forever* (1970).

While his broadcasting career on film was being established, he continued to campaign for the preservation of Georgian and Victorian architecture that, by the late 1950s in many British cities, was under threat from redevelopment. Both the Coal Exchange in the City of London and Euston Arch, at Euston station, were demolished in 1962 after hard-fought and very public 'Save' campaigns led by Betjeman (Hillier, 2004). During the 1960s and 1970s, he was also actively involved in the campaign to save London St Pancras station and the Midland Hotel from demolition. Combining his output with formal voluntary roles, he co-founded and became the vice chair of The Victorian Society, and later – in what must be regarded as official recognition of his expertise on the subject – the government appointed him as a member of the Royal Fine Arts Commission.

Among his output of almost 100 film and television works in the 1960s are shorter programmes and commissioned series, including: five further films for Shell (1964); *Betjeman at Random* (four films for the BBC, 1966); *The Picture Theatre* (BBC, 1967); *Tale of Canterbury* (Rediffusion, 1967); *Betjeman's London* (six films for Rediffusion, 1967); and two notable documentary series – 12 short films under the title of *Wales and the West* for TWW in 1962-63, and three programmes as part of the *Bird's-Eye View* series for the BBC in 1969-71. These latter two are worth examining in more detail since, in the case of the TWW series, the films were only rediscovered in October 1993 after having been 'lost' for 30 years. In the case of *Bird's-Eye View*, this series was shown in 1969 in colour on the BBC. It was the first series to pioneer the technique of aerial photography for television from a helicopter and was the most expensive series the BBC had ever commissioned at the time (see Chapter Eight), a mere 10 months following its previously most expensive series, Kenneth Clark's *Civilisation*. Both series offer useful glimpses of Betjeman's approach to filming, including his requirements in the directing of specific films, and his utilisation of subject matter to further expound his views on Britain, architecture and change. As Lycett Green notes:

> Coming fresh to the making of documentaries, which were not government-briefed but were his [Betjeman's] own creations, he found a new excitement. His passion to get things across came to the fare [sic] and he took inordinate trouble with his scripts, reading them through again and again over the images on the screen. He now saw a way of showing the beauty of his surroundings to the public, which might galvanise them into realising how wonderful England was. (Lycett Green, 1997, p 229-30)

Railway stations as supreme examples of Victorian architecture excited Betjeman: London Bridge station, originally two separate termini, rebuilt on several occasions since

But more importantly, Betjeman appears to have recognised at an early stage the advantages television offered for transposing prose and poetry into a filmic format. In an interview for the *Illustrated London News* in 1955, discussing the locations for filming he had visited around Britain in the previous two months, he stated: 'If I have a mission at all – and I am speaking quite seriously about television – it is to show people things which are beautiful so that they will very soon realise what is ugly. I really do want people to use their eyes as they go through life' (Betjeman, 1955). Betjeman thought that the most successful approach in making interesting arts-related films in a popular genre, that captured public attention, was through collaborative effort between the film crew and artist. Betjeman was not prepared to be merely an artist-as-subject for television arts programming, even in the 1950s. From the outset of television, he wanted to be actively involved. Betjeman himself, writing an obituary for his friend, the documentary filmmaker, Sir Arthur Elton, in January 1973, best summarises his approach:

What has not been mentioned is that the making of films, whether documentary or feature, and Arthur made both, is a co-operative effort and demands forbearance on all sides. Cameraman, sound man, editor, cutter, sound mixer and their assistants, and a person to be a successful film producer, such as Arthur was, must not only be a good mixer, but have a clear mind and an idea of the shape of the film right from the beginning. He must also be humane and humorous and prepared to change his opinions. (Betjeman, 1973)

This approach is confirmed by recollections from colleagues working on his television programmes. Kenneth Savidge, a BBC producer in the 1960s, remarked on how well Betjeman knew the television business:

He was always keen to think of the audience – "our readers", as he called them. He'd say: "Do you think our readers will understand this?" And he had a very just estimation of the place of television…. (Kenneth Savidge, interviewed by Bevis Hillier in 2000, cited in Hillier, 2004, pp 186-7)

His director for the *Wales and the West* series (Jonathan Stedall) and his producer/director for the *Bird's-Eye View* series (Edward Mirzoeff) also confirm this approach (see below for further discussion). Betjeman's biographer, Bevis Hillier, states that Betjeman already had 25 years of television experience by the early 1960s and was regarded as one of the leading pioneers of the medium but that, stylistically, he was quite unlike his contemporaries: 'He talked, not in carefully honed passages of prose, but as one might chat to a friend, with jerky inconsequences, asides and second thoughts' (Hillier, 2004, p 190).

It seems that Betjeman was advocating the artist being central to the shaping of the production, and although his opinions, quoted above, appear to refer to the role of the producer, they may also refer to Betjeman's role in carving out a film that would be successful on many fronts: as a film, as a commentary, as an artist's viewpoint and as a coherent feature. Having such close involvement with the writing, filming and editing of the series, Betjeman became, in many respects, an established authority, or at least appeared to do so, on his filmic subjects. It is no coincidence that some of Betjeman's most memorable films involved the same editor, cameraman and director. Jonathan Stedall also directed later Betjeman films for the BBC, including the two-part *Thank God It's Sunday* (1972) and a series

Sir George Gilbert Scott's Midland Hotel, St Pancras station; the station and hotel survived thanks to Betjeman's campaign against demolition plans

of seven films entitled *Time with Betjeman* (1983). Edward Mirzoeff went on to produce – with Edward Roberts' editing – some of Betjeman's most popular films with British television viewers: *Metro-land* (1973), *A Passion for Churches* (1974), *Summoned by Bells* (1976) and *The Queen's Realm* (1977). Both *Wales and the West* and *Bird's-Eye View* are discussed further below.

WALES AND THE WEST (1962-63)

TWW had commissioned John Betjeman to make 12 short programmes on West Country towns. The towns were: Devizes, Sherborne, Crewkerne, Chippenham, Swindon, Sidmouth, Bath (twice), Marlborough, Weston-super-Mare, Clevedon and Malmesbury. His director for the films was Jonathan Stedall, a young 24-year-old Harrovian, whom Betjeman took to immediately and, with Tony Impey on camera and Ian Bruce on sound, the team produced some memorable short films. Stedall and Betjeman visited each town in advance of filming to select appropriate places for film shooting but it was Betjeman who had the final say on the choice of locations, possibly because he was the one expected to write the original prose to accompany the films. In a letter to Stedall following a visit to Weston-super-Mare, he outlines his proposed treatment for the Weston film:

> Visually, there will be a temptation to do just one more film about the pleasures and fairgrounds and ice-lollies, kiddies' swings and roundabouts. We must resist this and make it Weston. The characteristics of Weston, apart from its mud, situation and donkeys, are its hotels and holidaymakers…. This is just a suggested treatment and I realize that Tony, Ian and yourself will have your own ideas. (Betjeman, Letter to Jonathan Stedall, 1962, cited in Lycett Green, 1994)

Stedall recalls in an article for *Camera: Cambridge University Film Quarterly* in 2002:

> Betjeman's commentaries were wonderful. He had a real sense of how to write to film, and when not to write. In other words, when to let the images speak for themselves. Betjeman was also a great

'Notice the delicate iron work': Bath's Lansdowne Crescent

mimic. He had various characters in his repertoire, one of which was a property developer. We did a film in Bath about a property developer showing Betjeman round the town and enthusing about the new modern buildings which were absolutely ghastly. Betjeman did both voices, with the property developer gradually shoving Betjeman out of the picture.... (Stedall, 2002)

Indeed, in the narration to the Bath film, Betjeman adopts the voice of a London property developer who is in conversation with 'Mr Betjeman' about the need for 'moderne' buildings and the demolition of 'Georg-ee-an' properties:

> Today, building must express itself honestly and sincerely, as for instance in this feature [shot of a concrete external lecture theatre on a new college development in the centre of Bath], which might be termed "the vital buttocks" of the construction. As you can see, it expresses its purpose, whatever that may be, sincerely, and this causes it to blend harmoniously and naturally with the Georgian on the left there. Each age should express itself as it really feels and you can see how this age feels about Georgian.

And then Betjeman, returning to his normal voice, replies: "Well, I suppose you may be right. You must know what you're talking about as you make such a lot of money as a developer."

As well as providing amusing and entertaining slants on important, serious and possibly even dull subject matters, Betjeman was able to undermine the credibility of those in authority but simultaneously make himself and his arguments appeal to television audiences, often in quite subtle ways. He became not only a champion of alternative forms of planning, such as conservation planning, but an expert in his own right, using humour and filming techniques to mock and ridicule the accepted planning wisdom of the day. Betjeman may not perhaps be regarded today as one of the great English poets, but he did employ a great deal of irony in his prose that is, in itself, a common feature of English literature. Antony Easthope remarks that irony in English literature:

> ... seeks to be an indirect means to refer to reality by inviting the reader to discard the offered significance as either understated (*litotes*) or overstated (*hyperbole*), and go straight to the "real" meaning.... The knowing reader is granted a pleasurable position of shared

superiority to whatever or whoever is the target or object of the reference. (Easthope, 1999, p 97)

Betjeman uses clear classic irony in his commentaries on developers and planners, as a way of suggesting to the audience that their perspective of new build, employing professional planning opinion and expertise, may not be correct. In essence, Betjeman uses irony as a form of mockery, but with the encouragement to the audience to continue questioning the accepted edict of the time.

Within the TWW series, what often started as a programme on local architecture would become a very different sort of film by the completion of location filming. Timothy Mowl, in his *Stylistic cold wars: Betjeman versus Pevsner*, suggests that Betjeman could not resist looking beyond the building's façade, to its occupiers and users, to further the viewer's interest (Mowl, 2000). In the Clevedon film, for example, hardly any footage is given over to the architecture of the town. Most of the film portrays old ladies taking tea in retirement homes and middle-aged couples arguing over lunch with a sympathetic but also slightly irreverent voiceover provided by Betjeman pretending to be one of the residents. The beautifully

'The vital buttocks': Betjeman's humour employed to the full in his commentary on Frederick Gibberd's Bath College external lecture theatre extension

filmed output, coupled with the amusing and interesting narration in that gentle bleating voice, holds the audience's attention on a – broadly defined – arts subject.

Stedall (2002) suggests that television film provided an opportunity for Betjeman to develop imaginary stories about people and how they use places. This enabled a more popular appeal to be developed with audiences on subjects that may not have otherwise attracted a significant television viewing audience, an alternative planning vision that focused on places and their meaning, rather than with construction and use. The resultant work on Clevedon is more about a day in the life of a retirement hotel than it is about a West Country town. It was certainly innovative and perhaps more daring as art output compared to all other arts programmes at this time. The series as a whole, with its fly-on-the-wall approach, also marks out its distinctiveness and precedes the time of drama-documentary/docu-soap by a number of years.

Bird's-Eye View (1969–71)

In 1968, the BBC approached Betjeman about the possibility of making a series about Britain that, uniquely, would be filmed entirely from a helicopter. The technique had not been used before and the idea was to use colour aerial photography to show how Britain had changed and was continuing to change, with an anthology of verse and prose chosen by commissioned authors, all accompanied by an anthology of relevant music. It was also an opportunity to exploit the possibilities of colour television, first transmitted on BBC1 in 1969, in visual spectacle. Thirteen programmes were eventually made and transmitted between 1969 and 1971, each of 50 or 60 minutes duration. Betjeman made three programmes: 'Beside the seaside', 'The Englishman's home' (both in 1969) and 'A land for all seasons' (in 1971). A 14th programme, 'The Queen's realm', broadcast in 1977 and narrated by Betjeman to commemorate the Queen's Silver Jubilee, was compiled from the 13 programmes of the 1969-71 period.

Betjeman was enthusiastic even before filming commenced, and wrote to the producer, Edward Mirzoeff, suggesting ideas for programmes within the series. He believed that the helicopter should play God – tracing prehistoric tracks along the tops of the chalk downs, looking down the swamps the Saxons had tamed and drained, seeing the winding lanes criss-crossing counties. Mirzoeff wrote to Betjeman asking for a list of places suitable for helicopter filming for one of the first programmes scheduled in the series, 'Beside the seaside'. Betjeman replied on 10 March 1969:

> I don't quite know how to treat the subject yet, without boring everyone to death, but I have an idea we should treat it rather on the lines of Edmund Gilbert's *Essay on the Holiday Industry and Seaside Towns in England and Wales*. We should start with the history and end with the threat to our shrinking unspoiled coast. In fact we should go from the Marine Villa of George III's reign to the caravan of Elizabeth II…. (Betjeman, Letter to Edward Mirzoeff, 10 March 1969, cited in Lycett Green, 1994)

Betjeman goes on to suggest: Cheltenham as an example of an inland spa; Brighton, Weymouth, Ryde and Torquay to represent the Georgian to Victorian periods; Ventnor for early Victorian seaside resorts; and Bournemouth and Frinton as Edwardian spas. He suggested interspersing shots of these locations with film of day trips by rail or pleasure steamer, concerts on the pier, advertisements for large and small hotels, escapism to non-developed coastal locations, old fishing harbours such as St Ives and Polperro, caravans, chalets and Butlins. It seems safe to believe that Betjeman had not written any prose for the film by the time of his letter to Mirzoeff, but by Christmas Day 1969, when 'Beside the seaside' was transmitted on peak time evening BBC2, the *Radio Times* trailed the programme with the following verse, penned by Betjeman himself:

> A swooping seagull takes its flight
> From Weymouth to the Isle of Wight
> From Cornish clifftops wild and bare
> To crowds at Weston-super-Mare…
> A scrapbook made at Christmas time
> Of summer joys in film and rhyme. (*Radio Times*, 1969)

Virtually the entire broadcast comprises colour aerial photography. The programme opens with shots of the cliff tops and then pans out dramatically to the sea, accompanied by Vaughan Williams' 'Sea Symphony' and Betjeman's recital of 'For those in peril'. We are shown long and close-up shots of a fishing trawler, the launch of a lifeboat and the wreck of an oil tanker beached along rocks, before focusing in on a lighthouse in calmer conditions, the return to the cliffs and inland to the countryside, as the music continues and Betjeman's prose commences, characteristically, in earnest:

> They feared it most, who knew it best
> The sea that hits the rocky west.
> To merchantmen, it might bring wealth
> But it was a danger to health.
>
> Far better live inland and warm
> Out of the perilous wind and storm.
> Safe from fresh air and such like harm
> In sheltered mansion, cot or farm.
>
> Quality sent its sons and daughters
> In search of health to inland waters.
> To Roman Bath or Cheltenham Spa
> Where the Chalybeate fountains are.

The film broadly follows Betjeman's plan, with images of Weymouth, Lyme Regis, Sidmouth, the Isle of Wight, Clevedon and Bournemouth. There are shots of pleasure steamers and ferries, games played by children on piers, and hotels and lodging houses, with Betjeman again adopting various provincial accents to mock make believe residents complaining about food, having nothing to do and the weather. We are shown trains heading west, Weston-super-Mare in a thunderstorm, a Salvation Army band playing hymns on the promenade, speedboats and water skiing, before moving to Cornwall for peace and tranquility. The music is appropriate for the film, ranging from Elgar to Walton to Bax and, later in the film, to Stravinsky and Shostakovich, as the themes depicted move away from gay little fishing ports and seaside resorts to the sprawl of holiday caravans and coastal commercial development. The final five minutes of the film depicts, as the menace of Shostakovich's Tenth Symphony score slips away to leave only the noise of the sea and seagulls, aerial shots of Betjeman himself walking along the undeveloped North Cornish coast. This allows him to return to his passionate interests in the narration, namely the protection of Britain from unbridled development:

> You know that Holy hush there is on Christmas morning, the roads almost empty, the skies free of aeroplanes, and you begin to see and smell and hear once more? Well, the seaside can be like that.... The

'Cornwall. Not another county. Another country': Betjeman's beloved Cornwall – St Ives

developers have had more than their fair share of the coast. A third of it is already completely built up. We must keep the rest of it for the good of our souls.

Another of Betjeman's programmes in 1969 for *Bird's-Eye View*, 'The Englishman's home', is even more polemical. He mocks planners for their visionary perspective of new housing. The images move away from English villages, Bath, Clifton and Brighton, and the music of Elgar and Vaughan Williams, to a depiction of the massive tower blocks of London's East End and Essex, accompanied by the more contemporary music of Goehr and Martinu, leading Betjeman to once again employ heavy irony:

> The planners did their best.
> Oh yes, they gave it all a lot of thought.
> Putting in trees and grassy rides
> And splendid views across to Richmond Park
> And landscaped streets and abstract sculpture.
> Oh, Roehampton won the prizes!
> It was all so well laid out.
> Just so much space from one block to the next.
> Perhaps this is the way we ought to live?

But where can be the heart that sends a family
To the twentieth floor of such a slab as this?
It can't be right,
However fine the views across to Greenwich and the Isle of Dogs.
It can't be right,
Caged half way up the sky, not knowing your neighbour
Frightened of the lift and who'll be in it
And who's down below.
And are the children safe?

New towns, new housing estates,
New homes, new streets, new neighbours,
New standards of living,
New financial commitments,
New jobs, new schools, new shops,
New loneliness, new restlessness,
New pressure, new tension.
And people,
People who have to cope with all this newness.
People who cannot afford old irrelevances.
People who have to find a God who fits in.

To say this is sensationalism, rather than prose, would be an understatement. But as a television spectacle, the force of the argument – irony, mockery, questioning beliefs, emotional vulnerability, combined with aerial colour imagery and rousing music – acts powerfully on the audience. Thanks to Betjeman and others who captured – and perhaps led – public imagination against the rationality of the accepted doctrine, what may be termed the 'planning wizardry' of the expert, the tide towards modernism and development had started to turn at this period.

Mirzoeff states that the polemical element of some of the films was strongly encouraged, and there was also an attempt to stimulate a debate about changing Britain. In interview, Mirzoeff recalls the affect of this agenda on the audience with reference to 'The Englishman's home':

The strongest images and writing were those high-rise flats near Greenwich, which was really quite counter to the accepted view of the time, and it brought quite a backlash for Betjeman. The view was, how dare this old buffoon criticize what we know is the best way of living, and it was the precursor of the now clichéd accepted

'It can't be right, however fine the views': Betjeman's comments on high-rise flats

view of the flats. People wrote letters to me saying it was absolutely outrageous we could say these things, and it was viewed as anti-working class; at last we have decent houses for the people and you are knocking it. But something clicked as a result of this and it was very much at the forefront of new ways of looking at tower blocks as evil, as places that people don't really want to live in. In terms of planning, that was probably the most important moment in the series. (Mirzoeff, 2003)

Press reaction to the programme reveals the extent to which Betjeman seemed to have hit a chord with the viewing public. The *Observer* of 30 March 1969 featured *Bird's-Eye View* prominently:

The Englishman's Home. A helicopter trip over the blessed plot with John Betjeman showing homes off like an estate agent who's got the muse. Humble viewers can look down on Blenheim, having for so long looked up, a novel experience…. Betjeman's commentary is a fusion of his and other people's poetry – "… the silvery shower/a dancing tribute to hydraulic power" (Chatsworth fountains, fabulously photographed) and sonorous phrases – a Wiltshire valley changed to

"Italy" (Stourhead) and trumpet obligato. Being Betjeman, he bites when you least expect it. The musical accompaniment is witty – Melba squeezing out her 1910 recording of "Home, Sweet Home" (vision: Wentworth Woodhouse) and admirably partial – Lawes and Scarlatti go with what's all right; modern work with what's not. (*Observer*, 1969)

Initial press reaction following transmission was very positive. Jimmy Thomas in the *Daily Express* of 8 April 1969 stated that the programme was 'one of the best TV features of the day' while the *Daily Mail* on the same day described it as 'a marvellous series'. Mirzoeff also reports hundreds of letters being set to the BBC by members of the public in support of Betjeman's views.

CONCLUSIONS

At times the urge to preserve the past, with which the Sixties were obsessed, took on the proportions of mania.... Often the name of John Betjeman was attached to appeals, and eventually Mr Eric Lyons, himself an architect, coined the phrase "Betjemanic depressives" to stigmatize collectively those who would preserve at all costs everything from the past.... (Levin, 1970, cited in Hillier, 2004)

One of the driving forces behind Betjeman's desire to broadcast his concerns more explicitly and prominently was to question accepted wisdom, particularly that of the rational professional planning expert. Betjeman, like Clough Williams-Ellis and J.B. Priestley, was not necessarily anti-planning, but rather concerned at its purpose, form and authoritarianism. By using literature, radio and television films to question the accepted wisdom, these individuals became prominent public figures in their own right, but their writings and broadcasts also had the effect of opening up planning and development debate to a much larger audience than government officials, landowners and local councils. At a time when public involvement in planning remained many years away (the Skeffington report calling for the introduction of public participation in planning was published in 1969), these individuals became – to borrow Gold and Ward's terminology, alternative planning wizards, championing what they saw as 'the people's view'.

Betjeman and others, by broadcasting their personal concerns, intended to initiate debate about a Britain of the future, and really had no qualms about using the BBC to make programmes they saw as being in the public interest. Of course, by utilising film to espouse his own views, one may argue that Betjeman was adopting a modernist practice himself by possibly convincing the audience that he too was a planning expert, albeit an expert with a perspective that went against the grain of other commentators at the time.

Betjeman's films, encapsulated by *Wales and the West* and *Bird's-Eye View*, are an important archive of a changing Britain, a Britain that, as Betjeman was all too aware, was disappearing before his eyes. The films are unique for their time, adopting a truly collaborative approach between writer and crew, and not afraid to be too serious or factually correct so as to interest and entertain the audience; they are a marked contrast to the documentary planning films of the Abercrombie era. Betjeman appears to have been uncomfortable with modernity, a trait shared by another English poet, Philip Larkin. But this may explain his reaction against professional and bureaucratic expertise. His films, associated with his more popular *Metro-land*, directed with Edward Mirzoeff in 1973 (an examination and homage to the suburb, an irony given that Betjeman had been concerned about suburbia in the 1930s), provided Betjeman with a broad canvas on which to carve out distinctiveness in prose and on screen, and to champion issues to a broader audience. The pioneering use of colour aerial photography for the *Bird's-Eye View* films, against a rich backcloth of rousing music and a gentle English voice, brought the arts to a mass audience and topical planning issues directly into the home that may have seemed unimaginable in the mid-1940s.

It may have been Betjeman's own interests, his friendship with the documentary filmmaker Arthur Elton, his years of writing and his broadcasting experience for the BBC after 1932, that provided Betjeman with an opportunity to produce arts features that could be popularised for a mass audience. To think that such a programme as 'Beside the seaside' could be shown on prime-time terrestrial evening television on the BBC on Christmas Day may seem incredible to us today, as one casual glance at present day Christmas television schedules reveals a dearth of documentary features. But the fact that the programmes have been repeated over many years indicates that they did capture public attention.

Simultaneously, analysis of the films, indeed of most of Betjeman's broadcasts, suggests that he knew exactly how to use television to capture public attention to further his own architectural interests and campaigns against modern developments. This also marks out his films uniquely. He was not only devising the narration and images on screen and was involved in editing, cutting and directing, but he was also employing television as a form of architectural propaganda in order to challenge the viewpoint of the experts. Betjeman's hard-hitting realism occurred through subtle means: a use of ironic prose, humour, conversation-style commentaries and carefully chosen images, interwoven with gentle pleas to save the special features of the places in which the individual lives and that matter to the individual alone. The use of irony and humour within debates on planning should not be regarded with disdain. As Antony Easthope remarks, 'The comic can be invoked not just to defy theory but because a mere presence can perform an act of terminal closure' (Easthope, 1999, p 162). Betjeman was not the first, and certainly not the last person to employ humour in serious discussion of town planning and its impacts. And if such humour strikes a chord with the audience, we need to understand these emotional reactions if planning as a profession is to be taken more seriously by the public in the 21st century.

Early television, the pioneering use of aerial and colour documentary photography, an ability to turn realism into irony and humorous observations and to make planning and development more accessible for a broader spectrum of the population, comprise the legacy of Betjeman and the film crews he worked with. We have become used to seeing the names of Abercrombie, Unwin, Geddes, Osborn, Holford and others as the major players in planning's history of the 20th century in Britain, partly because of their writings and partly because of their official positions as planning academics or practitioners. Perhaps it is time we concentrated on some alternative figures from 20th-century British history, figures from literature and the arts, whose work may have influenced the form, trajectory and perception of town planning in an equally robust but highly divergent way. This chapter has provided a window on just one of these figures; more research is required, however, to assess the relationship between key individuals in both planning and cultural history.

Surveying the magnificent roof of St Pancras: Betjeman statue

EIGHT

Taking a bird's-eye view: modern planning and the changing landscape

INTRODUCTION

The UK has witnessed a number of high profile and highly successful television series over the last 10 years using aerial photography. Among the most prominent have been several series entitled *Coast*, capturing Britain's coastline through a series of linear geographies, and *Britain from Above*, which considered such diverse subjects as the UK's infrastructure needs, urban development and natural landscape. And that is aside from the success of Google Earth, that uses aerial and satellite imagery to good effect. The success of featuring and transmitting aerial camera work to represent the changing landscape is not, however, a recent phenomenon. In 1966, the BBC discussed the possibility of making a series about Britain that, uniquely, would be filmed entirely from a helicopter. The series would use colour aerial photography to show modern Britain, how the country was changing, with an anthology of verse, prose and writing chosen or written by well-known authors of the time. The 13 programmes of *Bird's-Eye View*, produced and directed by the respected documentary filmmaker Edward Mirzoeff, were eventually made and transmitted between 1969 and 1971, and include: 'Beside the seaside', 'The Englishman's home' and 'A land for all seasons' by John Betjeman; 'Eastern approach' by Stuart Hood; and 'Man on the move' by Correlli Barnett. The focus for the series at this time was to record a rapidly changing Britain, with new housing estates, the motorway network, infrastructure provision such as nuclear power stations, and leisure patterns. The *Bird's-Eye View* films are an important archive of a changing Britain in the 1960s. The series became the most expensive series ever filmed, but since its programmes were transmitted over a two-year period and despite press and public reaction being extremely positive, its historic impact has been diluted by the lengthy three year transmission time.

The technique of making a television series on Britain's changing landscape filmed from a helicopter had not been used before. It was also an opportunity to exploit the possibilities of colour television, enacted on the BBC2 channel in 1967, in visual spectacle.

Bird's-Eye View was a series of programmes transmitted on the peak time evening 'arts slot' on BBC2 between April 1969 and April 1971. Championed by senior BBC management as a star feature in the BBC's galaxy of programmes in the late 1960s, the series was promoted as a symbol of the BBC's commitment to make and broadcast innovative, high quality television, simultaneously embracing new colour film and technological advancement. *Bird's-Eye View* cost a considerable sum to make at the time, some £250,000. It also proved to be one of the most difficult technically to achieve. Making a complete series of aerial films that captured the unique features of the landscape had never been achieved before for television and there was a lack of expertise both within the BBC and across Europe on filming techniques involving aerial photography. Furthermore, immense administrative difficulties occurred through programme planning and filming relating to the clearance for low-flying aerial photography in urban areas that had to be overcome and involved meetings at the highest level of government to ensure clearance. Finally, there was evidence that the BBC's organisational structure and its concern with programme costs might affect both the quality of filmmaking and the achievement of the sort of series that had been put forward.

What was achieved, cinematographically, was a feast, and BBC executives, press reviews and the audience were all enchanted both by a new perspective of looking at Britain and with the quality of the images, narration and musical mixture that was evident in most of the 13 programmes. What was also unique about the series was the combination of the new aerial perspective, a lack of location sound, carefully edited music and poetry and prose selection, and the involvement of a range of notable writers and actors to narrate the work. In this approach, the changing landscape was brought to primetime television in a new way and may have had the consequence of appealing to viewers who might otherwise have found geography and change uninteresting. The series was also unique in that it encouraged the viewing public to look at itself aerially for the first time on television and inform the public with regards to their everyday landscape, environments that had – for the most part – been largely taken for granted.

Bird's-Eye View accomplished some significant achievements with television filmmaking within the BBC. The success attributed to the series, judged by the media and audience, at the time of its transmission, associated with the series' ability to communicate environmental and development change to a more general audience, and in the pioneering use of aerial photography for television, are all reasons why *Bird's-Eye View* needs to be considered as a milestone series in the filmic depiction and representation of planning in Britain. And yet, compared to other BBC programmes of the period such as *Monitor* and *Civilisation*, *Bird's-Eye View* seems to have been largely forgotten or at least remains under-appreciated, even within the BBC itself.

They key question to ask, therefore, is, to what extent and in what way may we look at *Bird's-Eye View* as a landmark series in the development of planning and the modernist movement? This chapter is intended to provide an anatomy of the *Bird's-Eye View* series. Its purpose is to consider the origins, development, production and transmission of the series and to pose some broader questions relating to the:

- attitude of the BBC towards televising planning and environmental change during the so-called 'golden era' of television;
- difficulties encountered in producing a series devoted to the changing landscape when shot entirely from the air; and
- public and press reaction to the series concerning the changing face of Britain during modernity.

The chapter begins with contextual material centred on a debate relating to the history and origin of arts television in Britain and the role of arts documentaries. There is also a review of the development of BBC2 in the 1960s and a brief discussion of the innovative approach of the BBC channel towards arts programming. The chapter then focuses on the origins and purpose of the *Bird's Eye View* series, identifying the series' scope, title issues and topics to be addressed. It also includes a discussion on how the helicopter series idea came about. The costs of film production and plans for the total timing of the series are reviewed. A section is included on the practical and technical difficulties of aerial photography related to the series since the programmes were original in this respect. The contents of the programmes are reviewed, including their cutting-edge polemical style, and a few of the films are selected for further illustration. Scheduling, press and critics' responses to the series are debated, as are audience reactions. A final section provides some conclusions and overviews.

ORIGINS AND PURPOSE OF THE *BIRD'S EYE VIEW* SERIES

A television series about urban planning and the aerial filming idea

In the mid–1960s, as part of the BBC's new interest in technological advancement, interesting programming and a desire to capture on film appropriate subjects for colour transmission, channel controllers were asked to develop ideas for innovative new programmes that would demonstrate these attributes. David Attenborough, appointed controller of BBC2 in 1968, remarks in his autobiography of the

Aerial views reveal different perspectives of the land: Cardiff Bay

pressure from senior BBC personnel to think up new programmes that would reflect the new technology available:

> BBC2's job, as I saw it, was to innovate.… I proposed instead that BBC2's policy was simply to produce programmes of a kind that neither BBC1 nor ITV were showing and that these would be scheduled so that each would contrast as extremely as possible with what was being shown at that time on BBC1.… (Attenborough, 2002, p 202)

Attenborough goes on to state that a particular approach to programme selection was also adopted, with a determination to avoid carbon copies of existing programmes on other networks or bland features:

> We would take programmes from every category one could think of, and find new approaches and neglected subjects. One measure of our success, I said, would be the width of the spectrum that our programmes covered. (Attenborough, 2002, p 203)

Edward Mirzoeff, an up-and-coming television producer at the time and attached to BBC2 and who would go on to become the producer of *Bird's-Eye View*, also noted the pressure, but at the same time noted the excitement within the network at the prospect of being given a blank sheet – and, to all intents and purposes, a blank cheque – in order to make new television. He remarks in interview: "BBC2 had put a lot of money into it. BBC2 was very experimental, very new, very fresh, and colour was pretty new.…"

The origins of *Bird's-Eye View* can be dated back to 1966, when in preparation for the commencement of colour transmission of BBC2, programme planners were under instructions to develop features that combined innovation and uniqueness, opportunities to show off colour subject matter and technological advancement. The idea of using a helicopter for filming seemed appropriate, but it was not unique within film; as far back as 1954, for example, Alfred Hitchcock had used a helicopter to capture a speeding car travelling along the Cote d'Azur in *To Catch a Thief*.

The exact origins of who had the idea to use a helicopter for BBC filming purposes are difficult to ascertain. Mirzoeff maintains that the prospect of helicopter hire had originated in the first instance and only following this agreement was serious consideration given by BBC2 to generating a series of helicopter programmes as general or arts features. Scrutiny of BBC Archives at Caversham Park also fails to unearth the exact origins, but the files do contain development ideas for 'a helicopter series'.

The first BBC programme to utilise a helicopter for filming was a one-off documentary entitled 'Bird's-eye view over Britain', broadcast on BBC2 on 24 December 1967. There are no files available on this programme at BBC Archives and even the programme itself has not been tracked down. But it appears that the BBC controller and audience reaction to the broadcast on Christmas Eve 1967 had been extremely positive, and sufficiently innovative to embark on planning a more formal series devoted to aerial filming.

Mirzoeff suggests that another origin of the aerial filming series was because a contract had already been signed between the BBC and British Executive Air Services (BEAS) for helicopter hire for broadcasting purposes. But the idea of one series utilising all the allotted hours of the agreed use and hours of helicopter hire, as stated within the contract, had still not been agreed by the time the contract had been signed in June 1968. BBC2 had already commenced outside broadcasts at sporting events, such as the tennis championships at Wimbledon and football matches, and it was thought that the helicopter could be used by BBC Sport to provide an alternative, aerial, perspective of these live events, much in the same way as the BBC and other production companies use helicopters and airships today to film live sporting and other cultural events for television (such as the FA Cup, the London Marathon and the Boat Race). Unfortunately, BBC Sport was not totally convinced about using the helicopter for outside broadcasts of sporting events. It may have been nervousness on the producers' part toward helicopter filming for television (which was still very much in its infancy), or it may have been related to a lack of availability of outside broadcast colour television cameras, that was certainly apparent at the time; David Attenborough, for example, talks of the poverty of technology that affected programme planning and production in the early years of BBC2.

Whatever the reason for BBC Sport's low use of the helicopter, as a direct consequence and during the planning of the first year of helicopter hire in 1968, the schedule for helicopter use in filming was significantly below the expectation, and this started to have serious repercussions on costs for BBC Television.

As a result, the low usage of the helicopter combined with the reluctance on the part of BBC Sport to use the helicopter, may have been a major reason why thought was given over to filming an entire series of programmes on the *Bird's-Eye View* theme, rather than an occasional additional programme in the spirit of the Christmas Eve 1967 feature. Production planners within the BBC were set the task of developing a series of possibly at least 12, and not more than 16, 50-minute programmes along the theme of changing Britain. The proposed number of programmes in the series indicates quite readily the extent to which there was an overwhelming desire to make up the shortfall in helicopter hours use, as had been agreed in the BEAS contract. The series was going to become a large-scale production and Mirzoeff indicates that the £250,000 budget to match the scale was agreed to in principle by BBC2's controller.

Commissioning and selecting films

A document written by Antony Jay, dated 1 February 1968, indicates that agreement towards producing a helicopter series had been advanced to such an extent that themes, individual programme content and titles were being discussed at the time. The document outlines Jay's proposal for 16 programmes under the title of 'Bird's-eye view of Britain', and three principles for programme development were stressed at the outset. These are as follows:

A. All programmes should be national and not local. There are no divisions on the lines of "Dartmoor", "The Lake District", "The Great Wen", etc. Each programme follows its theme over the whole country.

B. In principle, the whole of each programme should be shot from the helicopter. To advocate ground shooting "because the subject can't be covered properly from the air" is to miss the point of the series. The series is not about "covering subjects". It is about seeing Britain in an entirely new way. The only reasons for leaving the helicopter are technical ones.

C. The programme subjects are divided along physical and not conceptual lines. There are no "theme" programmes like "Pleasure", "Our Heritage", "Work and Play". We may choose theme titles, but the basic content of each programme is physical: geographical or architectural features which over the course of the programme and the length of Britain are made to tell a developing story.

Capturing the historic landscape provided obvious subject matter, but not necessarily change: Ely Cathedral

Jay's paper then goes on to outline the 16 programmes. The topics suggested reflect the above principles, and comprise: 'The coastline', 'The rivers', 'The roads', 'Canals', 'Railways', 'Agriculture', 'Mining and quarrying', 'The sea around us', 'The crowded sky', 'The future', 'God's acre', 'Funspots', 'The deserted island', 'The spread of the city', 'Englishmen's homes' and 'Britain's battlefields'. In the spirit of the trajectory of the controller of BBC2 at the time, it is interesting to note the programme entitled 'The future' as this most closely relates to the theme of technological advancement, echoing a theme developed by Harold Wilson, the then Prime Minister, of the importance of 'the white heat of technology'. The synopsis for the programme outlined by Jay suggests the desire to look at how Britain would be shaped in the years ahead:

> A look at all the most modern developments, or the ones which are going to shape the future most. The Atomic power stations at Berkeley and Dounreay, the deep water container ports, the natural gas and oil pipelines, Fylingdales Moor. The newest buildings and a factory turning out prefabricated sections of flats. The new city centres – the Bullring at Birmingham, Coventry precinct, or the contrast between Welwyn Garden city and Cumbernauld. The new Universities still being built at Brighton and Colchester.

One can almost feel the excitement towards modernity in this paragraph, a desire to look forward rather than back, and for improvement and wonderment. This is put into even greater perspective in the present day by the fact that so many of these particular developments are now regarded as obsolete, have been mothballed, or are described as architectural and planning disasters. Overall, however, the programme topics suggested do convey some sense of history, of change, of technological and economic change, of industrialisation and the rise of the car, and – in turn – of a rapidly changing Britain.

Mirzoeff drafted some 'Supporting notes for the offer for the helicopter series' on 29 March 1968, which seemed to have amended Antony Jay's suggestions. This document appears to be the formal proposal to the controller of BBC2 for final authorisation to make a helicopter series. A small news feature reported in the Weekend Review of *The Sunday Times* on 25 February 1968 had already stated that the BBC were considering proposals for a further helicopter series, following the pilot transmission on 24 December 1967 entitled 'Bird's-eye view of Britain'. Mirzoeff's 29 March note requests permission to make 13 (rather than 16) programmes, to be made over three years for transmission in 1970/71, although **he** holds out the possibility that blocks of three programmes could be transmitted earlier as each programme was completed, with the first batch becoming available in January 1969. Mirzoeff stated that each programme would be of 50 minutes duration, would be shot in colour and largely shot from a helicopter. At this stage, the exact choice of 13 subjects was not stipulated in the notes, although seven topics were highlighted for illustrative purposes, and these comprise: 'The land', 'The sea around us', 'The Englishman's home', 'The rise and decline of Christianity in Britain', 'Transport', 'Britain as a fortress' and 'Artistic heritage'.

Mirzoeff, in interview, highlights one particular problem he faced immediately on embarking on the project: narrative. Securing relatively shake-free footage taken from a travelling helicopter of appropriate subject matters would be difficult enough in itself, particularly when one also thought about at what height subjects would becoming meaningless to television viewers. But trying to weave a narrative within each 50-minute film was also going to be a challenge; would a film tell a story or was it purely aesthetic? In this sense, it became obvious to Mirzoeff and others that pitching the programmes within a particular category of television (arts, documentary, general feature, etc) would also raise problems, not least organisationally within the BBC as to which section of BBC

Emblematic of the white heat of technology: Didcot Power Station, 1968

Television would take ownership, and financial responsibility, for the series.

A further potential problem related to the desire for national subject matter to be selected, rather than regional and local subjects. There might have been a complication here, since any subject matter – whether it be a castle, a house, a motorway or power station – was situated within a particular locality that might be recognisable to the audience even if each had a national significance. The decision to avoid sub-national subjects seems to relate to overarching themes alone; if a series was to be about castles, it would not focus on castles in Wales, for example. Programmes would attempt to illustrate the subject matter with as much footage taken from as many examples as possible representing all regions of the UK.

Eight days prior to drafting his March 1968 note on programme selection, Mirzoeff had organised a 'Helicopter lunch' at the BBC and a brief record of the meeting survives in the BBC Archives. Arranged on 21 March 1968, the lunch had brought together a number of prominent writers and broadcasters to further plans for a series and to flesh out narrative issues. Among those present were John Betjeman (later Poet Laureate and already a recognised face and voice on the BBC), Correlli Barnett, Patrick O'Donovan, John Terraine, Gordon Watkins, Paul Johnstone and Brian Branston. Magnus Magnusson and John Lloyd sent their apologies. We may be forgiven for not recognising many of these names today but, at the time, they would have been well known figures in broadsheet writing, in radio broadcasting and on factual television programmes. Both Barnett and Terraine, for example, had already worked on two landmark BBC series of the 1960s, *The Great War* and *The Lost Peace*.

Following much discussion, they had agreed the first four programmes for the series, these being: 'The romantic beauty of England' (focusing on painting and culture), 'The land' (geology), 'The sea around us' (the affect of sea on the land) and 'Invaded island' (the Celtic fringe). It was anticipated that each writer would contribute two or three programmes and the writers would have access to leading historians, geographers and other specialists to develop their subjects. John Betjeman would write the script for the programme devoted to the sea.

Development of the series continued throughout the spring of 1968 and had reached a stage by mid May for Mirzoeff to provide an overview of progress in a memo produced for the BBC Head of General Features (Television). It is possible that Mirzoeff may have also used the opportunity to scotch rumours about the series' pitch, since there remained some uncertainty within the BBC as to what exactly had been approved of and what was causing a demand for high expenditure. Within the memo, Mirzoeff stipulated that the series should not be seen as an historical pageant, nor 'a kind of ultra-expensive Schools programme', or for that matter a series of travel films about regions of Britain. Mirzoeff went on to state that:

> It is predominantly a series of hard stories, factual and informative, on subjects which best repay being filmed from the air. It is about the physical attributes of Britain – from this is what we see from above. About the sea and the land, and the effect of man [sic] on both. The traces of man [sic], in buildings and roads and landscapes, are the traces of our past; and these will form a large part of the programmes. So will the future, for as the actions and decisions of today have a determining effect on tomorrow, so will many of the programmes be looking forward....

Beside the seaside

The idea had developed to combine film with narrative (a script provided by the scheduled writer, but not necessarily spoken by him on film) together with music, allowing a hard narrative while the aerial footage would allow a lyrical and romantic approach. The availability of particular writers and directors dictated some of the programmes being produced earlier than others, and it appears from the scores of memos exchanged between Mirzoeff, the heads of various divisions in Television Centre, the controller of BBC2 and the Finance Division between 1968 and 1970 that the full amount of requested funding was not provided at the outset but would be reviewed once the earlier programmes had been transmitted. The series, as at May 1968, was provisionally titled *Britain Revealed*, and the list of 13 programmes in the series were recorded as the following:

'1.   Set in the silver sea' (writer: unidentified)
2.   'The use of the land' (writer: unidentified)
3.   'Town planning and urban sprawl' (writer: unidentified)
4.   'The conservation of the countryside' (writer: John Lloyd)
5.   'Transport' (writer: Correlli Barnett)
6.   'The wealth of Britain' (writer: unidentified)
7.   'The Englishman's home' (writer: John Betjeman)
8.   'Britain as a playground' (writer: unidentified)
9.   'The Invaded Island' (writer: John Terraine)
10.   'Britain as a battlefield' (probable writer: John Terraine)
11.   'Romantic Britain' (probable writer: John Betjeman)
12.   'Britain 2000' (writer: unidentified)
13.   'A land for all seasons' (writer: unidentified)

The allotted writers were not always used for particular programmes, for a variety of reasons, and with exception to film numbers 4, 5, 7 and 9, there still remained no commitment to film the other programmes suggested by title. A BBC writer supported each writer, and both worked collaboratively to produce a script that provided a lyrical element that was interesting, and which provided a defined position on a particular topic. This defined position is interesting because this is exactly the element that Mirzoeff was searching for to give the programme some contemporary relevance and thereby avoid the series receiving a travelogue or historical picture label. And given the range of topics suggested (the increase in car ownership and mobility, urban sprawl and town planning, the protection of the countryside, for example), there can be little doubt that these subjects did lend themselves to the formulation of particular agendas.

As planning of the series progressed, the topics identified for each of the programmes were revised. Mirzoeff explains in interview that some initial subjects became no-hopers:

> I remember the first time we put together an assembly of material that we thought of, early material for 'The Englishman's Home', and the original plan was to start with archaeology type of material – ruins and remains of buildings, and so on – and we shot 40-50 minutes of this stuff and we said to [John] Betjeman to come in to the cutting room, and we ran this on a sort of projector, and it ran and it ran, and there was nothing, complete silence from him. And after about half an hour, he said, "Oh God, this is boring, let's go and have a drink!" And, I thought, oh God, he's right, it is boring. And at that moment, we knew archaeology was out, it just wasn't going to work.

Given that production of each of the programmes would be dictated by the availability of the helicopter, the number of flying time hours that were available (no more than 320 hours per year), the weather conditions, the availability of a script and the availability of BBC finance (£33,000 per year for three years for helicopter use alone), it is not surprising that batches of programmes were made, and it was inevitable that all 13 programmes in the series would be produced over a much longer timescale than originally intended.

Focusing on the themes of the series

By November 1968, the first programme in the 'helicopter series' (as it was still labelled) had just completed its editing period, and there was the rather urgent requirement to select a more appropriate title. The urgency was to design opening titles and graphics, film opening sequences and make opticals. In a memo between Mirzoeff and the BBC Head of General Features dated 11 November 1968, the title *Helicopter Britain* was put forward as the preference of the production team, and Mirzoeff outlines his justification, asking for formal approval:

1.   The need to tell the audience that these films are taken from a helicopter giving an aerial view and a new perspective of Britain.

2. The helicopter will never appear in the body of the film but there is, I believe, an audience interest in the way that these films have been shot. The opening titles consist of specially shot, fast moving film of the helicopter in action, and the title "Helicopter Britain" will fit very well with this film.

3. It seems to me important that while the title of the series should be informative and memorable it should not detract from the individual titles of the programmes themselves. I feel that with a title like "Helicopter Britain" equal emphasis can be put on individual programme names. It is a series title, which is in effect a symbol. Indeed, we have a designed a graphic symbol to be incorporated with the word "Helicopter", to be used also in the end credits.

But there appears to be reluctance with the *Helicopter Britain* title, and in a memo to Gordon Watkins written just four days later, Mirzoeff puts forward alternative titles, including *Sky View Britain*, *The Face of Britain*, *Skies Over Britain*, *Something in the Air*, *Above It All*, *The View of the Land* and *The Sky's the Limit*, but adds that 'Helicopter Britain remains the best.' Eleven days later, on 26 November, Mirzoeff – in a further memo – suggests *View from the Air*, but asks for the billing to be done in the style of *Towards Tomorrow* (a BBC documentary series from 1967-68), 'a series title followed by a few words or description, followed by the individual programme title and author'. The individual programme titles had, of course, already been worked up in draft form, as the list identified earlier indicates.

The written archives do not record the taking of the final decision for the series but it seems safe to believe that this occurred in one of the BBC's Officers' Meetings rather than through written memorandum. The final choice of title for the series was *Bird's-Eye View*, and the final list of all 13 programmes are outlined below, although it should be remembered that many of the latter titles were not chosen until quite late in the 1969-71 series history.

Table 8.1: Final choice of programme titles for *Bird's-Eye View*, transmitted on BBC2, 1969-71

Programme title (writer)	Original transmission date
'The Englishman's home' (John Betjeman)	5 April 1969
'Man on the move' (Correlli Barnett)	22 May 1969
'A green and pleasant land' (John Lloyd)	22 June 1969
'The island fortress' (John Terraine)	26 October 1969
'John Bull's workshop' (Correlli Barnett)	30 November 1969
'Beside the seaside' (John Betjeman)	25 December 1969
'The Highlands and Islands' (Magnus Magnusson)	25 January 1970
'What a lovely day' (John Lloyd)	22 March 1970
'Eastern approach' (Stuart Hood)	17 May 1970
'From Bishop Rock to Muckle Flugger' (unassigned)	25 December 1970
'Wales – The Western stronghold' (Renee Cutforth)	28 February 1971
'Innis Fail – Isle of Destiny' (James Plunkett)	17 March 1971
'A land for all seasons' (Correlli Barnett/John Betjeman)	18 April 1971

As can be noted from the titles above, some of the themes come through quite strongly – with a concentration on housing, transport, the countryside, industry ('John Bull's workshop'), the coast, defence ('The Island fortress'), and playtime ('What a lovely day'). Other programmes, however, do focus in on particular regions – the Scottish Highlands and Islands, Wales, and Eire ('Innis Fail'). The three remaining programmes take alternative linear geographies, with 'Eastern approach' looking at the east coast of Britain between Montrose and the Thames, 'From Bishop Rock to Muckle Flugger' that travels between Britain's extremities off Land's End and John o'Groats and 'A land for all seasons', that concentrates on rural life and agricultural production, predominantly, looking at how the seasons affect the landscape.

Edward Mirzoeff became the series editor while individual programmes were allocated to different producers. This allowed an individual approach to the programmes, even an experimental path, over a two-year period that allowed different types of narrative to the explored. For example, 'The Englishman's home', 'Man on the move', 'A green and pleasant land' and 'Beside the seaside' are all polemical while lyrical, with one writer providing an overview and lively commentary. By contrast, 'The Highlands and Islands' and 'Wales – The Western stronghold' are reportage in style. 'Eastern approach' and 'Innis Fail' are rather more personal films, with a writer (through the narrator) providing a commentary that takes the audience directly to places and features that the writer recalls from his youth. 'What a lovely day', meanwhile, takes a very alternative approach, with two narrators arguing in a jocular way over the appropriateness of different forms of leisure depicted in quite a high-handed, almost class-ridden, way; it was one of the least successful films. Finally, 'From Bishop Rock to Muckle Flugger' tells a story of the helicopter's journey from the South West to North East of Britain, with shots of the helicopter in the film en route, commentary linking places to fuel stops, the public's curiosity and interest in the helicopter as it landed at remote locations, and the sheer ambition of the journey.

So even though at the planning stage of the series there was no intention to focus on particular regions by title or to include shots of the helicopter within the footage, particular producers did manage to find their own voice and expression. Mirzoeff, in interviews, recalls that this mix in style was seen as essential, providing a degree of variety (which sometimes worked but on other occasions did not), and an experiment in television filming:

> Writers were encouraged to put across a balanced personal view. They were political, with a small p, views. It would also make people look at Britain, get us to look at Britain…. It was an education on heritage and what was happening to the land and what planning was doing. We were tackling the issues in a way that hadn't been done before.

By the time the final batch of programmes was being filmed, attention turned towards whether to undertake a commitment to film further programmes either within the UK or overseas. The total cost of the series of 13 programmes had already escalated to over £250,000, and became – as a result – the most expensive series ever to be commissioned by the BBC; it had even surpassed the costs of the landmark BBC2 series, Kenneth Clark's *Civilisation*, broadcast over 13 weeks between February and May 1969, which overlapped with the commencement of *Bird's-Eye View* by a few weeks. Files at the BBC Written Archives indicate that the running costs of the series was a continual headache, and some of the features of the series had to be changed as a consequence of the squeeze on expenditure; among these, for example, was the decision to abandon plans for original specially commissioned music for each programme, and the choice of actors to provide narration.

Transport interchanges transformed urban centres: Bradford

Mirzoeff remarks in interview that, by 1971, members of the helicopter unit were exhausted from the experience of making the 13 programmes for the series and were extremely reluctant to pursue further *Bird's-Eye View* ideas. This is hardly surprising if one takes into account the logistics involved in selecting appropriate subjects in the first instance, securing permission for filming rights from every landowner for every location, the pressure to undertake the right shooting at the right locations, to avoid undue time delay and expense and maintain the minimum hours flying time, and then assemble narration and musical accompaniment to the images in as near a perfect way as possible. Accordingly, a decision was taken not to commission any further programmes.

EXAMPLES OF PROGRAMME CONTENT

Overview

As indicated earlier, because a number of different producers were allocated to the series over the 1968-71 period, and there was a degree of flexibility in the form of filming and style of narrative, many of the programmes did not fit into the same genre. As discussed earlier, some of the films were polemic and poetical (such as those of John Betjeman), while others were more report-like in style, and others more personal. This makes it difficult to label the entire series – could it be described as arts, general features, documentary or geographical? Certainly the series scheduling, in the evening 19.30 hours slot on BBC2, did lend itself in this period to be a serious feature (see the next section for further discussion). But on analysis of all 13 programmes, it is possible to divide up the films into several sub-genres. These are indicated below, in Table 8.2.

Table 8.2: Sub-genres of *Bird's-Eye View* (1969-71)

Programme	Transmission date	Sub-genre
'The Englishman's home'	5 April 1969	Polemical, artistic
'Beside the seaside'	25 December 1969	Polemical, artistic
'A land for all seasons'	18 April 1971	Polemical, artistic
'Man on the move'	22 May 1969	Polemical, journalistic
'A green and pleasant land'	22 June 1969	Polemical, journalistic
'The island fortress'	26 October 1969	Factual, journalistic
'John Bull's workshop'	30 November 1969	Factual, journalistic
'Wales – The Western stronghold'	28 February 1971	Factual, journalistic
'The Highlands and Islands'	25 January 1970	Factual, journalistic
'Eastern approach'	17 May 1970	Personal, travelogue
'Innis Fail – Isle of Destiny'	17 March 1971	Personal, travelogue
'What a lovely day'	22 March 1970	Fictional narrative
'From Bishop Rock to Muckle Flugger'	25 December 1970	Documentary

These six sub-genres are now defined in a little more detail.

Polemical, artistic refers to programmes that possess a defined agenda within the narrative, either indirectly or directly making reference to the changing state of Britain; this includes, for example, statements on housing provision, on the protection of the coast and countryside; it is artistic because the narrative utilises prose and poetry to communicate to the audience.

Polemical, journalistic refers to programmes that also possess a defined agenda within the narrative, either indirectly or directly making reference to the changing state of Britain; this includes, for example, statements on the increase in car transport, the future of the countryside and the changing face of industrial Britain; it is journalistic because it contains a degree of statements on facts and figures, and is devoid of poetry and prose.

Factual, journalistic refers to programmes that are not so polemical in character but which nevertheless provides the audience with a description of a changing landscape and a changing society; programmes are almost travelogue in format, and are partly conversational in the narrative.

Personal, travelogue refers to programmes that possess a narrative that is personal in style, usually authored by a writer with direct experience of the places and locations used; a form of reminiscing about childhood days and places, and experiences in travel and employment. Sometimes an actor speaks the dialogue, but the dialect is meant to reflect the particular region at the centre of the film.

Fictional narrative refers to programmes that possess a narrative that is weak, and relates more directly to the images shown; this category only contains one film, and the dialogue for this was a fictional conversation between two people (possibly husband and wife) commenting as voyeurs on the sequence of shots on display and making judgemental statements about activities. The programme was scripted but acted out to a greater extent.

Documentary refers to programmes that do not hide the fact of filmmaking from the audience, and the experience of making the film is as much a part of the programme as the shots and commentary devoted to places. The one film in this category contains, for example, footage of the helicopter taking off, flying and landing, and the curiosity of the public towards the helicopter landing at remote locations.

Some of these sub-genres are explored further with illustrations taken from the films.

The polemical and artistic films

John Betjeman made three of the programmes for *Bird's-Eye View*, these being: 'The Englishman's home', 'Beside the seaside' and 'A land for all seasons' (see also Chapter Seven). These were some of the most popular programmes of the series, as may be gleaned from press reviews and audience reaction, discussed later.

'A land for all seasons' was Betjeman's third programme, and it was to be the last programme in the *Bird's-Eye View* series of 13. The focus on this film was on the seasons and on the countryside, especially farming. The film was shot over a 12-month period at similar locations to provide the viewer with an aerial perspective of the changing seasons and their affect on the landscape. In contrast to his two previous films, it was decided that the film would be an anthology, with some newly commissioned poetry by Betjeman, accompanied by other poets' work selected by Betjeman but read out by a number of actors. The script was originally formulated by Barnett and developed by Betjeman, while John Bird produced the programme. Betjeman was not first choice; Correlli Barnett developed the key themes, as is evident in a letter he sent to Mirzoeff on 12 August 1969:

> The central theme of the programme would be to combine and contrast the townsman's sentimental view of the land as picturesque scenery to drive through and picnic in, with the reality that agriculture is one of our most modern and efficient industries – perhaps the single economic activity where we hold a huge lead over foreign rivals.

Betjeman was approached only after the Gloucestershire author, Laurie Lee, declined the invitation to develop the script. Betjeman viewed the film after completion in late December 1970 and agreed a fee of £355 for both narration and the new material. But by the time of the programme's production, Betjeman's health had deteriorated, and he was in the early stages of Parkinson's disease. This may account for the lack of sparkle in the verses that were present in his previous films, but the overall work is nevertheless impressive.

This film is probably one of the most artistic in style, with a mix of music and poetry, rather than prose, containing a romantic and lyrical rhythm. One gets the feeling that the difficulties of helicopter filming have been overcome and that the whole ensemble is as near as the producers are going to achieve to a perfect aerial film. Among the shots are: the same cluster of trees in each of the four seasons; cherry blossoms; a summer wedding; the countryside covered in snow; a winter funeral; the mountain ridges of Snowdon; a windswept hill farm in North Wales; a pheasant shoot (filmed at ground level); swans in the Norfolk Broads; horses in the New Forest; women picking daffodils in Spalding; tractors assisting with the harvest; children playing around the Maypole as part of a village's celebration of May Day; fields of yellow rape-seed oil; old ruined cottages and electricity pylons; sheep dipping; helicopter crop spraying; crowds flocking to Beaulieu Motor Museum in Hampshire; stubble burning; the Wye Valley in autumn colours; a fox hunt; and children and cars in snow drifts.

Betjeman wrote over 17 original verses for the programme, and these have been published only recently (Games, 2006). Accompanying the images of snow-capped mountains of Snowdonia, for example, Betjeman recites:

> On yon unsheltered mountain height of Wales
> The stalwart precipices face the gales,
> While gathering clouds assume a threatening form
> And valleys wait th'inevitable storm.
> Under the winter's unrelenting sky
> Caernarvonshire and Merioneth lie.
> And few will think that there can ever be
> An end to winter's reign of tyranny.

Later in the film, during a series of shots of harvest time, Betjeman provides some characteristic acerbic poetry, incorporating humour and bite simultaneously:

> We spray the fields and scatter
> The poison on the ground
> So that no wicked wild flower
> Upon our farm be found.
> We like whatever helps us
> To line our purse with pence;
> The twenty-four-hour broiler-house
> And neat electric fence.

> All concrete sheds around us
> All Jaguars in the yard,
> The telly lounge and deep-freeze
> Are ours from working hard.

Personal travelogue: 'Eastern approach'

'Eastern approach' was written by Stuart Hood and depicts an aerial journey down the East Coast of Britain between Montrose and London. The narrator for the programme was Gordon Jackson. Hood develops his script from a personal perspective; he was born and raised in Montrose, and the narrator weaves a story based around reminisces of boyhood and adolescent journeys on fishing

Doom scenarios: the implications of rising car ownership were raised in the 1960s

trawlers between Scotland and the Thames, cherry-picking places en route of historical and geographical significance.

The opening shots are of Montrose and its surroundings, followed quickly by Arbroath and – further down the coast – Dundee. The dialogue accompanying the film states:

> The horizons of childhood. The hills – the Basin – the lighthouse on the point – the Bell Rock Light out at sea. The aerodrome where Cobham and Mollison and Amy Johnson came with their flying circuses and I saw my first helicopter. From this enclosure area we lift off to fly over the sandstone coast to Arbroath. In its red Abbey Robert, King of Scots, and his nobles took a great oath to fight the English seeking neither glory nor honour nor riches but that freedom which no man lays down but with his life. This was my metropolis: a Dantesque city stratified in layers on the hill above the Tay – from the tenements round the jute mills to the millowners' mansions on the slopes of the Law. It was a vantage point from which you could see a wider horizon – the Highland hills, fire sticking its tongue into the North Sea – the cargo boats laden with jute from India – the steamer for London passing the lightship at the mouth of the river.

The footage depicts various places along the coast, from Leuchars naval air station, to the abbey at St Andrews, the Tweed at Berwick, Lindisfarne, Bamburgh Castle, the sea collieries in Northumberland, the Cook statue at Whitby, the beach at Bridlington, an oil rig at Holderness Bay, the Lincolnshire coast and fenland, the Second World War anti-invasion stones on East Anglia, Lowestoft, Harwich port, and Canvey Islands and the approach along the Thames, finally finishing at Tower Bridge. The narrative provides a novel way of linking the disparate places together and the variety in type of images and locations shown keeps the viewer sufficiently interested.

From an historical perspective, and viewing the film today, it is amazing to see how much of Britain has changed over a 40-year period. The ports and harbours are but a shadow of their former selves, coastal waters are cleaner and the more industrial plants on the coast have all but disappeared. Even London's docklands in the film resemble a busy, working industrial environment unlike the high-rise financial sector offices and expensive apartments that exist there today.

Mirzoeff states that the producers and editors of the programmes wanted to achieve a mix in the musical accompaniment, and there was no hesitation in using more contemporary music of – at the time – living composers, such as Shostakovitch, Stravinsky, Britten and Tippett. The use of the music in 'Beside the seaside' illustrates the careful editing and musical choice, with high usage of music by composers ranging from Elgar to Walton to Bax and, later in the film, to Stravinsky and Shostakovitch. Mirzoeff states that the polemical element of some of the films was strongly encouraged, and there was also an attempt to stimulate a debate about changing Britain. This polemical, agenda-setting purpose of the series is also reflected with reference to a six-page document prepared by David Collison to Gordon Watkins, BBC Head of General Features (Television), relating to the proposed programme on the countryside, and very much reflecting the opinions of Ian Nairn from the mid-1950s. Collison states:

> I believe the subject to be of major importance and that television can help to alleviate an increasingly alarming situation; that is to say that if the present trend is allowed to continue there could be little or no natural scenery, no flower, insect or animal life left in these islands in 40 years' time; I do not think this is overstating the case.... The BBC, by providing this public service but providing it entertainingly and critically, could be the strongest agent in ensuring that Britain in 2000AD does not resemble Slough Trading Estate from Land's End to John O'Groats.

Changeless but changeable: the view from Richmond Hill

PRESS AND PUBLIC REACTION TO *BIRD'S-EYE VIEW*

In order to meet the expectations of the BBC's higher echelons that *Bird's-Eye View* could become a significant series, considerable effort went in to promoting the series. A press release issued in late March 1969 just prior to the transmission on 5 April of the first programme in the series, 'The Englishman's home', announced some of the principal features of the programme but also took the opportunity of announcing some of the themes to be addressed later in the series. *The Daily Telegraph* took up the story of the new series on 29 March, *The Guardian* on 3 April; both newspapers published accompanying photographs. The BBC organised a press event at Battersea Heliport on Wednesday 2 April 1969, to show off the helicopter, and offer reporters the experience of short rides over South London. Journalists from the *Evening News*, *Evening Standard*, *Daily Telegraph*, *The Sun*, *The Sketch*, *The Sunday Telegraph*, *The Guardian*, *The Times* and *Sunday Mirror* all went aloft, according to

BBC Archive records, and the event was regarded by the BBC as a success for the publicity generated.

Initial press reaction following transmission of 'The Englishman's home' was very positive. Jimmy Thomas, in the *Daily Express* of 8 April stated that the programme was 'one of the best TV features of the day' while the *Daily Mail* on the same day described it as 'a marvellous series'. And so the press reviews continued with subsequent programmes, although rather more mixed in tone. In the *Daily Express* on 23 June 1969, Jimmy Thomas remarks, following the transmission of 'A green and pleasant land':

> To all those readers who wrote agreeing with my condemnation last week of the rubbish dished up on Sundays by the two major channels, I can only suggest an immediate move to BBC2.
>
> And in colour it is worth the price of four packets of cigarettes a week.
>
> Last night up came the enterprising infant again, with one of the best TV features for many a day, "Bird's-Eye View". In three attempts at the unusual, this series has given sheer enchantment as its helicopter-borne cameras reveal an entirely new view of Britain.
>
> Last night's was about the preservation of the countryside – splendidly done, bursting with questions for a Government and a people too unconcerned as industry, boxhousing and motorways, gobble up our heritage.

The transmission of 'John Bull's workshop' caused *The Times* of 16 November 1969 to print a four-column aerial picture of Telford new town, reporting that the social relations officer of the town corporation was not 'entirely flattered' by the BBC's description of the town. The programme itself was actually transmitted 14 days later. A similar press report had cropped up in the *Brighton Evening Argus* and *Brighton and Hove Gazette* on 6 December 1968 with Peacehaven Parish Council expressing concern to the BBC about how Peacehaven, a not-so-successful display of planning located on the South Down cliffs, might be portrayed on film.

The broadcast of 'What a lovely day' in March 1970 also caused consternation, partly because of its high-handed narration between a man and a woman commenting on the film. Jimmy Thomas, again, in the *Daily Express* of 23 March, claimed that the 'BBC made a tremendous success with *Bird's-Eye View* – where the now famous helicopter took a look at Britain at leisure.... I cannot think of any feature programme which gives me this much pleasure...', whereas

The South Downs; leisure was an emerging theme of the early 1970s but with environmental implications

Nancy Banks-Smith in her *Guardian* review of the same day takes a rather different perspective:

> *Bird's-Eye View* (BBC2) made my toes curl because of the condescending commentary…. Perhaps seeing things from above does give you a rather diminished opinion of your subject. The commentary was shared between three speakers, whom I like to think of as Cyril (who was suave), and Dai (who was bluff) and Dai's Mrs (who was a little potty and so tended to get sat on). Well, I'm sorry, but condescension does tend to make me come over all-coarse. I think they were meant to be the common man and his mate, and a chap from the BBC, who were escorting them around ill-concealed ennui. Pretty pictures, jolly songs, incompatible company.

Gerard Garrett, in *The Daily Sketch*, the same day, also found the programme commentary 'out of proportion … eccentric … with embarrassment'.

The transmission of 'Eastern approach' in May 1970 also attracted considerable attention. The *Observer* of 17 May 1970 called it 'one of the best *Bird's-Eye Views* yet … history gently told, affection transmitted', a view echoed in the *Daily Mirror* on 18 May: 'the best *Bird's-Eye* films that I have seen'. *The Sunday Telegraph* also remarked on Stuart Hood's 'outstanding' commentary at the beginning and end, although complained that the middle of the film was 'rather guide-bookish', adding, 'But why does this series ... so distrust its contributors that it hires actors to read their words?' The *Birmingham Post* of 18 May also remarks, 'The *Bird's-Eye View* series has not always come up to expectations. Sometimes bad lighting conditions have made the photography dull; sometimes the commentaries have been irritatingly "bright". Last night's film was a winner.... Imaginative photography, exploiting ever-changing light on sea and land emphasising this sense of variety. This is the sort of programme where colour counts.' *The Sunday Times* of 24 May, meanwhile, offers remarks on Stuart Hood's penned commentary: 'A bit dour, not frivolous enough for my weaker self, but admirable, perceptive, with its proper poetry. I'm not at all so sure about the value of the helicopter, though. The first revealing flip is fascinating, but you get to wishing the darned thing would touch down for a minute while you digest a view. You need to stand still.'

Finally, the transmission of the last programme in the series, John Betjeman's 'A land for all seasons', on 18 April 1971, attracted very positive reviews. Richard Last in *The Daily Telegraph* of 19 April states, 'One of the joys of the format has been its total exclusion of all those normally mandatory interviews ... for some, the combination may have been too soft-centred, and Sir John's own poetry can have a slightly bathetic effect. But it was a splendid celebration of what is still, despite the developers and polluters, our green and pleasant land.' Ivor Jay in the *Birmingham Post* of the same day is more lyrical in his praise: '... one of those rare delights of visual and verbal beauty which rebukes the easy sneer that television is a wasteland. One wallowed in it like a fragrant bath of restorative and healing powers.' Peter Black's television column in *The Daily Mail*, also on 19 April, provides a criticism of 'Too much hunting and slow motion running about sentimentalised scenes, and there were too few familiar poets in the commentary,' but adds that: 'The combination of imaginative pre-selection by producer John Bird and cameramen Mulligan and Vincze, and lyrical editing by Peter Barber, set out a breathtakingly beautiful view of the English and Welsh countryside, as of an inspection of his work by a kindly creator.'

The Sunday Times displayed a more thorough overview of the programme and series in the Maurice Wiggin column of 25 April:

> John Bird in his *Bird's-Eye View* series, shot from a helicopter, has very perceptively used those very factors – the flux of images, the whirlybirds of time – to create a new and mesmeric, hallucinatory

sensation, as different as possible from the isolated moment of the still photograph and equally remote from the pedestrian travelogue.... The *Bird's-Eye View* is complementary to other modes of recording and observing. It does not pretend to be exhaustive. The watcher has to agree to surrender the "right" to certain sorts of factual information, which can be got at ground level, in exchange for a certain swoony sort of dreamlike, godlike sensation, swanning high in a trance of freedom.

Finally, *The Listener* of 29 April 1971 asks, rhetorically, 'Has it paid off, this spending of 10,000 colour licenses?' It states it thinks it has and was 'breathtaking in its images', but adds that the real time to judge the series would be in 50 years' time.

Audience reaction to the programmes was quite positive. I will deal with individual responses in a moment, but for the present, I wish to analyse the BBC's own Audience Research Reports for some of the programmes. The four reports assessed are for: 'Man on the move', 'A green and pleasant land', 'Eastern approach', and 'A land for all seasons'. These reports produced confidentially by the BBC provide figures for the percentage share of the audience gained, the audience reaction (based on completed questionnaires from the viewing public), together with additional comments with preferences and views. Copies of the reports were discovered within the files for each programme at the BBC Written Archives at Caversham Park.

As already noted, 'Man on the move' was broadcast on Sunday 25 May 1969, on BBC2 between 19.25 and 20.15. The estimated audience for the programme was 2.9 per cent of the viewing public, and compared to shares of 16.4 per cent for BBC1 and 23.0 per cent for ITV for similar times. A sample of 41 members of the viewing public was asked for its reaction to the programme, and the reaction index was 78 per cent. The report notes that the audience response rate for the first programme in the series, transmitted six weeks previously, was 80 per cent positive. The viewers were 'enchanted' by the programme but the criticisms that exist appear to relate almost exclusively to the commentary. Some viewers were 'irritated' by the narration, and some of the pessimistic scenes (motorway building, for example) they maintained did not require constant commentary as the images conveyed the message clearly in their own right. The advantage point was appreciated, particularly to convey the history of old tracks and rights of way, and the majority of the audience thought the helicopter journey 'unique and probably ideal'. The

Radio, television and mobile phone transmitters remain contentious forms of development.

background music was described as noisy or distracting on times, but overall, 'satisfaction was the order of the day'.

The audience research survey of 'A green and pleasant land' again shows an overall positive attitude among the surveyed viewing public, although the audience reaction index had dropped slightly, once again, to 75 per cent, and share of the viewing public for the programme, transmitted on Sunday 22 June 1969 between 19.25 and 20.15, was a mere 1.2 per cent. The audience seemed to appreciate the focus and pitch of the programme, particularly its direct attempt to convey the urgency of the need to act to protect the countryside from urban encroachment. Criticisms related to the viewers not being able to identify the interesting places from the narration, and there was too much of the latter in places to detract from the excellent photography. A further criticism emanated from those watching in black and white and what was being lost in terms of viewing, and a tendency for the image to jump about suddenly from place to place rather than dwell on particular locations for lengthier periods, leaving some members of the public feeling 'dizzy'.

'Eastern approach' was broadcast on Sunday 17 May 1970 between 20.15 and 21.05. The audience for this programme was 3.9 per cent of the BBC2 viewing public. The audience reaction was the highest in the series, thus far, at 81 per cent. The personal commentary was appreciated and this made 'a particularly interesting and unusual documentary, it was said – a change from the run-of-the-mill, impersonal travelogue'. There was high praise for the narration by Gordon Jackson and for the photography, while the accompanying music was considered to be 'appropriate and well married to the film'. Some thought the music too loud and obtrusive and the notion that too much geography was covered in a short space of time. A minority considered the programme to be 'superficial' or 'sketchy'.

Finally, the audience reaction report for 'A land for all seasons' indicates that the programme had a viewing public of 3.7 per cent. It was broadcast on Sunday 18 April 1971, between 20.15 and 21.05. The reaction profile is different for this time than previous reports and, rather than an audience reaction index, the audience was asked to make judgements on a five-point scale of their perceptions on five indicators. Of the 92 questionnaires completed, 86 per cent considered the programme to be completely gripping, 76 per cent thought it highly informative, 89 per cent regarded it as completely clear, 72 per cent thought-provoking, and 89 per cent rewarding. The reaction was extremely positive and the audience were appreciative of the beautiful shots of the countryside, the blending of the poetry and music, and the effect of the programme was 'soothing, relaxing and moving, and had evoked feelings of nostalgia'. Interestingly, several respondents asked to see the programme repeated and some had asked for more programmes to be made in the series ('A land for all seasons' was the final film in the series of 13). The quality of the pictures and sound were rated 'exceptionally good' and aerial photography warmly praised. One or two remarked on the colour spectacle: 'This is the type of entertainment which makes a colour TV worth having', whereas others who still had a black and white set were disappointed: 'For once I wish I had a colour TV.' There were complaints though that the music had occasionally drowned out the poetry, and again there were criticisms that the public were not able to identify the places depicted: 'I knew a lot of the views shown, but not knowing the others left a slight feeling of frustration.' Finally, the film had taken an uncompromising view of the countryside life, including a pheasant shoot and a foxhunt, and some thought the inclusion of the scenes depicting the killing of a hare to be unnecessary. Some also did not appreciate the combination of poetry and music; as one of the films of the series to possess some

Bird's-Eye View has been mirrored recently by *Coast* and *Britain from Above*

of the most artistic in content, it was commented that, 'Poetry held little appeal or the music had not made much impression....'

CONCLUSIONS

Bird's-Eye View provides an interesting illustration of the development of technological developments to British television during a period of rapid change. The commissioning of an aerial photographic programme was ambitious, not least because of the dearth of skills relating to aerial filming apparent within the BBC in the late 1960s. Ironically, although senior BBC executives could champion the series by the time of the transmission of the 13th and final programme in April 1971, the series seems to have been developed in response to the need to find a principal use for a helicopter that the BBC had contracted to use for a three–year period from 1968. BBC2 was already establishing itself as an arts channel by 1968, and possessed an enthusiastic controller at the helm who was interested in pushing the possibilities of colour broadcasting to a wider audience and showcasing BBC2 for its position at the forefront of technological advancement. But the idea of developing a documentary series on planning, landscape and modernity, filmed virtually entirely from a helicopter, was experimental and risky.

As John Walker (1993) and John Wyver (1989) both outline in their seminal works on arts broadcasting in Britain, arts programmes by the late 1960s were either studio-based examinations, specially commissioned films, or – with *Civilisation* – expert knowledge communicated by a presenter. *Bird's-Eye View* would introduce a new form of programme to BBC2, with its concentration on prose and music for commentary and sound, and a rapidly changing succession of montages to provide the viewer with a new, aerial perspective of Britain. Planning and change would be brought into people's homes at primetime in a very new way; *Bird's-Eye View* would enable these matters to be communicated directly to the audience without an expert or academic explanation for the photography or the prose, without panel discussions, and without any studio or indoor filming. The fact that the press and audience seem to have, on the whole, taken to the programmes, suggests that the risk paid off and there was a great deal of appreciation for the direct way in which the subjects were being presented to the viewer. The combination of the personal in the narration, the prose, the music, the colour images and the new aerial perspective had provided viewers with a unique television experience and certainly, what we may now think of as, a landmark television series.

The transmission of the series over a two-year period was unique in itself, but this permitted some flexibility in narrative development and in photography, that may not have otherwise been possible. The colour transmission allowed the series to happen; one doubts whether such a series could have worked or would have been commissioned for black and white television. Watching the programmes today, one is struck by the poor quality images within some of the films, caused by relatively poor weather conditions. The series editor and producers were under pressure from BBC executives to complete filming even during adverse conditions when light was low. It is unfortunate that BBC financial expediency resulted in poorer images being used in some cases, but at £250,000, we should be grateful that the BBC decided, rather boldly, to commission what would become the most expensive series ever filmed in the first place.

Given the financial constraints, the experiment with aerial filming and the 'learning-as-you-work' ethic that was required by the helicopter team, the difficultly of securing permission to fly at low altitude, and the uncertainty of how the assemblage of film and sound would work in the cutting room, it is little wonder how a series of 13 programmes emerged at all. But the fact that the 13 programmes were applauded suggests that, somehow, the series worked. The development of a team culture within the BBC, with many staff hired specifically to work on the series alone, also contributed to its success. With uncertainty present as to whether the series would work at all, there was a commitment to 'go for it' and pull out all the stops.

The content of the programmes are also unique and are of current historical significance. They depict a Britain undergoing rapid technological change, the birth of cities and motorways, of high-rise flats, of the dawn of leisure time, and the commencement of the decline of manufacturing industry and agriculture. Mirzoeff explains this in interview:

> The films are special because it gave you a view of Britain at the beginning of the '70s and something changing. You can look at motorways which are only just being constructed, houses which aren't there yet.... Thamesmead only being built....

There is no doubt, in my mind, that most of the films in the *Bird's-Eye View* series provide an important historical record of

Britain in the middle of a modernisation ethos, while also on the brink of the breakdown of parts of the establishment and traditional forms of working, the onset of industrial competition that would lead very shortly to the collapse of British manufacturing industry. Perhaps, more intriguingly, the series is in stark contrast to most film and television from this period that possess, what we have become used to seeing as, an identifiable stamp of the late Sixties (swinging London, the Mini, fashion, the summer of love, for example). The *Bird's-Eye View* programmes contain virtually no display of this era of the Sixties. If anything, this makes the films even more of a landmark series in British television history; how many other colour television series from the late 1960s focus on the Britain that was fast disappearing, that owed its existence to pre- and postwar customs and constraints? And yet, paradoxically, the series used the most modern technological developments in order to capture the changes.

We may view *Bird's-Eye View*, these days, with nostalgia and lament in some instances at what Britain was losing; we may look in wonderment at parts of the country that have changed beyond all recognition, and how people 40 years ago treated the environment; we may also be thankful that events and conditions have improved, or we may be astonished to see how little has changed in ethos with regards to some of the best landscapes that we possess. What is undeniable, though, is the pace of change and, when filmed from a helicopter, how different landscape and places appear, providing us with perspectives on what we often – day to day – take for granted.

Bird's-Eye View may be viewed as the product of a particular age and of a particular way of filmmaking in television. As Mirzoeff remarks:

> I have a very strong belief that the best television comes up with very strong closely-knit teams working together who think of themselves an elite outside the rest of television. *Arena, 40 Minutes, Bird's-Eye View* were all just gangs of people who were close and who did all their things together. We worked hard and played hard. The intensity paid off. We knew it was risky and new and that it could all be a disaster. But it encouraged you to push harder because of the risk. It was television that worked, but the team thing has gone now sadly.

NINE

"Planning turned out to be war by other means"

Caravans and chalets sprawled along the coast in the 1960s and 1970s

New civic buildings, and pedestrians separated from the traffic by subways

Social housing programmes replaced Victorian and Edwardian terraced housing: Kensal Green

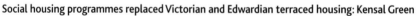

The Royal & Sun Alliance, Liverpool, 1972-76; it incorporates the elevated walkways promoted in the 1965 city centre plan

Former court buildings with severed pedway: Bristol's Rupert Street

Library, diagonally opposite the 1890
neo-classical Portsmouth Guildhall

Queensway, Birmingham, part of a concrete collar around the city

Brighton, part of the Conference Centre redevelopment

Kingsway Tunnel ventilation tower,
Liverpool, 1971

Wyndham Court, Southampton, 1966 69, intended to attract young professionals to reside in the city centre, now Grade II listed

Accommodating the car; a road since 1013 and formerly the site of Tudor courtiers' houses, the modern Upper Thames Street necessitated demolition of older buildings in the 1960s

Places of fear, crime or art? Beneath the A102(M) interchange

Hotel adjacent to Tower Bridge, London

Central House,
Bradford, opposite the
Kirkgate Centre

Alternative uses for abandoned concrete spaces

'Academy for the training of secret police': The Prince of Wales' comments on designs for Sir Colin St John Wilson's British Library

The changing
city skyline:
Richard Roger's
Lloyds building
and Richard
Seifert's Nat
West Tower

In everything, accept the genius of the place: Towards a new respect for place in planning

TEN

A multiplicity of meanings of space and place

INTRODUCTION

This book has explored the position of urban planning, and the image, representation and depiction of planning in film and photography over the last 80 years or so. It has essentially attempted to work on several levels: as a narrative of urban planning's remarkable ability to change and adapt to different conditions, political expectations and public desires over time; as an alternative history of places and change in the built environment and – more pertinently – reactions to that change, using sources from the arts and humanities; and as a prompt to those interested and involved in urban planning to consider the story of places in ways that the public, the media and others understand. It is intended to facilitate a wide-ranging debate on these subjects at the beginning of the 21st century, and one that has been lacking for many decades. From a personal perspective, although I have worked in the field of urban planning for many years, I have always found these aspects of planning – the image and representation of planning and places, the role of planning in achieving wider societal benefit and the depiction of cities through history – the most interesting and challenging, and sometimes the most difficult, to analyse and comprehend.

The fact that my dilemmas and uncertainties about these issues still exist today, two decades after I first graduated, perhaps lie at the root of the problem of urban planning and places themselves. My uncertainties with planning correspond to questions of planning as a self-perpetuating activity, devoid of a philosophical core, lacking a strong concern with place meaning and identity, and a continual source of criticism politically and in the media. I have not suddenly developed these uncertainties, and other commentators over the years have debated these questions far more effectively. But the opportunity to provide a critical viewpoint of urban planning and place narrative as part of a contribution intended to both promote and develop visionary, creative and progressive debates about the future of our environment and of places, has necessitated an analytical scrutiny of the subject matter I have immersed myself in since the mid–1980s.

My critical perspective for this book has emanated from a growing frustration with planning, particularly with planning's representation, with some planners' inability to consider planning as a contested political and powerful activity that originates from people's perceptions of change as both fact and fiction, and with planners content not to reassert their position in broader socioeconomic and environmental change. Although we live in different times with a very different role for the state, planners seem to have forgotten the 20th-century visionary ideals, and how urban planning can actually not only contribute towards but shape social and economic restructuring. These concern the wider societal benefits that urban planning has to tackle, as well as a more critical understanding of urban planning, place history and even townscape. At the present time, with urban planning constantly being subject to political and legislative reform, and with a growing list of purposes attached to it, there is a real danger that planning will become increasingly devoid of intellectual discourse concerning broader spatial or strategic questions, and will rather concentrate on its role as very little more than a neighbourhood protection service. There is debate, of course, on sustainability issues, on community desires, of health inequalities and regional economic differentials. But when allied to urban planning, they seem to take on an air of rhetoric.

By considering the visual representations of places and the achievements of urban planning, both the good and the bad, an alternative history of planning can be developed that allows links to be made between planning and place-based contentions. For those of us actively involved in the analysis, interpretation and design of places, I think it is fair to say that we often neglect the meaning and representation of places, to look at places how others see them, rather than through the eyes of experts or professionals.

Edinburgh Castle, leading up to the Camera Obscura, where Sir Patrick Geddes, sociologist and planner, surveyed the city

We can say that cities are physical constructs, but as Lefebvre (1974 [1991]) remarks, the social construction of cities and places is a vital element in how people see the environments that surround them. Representations evoke the real and the imagined and can 'challenge

A palimpsest of styles, the City of London

the prevailing structures of expectation' (Hall, 1997). To this end, work that examines the origins, the full extent and the possible impacts of these perceptions of the built and natural environment in Britain, and by implication, public attitudes towards development and change, is – I think – both useful and timely.

FILMIC NARRATIVES AND A SENSE OF PLACE

This book has demonstrated how the city and the way it is represented in film and photography can provide a unique perspective for us to consider urban planning and places in ways that traditional social science often fails to do. Some of those perspectives are real, some are imaged, and some are constructs. Globally, we may think of the way Chicago masquerades as Gotham in Batman films, Woody Allen's Manhattan backdrop or Hitchcock's use of San Francisco in *Vertigo*. The key point here is that the camera lens is well positioned to provide an holistic interpretation of interventions in the urban. Film provides an opportunity for an alternative critical perspective, gleaned from celluloid representation, which might explain the prevalence and significance of people's perceptions of places that often planners feel remote from or unable to discern. Film generates emotion about the here and now, and on what has gone before – the ubiquitous city skyline, serving to represent progress and the future, of urban bridges, gateways between different communities, or living on the right or wrong side of the tracks, of car chases and crime caper getaways. All these are employed in film narratives and the city as filmic location can be as important as the storyline itself. But film can also evoke a sense of history, of nostalgia for things past. Terence Davies' recent *Of Time and the City* (2008) is a remarkable homage to a long vanished Liverpool, one not only devastated by the collapse of manufacturing, but also by what the planners and architects did to the city in the name of progress between the 1950s and 1970s. And we sometimes forget in our rush to create modern places, with the best architecture and most rational solutions to urban form, that there is a desire often in the public's mind to look backwards for comfort, to familiar and cherished scenes, and awaken conservation and heritage sensibilities.

Blue plaques littered liberally around London are but one testament to this desire to remember what or who went before in very specific locations of the city. Or the popularity of walking or photographic tours around cities to capture fragments of the past,

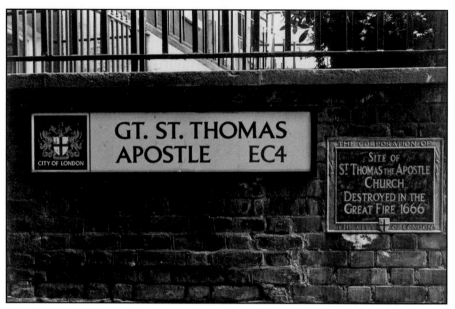

Fire offered the chance to build a grand city, but Wren's plans were turned down

or specific events that caused upheaval in our urban landscape. The sorts of architecture and planning we created after these upheavals create their own sets of emotions with public and audiences, relating to postwar housing, civic buildings or shopping centres. They seem to be either loved or loathed, illustrated perhaps by the fact that in a recent BBC poll to find the best and worst 20th-century buildings in Britain, the Barbican complex in London came top in both categories.

Emotions run high when modern buildings are juxtaposed with historic buildings in civic settings, or when views across the urban terrain seem to be compromised in some ways by new developments. And it reflects the subjective opinions that people hold about our ever-changing urban landscape. This is epitomised by the case of the Gateshead car park, a brutal modern construction that featured in the Michael Caine film *Get Carter* (directed by Mike Hodges, 1971). Its portrayal in the film captured public imagination, prompted the formation of *Get Carter* re-enactment scenes in the vicinity, and an active campaign to save the Grade II protected building from demolition in 2010 simply because of its filmic representation. It has since been demolished.

Our view of the urban is also affected by our use of transport. Even here film plays a role, certain forms of transport being synonymous with certain cities, the Paris Metro, the cable cars of San Francisco, yellow cabs with New York, or the red Routemaster bus with London, as mentioned in Chapter Four. These evoke notions of place identity – you can associate them with certain cities, and that is why they still have a role in film and television today as iconic symbols of places, in the face of globalisation that often creates identikit cities with the same shops and chainstores and motor cars.

Film can also serve to represent not only the city as exciting and entertaining places to be, but also places of play and leisure, whether that is organised or informal in nature, against a backdrop of city parks, that bring together a diversity of people. Think of how often Central Park, New York, has been used as a filmic location, or (as discussed in Chapter Five) the hills overlooking some polluted northern city, used to represent some sort of romantic escape for working-class characters from their mundane lives. We walk through the city using particular paths that we are used to, navigating our way through the urban streetscape, all of which creates its own sense of identity for us, where even footbridges, paths, street furniture and street signage contribute to a sense of belonging and familiarity because we know they are somehow different to other places. But it is also about the everyday places that we encounter routinely, of parking lots, backstreets, derelict land and boarded-up premises. These are areas of transition in the city, places that are neither here

'Heritage bus'

Whose city I: controlling the urban realm

nor there, places that once had a social and economic purpose, but perhaps today are less successful and subject to regeneration.

Patrick Keiller's films (*London*, 1994; *Robinson in Space*, 1997; *Robinson in Ruins*, 2010) demonstrate an eye for detail at capturing conditions of places, through entertaining journeys and oblique perspectives of change. Echoing the literary work of J.G. Ballard and Iain Sinclair, and a fascination for psycho-geography, the films evoke, to quote Sinclair, a 'quiet provocation' to audiences, noting in the film essay accompanying the DVD release of the first two films by the BFI: 'The truth of a city, divided against itself, can only be revealed, so Keiller believes, through a series of obscure pilgrimages, days spent crawling out on to the rim of things. The transcendent surrealism of airport perimeter roads, warehouses and reservoirs.' Keiller's films provide an imaginative capture through the lens of the direct impacts of urban planning and of the places the planners have left behind or even forgotten about. These images are not the stuff of picture postcards, of architects' and urban designers' glossy portrayals of possible bright shiny new spaces, palaces of capitalism. They are, rather, images that capture fragments of place history and place memory – 'liminal spaces', to use Andrew Higson's phraseology from Chapter Five – a poke in the ribs for those of us who transcend the city daily: look at places that we might otherwise regard as routine or irrelevant. To those of us involved in urban planning and place contentions, the resultant work is both equally familiar and baffling; Dave (2000) has commented that when released, *London* and *Robinson in Space* received hostile reception from critics since they were regarded as pretentious, nonsensical and even boring, dealing with capitalism, history, modernity and place. And perhaps this says something more about the difficulty of representing and communicating urban change to a cinematic wider audience. The films are certainly 'very English' in their liberal use of humour, whimsical observation and intellectualism (Andrew, 1997; cf Easthope, 1999). A similar style can be found in films by Paul Kelly for the pop group Saint Etienne. *Finisterre* (2002), an imaginary 24 hours in London, owes some of its ideas to aspects of Keiller's work but is also guided by a previous London-centred documentary, *The London Nobody Knows* (directed by Geoffrey Fletcher, 1967) and to Ian Nairn's work on London.

And what of the people left behind in this rush towards regeneration and property development, of the communities that might not benefit directly from a new shopping mall or entertainment complex, or living cheek by jowl in deprivation next to major pockets of wealth? These filmic images remind us that we need to consider who is benefiting from urban transition, or who is excluded from the opportunities, the costs, socially as well as financially, of regeneration opportunities. Paul Kelly's follow-up film in collaboration with Saint Etienne, *What Have You Done Today, Mervyn Day?* (2005), goes to the heart of this issue with an examination of dilapidation in the Lower Lea Valley, London, the location of the London 2012 Olympics.

We recognise buildings instantly from filmic images, and where they are located, what they serve to represent, from what period of history and how they are symbolic of changing times. Twentieth-century planning failed to see cities as living places, places of work and of homes, of interactions and communication, of the base as well as the sublime. Urban planning has to change to meet new times and demands, to think about the meaning of places, about how people use and think about places and how places can capitalise on their own identities and distinctiveness, to deliver better quality places to live and work within.

Whose city II: new apartments under construction in Deptford

GRASPING THE SPACE–PLACE–PLANNING NETTLE

As discussed in Part One of this book, urban planning has undergone a metamorphosis into a very different activity than in 1945, 1960 or even 1980, as it has ebbed and flowed within a political arena. It survived the New Right period, the Blair New Labour period and, if anything, was strengthened between 2004 and 2010. Presently, it has been suggested that planning now lacks a central paradigm or guiding principle, particularly since the demise of comprehensive planning (Beauregard, 1990). Instead, it is suspended between modernism and postmodernism (Wadley and Smith, 1998; Allmendinger, 2002), although to some extent this criticism has been apparent within planning since its instigation over a hundred years ago. One important by-product of planning and planners' incorporation into the state apparatus has been that since the 1960s, if not before, practising planners and the planning discipline have been acutely aware that their art – alongside that of politicians – is the art of what may be possible. As Bruton was able to note, the planning profession has been torn between the comprehensive ideal of grappling with the complex interrelations between economic, social, environmental/physical issues on the one hand, and the practical expediencies of its centrality to the policy-making process and the political and administrative machinery of the state on the other (Bruton, 1984, p 9). As such, 'it is not always easy to distinguish between professional input and political outcomes, and this is one reason why "the planners" are a group that are blamed when things go wrong' (Grant, 1999, p 5). Since the 1960s in particular, planning and planners have become acutely aware of the fact that 'failure' or, perhaps more generously, 'unintended consequences' are endemic in the policy process. This is a point that is made well by Scott and Roweis, who note how 'state intervention, *qua* urban planning, is reduced to never ending rounds of reactive, palliative, and piecemeal measures' (Scott and Roweis, 1977, p 1106). In part, such contradictions or unintended consequences of planning can be traced to utopian elements at the heart of planning: 'in exactly the same way that materialization of spatial utopias run afoul of the particularities of the temporal process mobilized to produce them, so the utopianism of process runs afoul of the spatial framings and the particularities of place construction necessary to its materialization' (Harvey, 2000, p 179). And, as a result, 'perhaps utopia can never be realized without destroying itself' (Harvey, 2000, p 167). The same point has been returned to recently by Bruegmann (2005) in his writings on urban sprawl. Echoing the thoughts of Jane Jacobs, he argues that the actions of planners have had paradoxical or unintended consequences. That does not mean to say that urban planning has no role to play, but rather it is the case that the sorts of solutions provided by urban planning must necessarily be seen as partial, piecemeal and temporary fixes to problems. Problems will change, the interventions will need to be reconsidered and further problems and interventions will need to be identified.

Since 'modernist narratives suppress the full impact of the spatial' (Massey, 1999, p 272), Doreen Massey (1999, 2005) has argued persuasively that what is needed is a relational politics of space-time based on the fullest conception of the geography as 'the sphere of the existence of multiplicity'. Here 'space is not stable, not a cross-section through time, it is disrupted, active and generative' (Massey, 1999, p 274). With space as the product of interrelations and the sphere of multiplicity, interventions in the urban will be temporal in nature and of course partial. But the perceptions of space, of theorisations and of imaginations will be multiple too. And that is the dilemma for urban planning that seeks to fix, legitimise and act politically in a particular direction. Before we begin to even consider urban planning interventions, we need to revisit the multiple imaginations of space held by individuals. And film and photography provide a means by which those multiple identities and understandings can be revealed. These filmic images of space and place are selective too, but they can be viewed as a prompt to consider less static, less fixed forms of space and place perceptions.

As planners recognised decades ago, and as we have witnessed visually throughout this book, urban planning intervention will

Political graffiti

always be accompanied by success *and* failure, or by the prospect of failure as history judges past urban planning decisions and comments on the physical manifestations. And so the search for planning perfection and the most optimal solution to an urban problem can never be ultimately achieved ad infinitum. The same postmodern sensibilities that highlight the partial nature of theoretical understandings of phenomena have also immobilised geographers into a search for perfection – or sensitivity – to all potential constituencies affected by policies. As Sayer and Storper describe, 'the concern with situatedness and diversity is coupled with a utopia of sorts – that of "radical democracy". The utopia of full, non-hierarchical expression of postmodern complexity is rarely questioned, either in philosophical or in practical terms' (Sayer and Storper, 1997, p 4). In this way, postmodernism can result in a 'passive cosmopolitanism' (Bridge, cited in Massey, 2005, p 186) – sensitivity to a sense *of* the other without sensitivity to a sense *for* the other (Cloke, 2002). And as such, 'it almost seems as though as we have become theoretically more sophisticated in identifying difference and differentiating identity, so our ability to offer imaginative and practical guidelines for doing something about anything appears to be diminishing' (Cloke, 2002, pp 588-9). The resonance with Harvey's now famous lament of positivism over 30 years ago is striking. There may be a case here for suggesting that some in the urban realm have become paralysed by the knowledge that, to intervene will necessarily be to intervene most likely on behalf of one group in society over another or, worse, to have failed one or more groups.

The problem here is that our postmodern sensibilities are in direct contradiction to the modus operandi of the corporate state apparatus it might seek to influence. While geographers, and to a degree planners, have rejected essentialist understandings of phenomena, the corporate state apparatus – for its own reasons – continues to operate in the world of essences. The postmodern sensibilities that have infused geography and, to a lesser extent planning, are directly opposed to the modernism of states which 'see' and act on phenomena in essentialist terms (Scott, 2000): 'States have no interest … in describing an entire social reality…' (Scott, 2000, pp 22-3) and 'no administrative system is capable of representing any existing social community except through a heroic and greatly schematised process of abstraction and simplification' (Scott, 2000, p 22). Instead, as we know all too well from the failures of the modernist planning movement, states impose spaces on places (Taylor, 1999).

Postmodern ideas

The Sage, Gateshead

LIMINAL SPACES: BETWEEN THE BASE AND THE SUBLIME

> ... the world of low density mess... a mean, middle state, neither town or country. Subtopia is the annihilation of the site, the steam-rollering of all individuality of place to our uniform and mediocre pattern. (Nairn, 1955)

Britain has heard almost apocalyptical warnings about the impact of capitalism and urban development on the landscape for over 100 years. Ian Nairn's warnings about the onset of unrestricted urbanisation and sprawl across the country link neatly back to similar warnings by H.G. Wells at the turn of the 20th century, with the polemical writings of Thomas Sharp in the 1930s, and with the literary contributions of J.B. Priestley in the 1930s and John Betjeman in the 1960s. The fact of the matter is that the landscape apocalypse has not happened. The proportion of the land developed remains at approximately 10 per cent of the UK land mass, an aggregated figure that has only increased marginally over the last 70 years (Government Office for Science, 2010), even if there are often significant local impacts from individual developments. One of the most significant periods of urbanisation occurred in the 1920s and 1930s through suburbanisation around towns and cities. Even in the deregulatory urban planning period of the 1980s, urban development expansion into the countryside did not materialise in the way that perhaps the house builders and some within the government had hoped, directly as a consequence of public reaction against housing development proposals in the countryside. We may therefore conclude that the planning process has been successful in preventing urban sprawl and achieving containment, some of the principles of the postwar planning consensus. But what is more interesting is the public perception of urban development.

In a survey carried out as part of the Barker Review of planning and housing commissioned by the Treasury in 2005, when people were asked how much of the land they thought was developed, well over 50 per cent of respondents believed that at least 50 per cent of the land had been built upon. The figure is in marked contrast to the actual figure of 10 per cent (Government Office for Science, 2010). The reasons why there is such a significant difference between the actual and the perceived are difficult to ascertain. Ninety per cent of the UK population live on 10 per cent of the land. Could it be because we are continuously surrounded by the urban fabric? Or could it relate more to issues of identity and a longing to keep the countryside untainted by development? We need to be concerned about this difference because it is bound to have an effect on emotional responses to what happens to the land, the pressure for economic growth and infrastructure provision and public perceptions towards planning and the role of the urban planning process in attempting to mediate between conflicting uses of the land.

Ian Nairn identified the process of urbanisation occurring in Britain in the 1950s as 'subtopia', and the emergence of places that are 'neither here or there'. Similarly, Thomas Sharp referred to exactly the same sort of process underway in his 1940 book as 'neither town or country'. The perception of urban sprawl must therefore be regarded as one of the subjects that raises the most significant emotional responses among commentators, the literati and the public, and has been prevalent for more than a hundred years of urban planning's existence. It may be described as rational in reflecting individuals' desires to be protective of the British countryside, or of a nostalgic perception of rural areas or of rural society. But it is surprising to reflect on the extent to which these perceptions translate into spatial imaginations of town and country, and of the urban planning process that strives to contain the physical extent of towns and cities. These imaginations then hold considerable sway over political contentions over space and how it changes or is perceived to be subject to change. The imaginations even fly in the face of evidence to the contrary. Raymond Williams, writing originally in 1973, talked of 'our real social experience is not only of the country and the city, in their most singular forms, but of many kinds of intermediate and new kinds of social and physical organisation' (Williams, 1985, p 239). The urban and the rural are inexorably linked, in terms of services, communication and resources, but these are not always acknowledged in the more passionate expressions against planning or development. The battleground between the urban and the rural and the perceptions that this creates appear to relate more to the values of the city and the values of the country; between the two is a sort of no-man's land of differing and contentiously valued cultures.

Debate today is still focused disproportionately on the perceived threat to these spaces between, of 'liminal spaces' (Higson, 2000), such as the greenbelt, not only from possible housing development but also from an array of other urban paraphernalia, including telecommunications and mobile phone masts, wind turbines, logistics and distribution sheds, retail units, freight termini, the motorway network and motorway intersections, high speed rail links and airport services. Many of these features are, according to Antony Gormley, 'the most permanent unconscious memorial to the age of mobility' and of a new landscape formed by the dominance of information and distribution rather than production (Gormley, 2007, p 7), exactly the same architecture captured on film by Patrick Keiller and in photographs by John Davies. Jonathan Glancey has also noticed the 'continuous roll of new executive houses, distribution depots, trunk road intersections and superstore car parks – a superfluity of man-made banality reeling by at two-miles-a-minute' (Glancey, 2006, p 5) as one speeds down the motorway by car. The sense of bewilderment, even depression, at the sight of these landscape interventions and liminal spaces evokes nostalgia in our sensibilities and perhaps wonderment at our modern age. Nothing is sacred, however, since even the countryside has been subject to change and has been fabricated by human activity (Matless, 1998; Matless and Short, 1998). Perhaps the highly charged emotions that landscape change and urban development seem to awaken in individuals relate to attitudes and identity. As Gormley (2007, p 7) remarks: 'The English national psyche has been a victim of the past, binding us to a reverence for the old things. But this acceptance of an imagined world, constituted and given value from the deeper past, also commits us to the role of victims; victims of choices made on our behalf by planners, architects and the government.' As such, the psyche may be as much affected by uncertainty in how to cope with modernity and the process of urban change as much as a concern for landscape aesthetics. It is perhaps no surprise, then, that the process charged with managing these processes of change – urban planning – should itself be subject to criticism and emotional outpouring.

SPATIAL NOSTALGIA: A VERY BRITISH DISEASE?

> Modernism at its best was meant to make the world brighter, lighter and healthier. Yet it failed to answer some strong instincts in the British – the love of privacy in a crowded island, a quiet suspicion that the past for all its faults may have been a nicer country. (Marr, 2009)

The nostalgic attitude towards the loss of old spatial coherences has been discussed by Massey (2005). The backward glance to a long vanished past is not backward looking at all, since it is a reference to a past that probably never was: 'The past was no more static than the present' (Massey, 1992, p 113). Individuals experience postmodern

A late 20th-century phenomenon: retail sheds, reliant on car journeys

feelings of nostalgia in order to fix or make sense of change in particular places. Such an emotional response finds expression in power and contestation on individual urban projects and proposed landscape interventions. And these contestations are part of the ongoing story and history of places, of place making and of change. The power element here centres on the fact that one individual's desire for spatial nostalgia can be a barrier to other people's desire for spatial history. What we often forget in this ongoing cycle of planning and resistance is that every place is actually an amalgam of previous space contestations; what we see is merely the surface snapshot of a place that hides previous buried histories. A memorial here, a blue plaque there, layers of different architectural and planning styles, aspects of dereliction and renewal, are all testaments to space and place contestation and arguments over the form and role of urban planning and the use of the land. This also explains an ongoing fascination on the part of some to unearth buried histories or to recall the significance of particular places for figures of the past or prior events. As Calvino (1974) reminds us, 'The eye does not see things, but images of things that mean other things.'

The ancient and modern: Southampton, viewed from the town walls

Urban heritage seems to be made up of narratives of change, reflecting spatial layering and place and planning histories. Like all histories, there are elements of fact and story in every development or land use change case, of the perpetuation or dispelling of myths, and the reassembling of narratives to reflect emotional responses and entrenched agendas. That is why the subject makes for great filmic subject matters, both documentary and fiction. David Harvey talked some time ago of these processes at work in an era of globalisation: 'The contemporary city has many layers. It forms what we might call a palimpsest, a composite landscape made of different built forms superimposed one upon the other with the passing of time' (Harvey, 1988, p 21).

With a desire for nostalgia moving on unabated, it seems reasonable to posit that sooner or later a great deal of 20th-century urban change will be regarded as heritage. Already, a significant amount of postwar modernist buildings have been subject to listed building protection; interwar suburban housing estates are also being designated conservation areas. In other places, the extent of urban demolition and rebuilding is shockingly fast; parts of the city of London, for example, appear to be on a 25-year redevelopment cycle with some buildings from the 1970s and 1980s already subject

Memorial, St James' Square, London

to redevelopment proposals to meet 21st-century office and energy technological requirements, or simply because there is an element of cache attached to the best, the most prominent and the most desirable new developments. This is the language and space of profit. The will of some individuals to fix space and attempt to stop the bewildering pace of change in the name of heritage will be matched by a relentless pursuit for economic development, housing need and infrastructure improvement. Urban planning, as a process charged with managing those different space contentions, will be subject to even greater pressures in the 21st century as a mediation exercise. Urban planning will only play a role in this game if it becomes more conditioned to space and place contentions, both real and imagined, and planners start to acknowledge the fragility and vulnerability of being caught and suspended between modernism and postmodernism.

St Pancras

ELEVEN

"A sense of beauty, culture and civic pride"

Greenwich

Liverpool fountain

Belfast's waterfront

Fournier Street, Spitalfields

Wales Millennium Centre, Cardiff Bay

Imperial War Museum North, Salford Quays

Scottish Parliament, Holyrood

South Bank

Bridgewater Hall, Manchester

Footbridge over Leith Road, Edinburgh

Bordeaux Quay, Bristol

Salford cranes

Hope Street, Liverpool

Canary Wharf

Prince's Dock, Liverpool

Beach huts, Bournemouth

Portsmouth, Spinnaker Tower

London 2012 Olympic stadium, Stratford

The Hayward Gallery, South Bank

Spital Yard E1

TWELVE

Fearful symmetries: the spirit and purpose of modern planning

INTRODUCTION

Planning in the UK has changed beyond all recognition over the last 100 years. It has shifted from a garden city movement, a process to deliver better quality housing, a proactive and interventionist campaign, stemming from a predominantly socialist and modernist ideology, through a period of deregulation and market dominance, to a process enabling local democratic involvement in political decisions, and onwards to a period of local space-and-place sensitivity and spatial integration. Despite political parties of all persuasions tinkering with urban planning continuously over the last 20 years in particular, it has broadened out from a narrow regulatory core. It is now charged with coordinating the spatial aspects of a range of policy agendas at local and regional scales, and to provide a mediation forum for various interests, responsive to changing conditions. And yet the image and popular representation of urban planning may have stalled in the 1960s when the modernist movement was at its height. Not only did this time pre-date any democratic public involvement in planning decision making, it also involved only the state, as opposed to the market, in urban planning interventions.

Accusations continue to abound, especially in the media, that urban planning is the full force of the Goliath bulldozer against the David community, alongside a perception that it is somehow Stalinist in form, a legacy of command and control, involving overt bureaucracy.

Perhaps this says more about attitudes within a largely politically right-leaning press towards the state, the public sector and intervention generally than it says about urban planning in its own right. And of course these accusations make urban planning a particularly easy target for successive waves of politicians to promise to 'do something about it'. Despite the inaccuracies about what planning is all about today, one thing seems to be guaranteed: political frustrations with urban planning are likely to continue long into the future, feeding on particular media and public perceptions of planning and a desire to enhance individual and business freedoms. If politicians really did want to do something about planning, the obvious areas to target would be landownership, recognition of land and environmental capacity and thresholds in different areas, and urban and regional differentials in wealth, poverty, access and property acquisition. But here we would be reinvigorating a principled and ideological debate about the spirit and purpose of planning in the 21st century. Such a debate, tragically, seems light years away. Interventions in land decisions still occur, of course, but ironically enough, virtually all of the investment and development decisions are made by the private sector. The urban planning process is intended to provide a supporting and enabling role to the property sector when the market identifies development opportunities. But urban planning also has to ensure democratic legitimacy in proceedings and opportunity for local community involvement as the projects proceed. Similarly to planning becoming a compromised legal process in the 1930s in seeking simultaneously to promote urban development and growth while protecting rural land from urban encroachment, so it attempts to satisfy the market while attempting to enhance social opportunity and civic engagement. Since the 1990s, urban planning has also had to not only balance economic and social interests, but to play a strong environmental role too. Planning is also a function of the private sector and the public sector. The planning profession comprises employees based in both sectors. And all these aspects make up the urban planning of today. It is little wonder that public, media, even political perceptions of urban planning are clouded in mystery and muddled by history.

And so the post-1997 reformed planning system reflects both continuities with and radical departures from the past. Planning can no longer be understood as a single entity (as is often perceived by those outside planning) but rather as turbulent, fluid and adaptable processes. What we have today are diverse activities of intervention, coordination and delivery that vary geographically and politically.

Bristol

Planning has been strengthened but within an increasingly complex and demanding environment that only serves to question its purpose and activity. Since the 1980s, local government functions have diversified from direct service provision to a much broader range of activities involving regulation, leadership and enabling. Governments globally have promoted an agenda of state infrastructure revitalisation, decentralisation and local responsiveness, cooperation and partnership with civil society, together with social responsibility. The planning reforms introduced in the UK since 2001 by different governments are set within this wider and fluid context. These planning activities are not deterministic, but rather embrace flexibility and difference; these are strengths of planning in the UK, especially to meet short-term political expectations, but can also serve as an ongoing uncertainty for planning's purpose. Change within planning is not new: planning in the UK has endured in various guises since its statutory inception in the Housing, Town Planning etc Act 1909 and its rebirth in the Town and Country Planning Act 1947. Planning possessed an elevated status as a modern forward-thinking and visionary discipline and practice in an era of the comprehensive redevelopment of cities during the period 1945-70 (Reade, 1987), reflecting its ideological status as part of modernity and social reform.

Urban planning has accommodated the agendas of divergent political administrations as well as major shifts in the national and international economy (Hall, 2002). By the 1980s successive governments had politically reduced the professional purpose and activity of planning to little more than an administrative exercise dominated by neoliberal agendas (Thornley, 1991), this in turn reflecting a new politics and market primacy over planning. The utopian ideals in the postwar period associated with the professional experts' desire to create more beautiful places (Fishman, 1977) appeared increasingly archaic in the Thatcher era, as the purpose and status of planning began to be undermined within the broader political campaign to bypass, centralise or remove local government powers, and roll back the state and rely on the market. Planning has yielded important successes in policy terms (Bruton, 1974) but, crucially, planning has become a system beset by trade-offs – between participation and resources, participation and speed, and resources and speed (Reade, 1987) – simultaneously to urban planning losing its ideological and philosophical heart with the demise of both the welfare state and the modernist movement. The trade-offs, to some extent, reflect differing attitudes to, perceptions of and expectations from urban planning, among politicians, developers and the public, groups that have often criticised planning for a variety of reasons. For some, planning is too slow, over-regulatory and thwarts necessary development. For others, it is intent on despoiling what is left of the countryside. Such criticisms have dogged urban planning since the 1920s in various guises and reflect the compromise nature of planning – that there is no 'perfect' or ideal system to suit 21st-century demands when everyone's philosophy of planning is treated equally.

The variety of elements and the trade-offs that now characterise planning have been easily accommodated within a system that is highly dependent on short-term incremental and politically infused changes to give it both objectives and process. The Thatcher years of 1979-90 did not entail a great deal of legislative change in order to shift the scope and purpose of planning while the culture of planning was changed under the Major governments of 1990-97 through the emphasis on competition and targets within local government. After 1997, the New Labour government made concerted efforts to modernise the planning system as part of a political programme intended to renew various public institutions and policy areas. This renaissance did not return urban planning to its socialist origins, but rather – like the Labour Party's makeover itself – attempted to improve the effectiveness, efficiency and relevance and, to some degree, ownership of the planning process to a range of stakeholders that extended beyond simple notions of the public and the private (Healey, 2007). More significantly, the post-1997 reforms awakened the strategic role for planning, beyond its narrow regulatory focus. The Labour government reforms culminated in a radical planning overhaul and the emergence of spatial planning, intended to encourage a broader perspective of planning into notions of place, space, community, governance and strategic integration, coupled with the introduction of regional and sub-regional spatial tiers of policy making, and a strengthening of local planning and community strategy making (Tewdwr-Jones et al, 2009). Under the third term administration, the government stressed the need for planning to be concerned with 'place-shaping' as a cornerstone of local governance (Lyons and HM Government, 2006). New forms of planning now exist at national, regional, local and community levels, allowing for different types of urban planning to co-exist, a marked contrast to older notions of central and local statutory planning. Overlaying these various scales of planning are significant policy areas that require addressing, including the impact of climate change, biodiversity and sustainability issues, and the impact of economic competitiveness and growth priorities, particularly in the context of the recent economic recession. Since 2010, further reforms to the planning system are being enacted as part of the Coalition government's localism agenda which will, ironically, disestablish the recently introduced strategic component to urban planning but refocus the purpose of planning to local space and place concerns.

Hawksmoor's Christ Church Spitalfields

All these changes and reforms to planning necessitate some reflection as to the form and trajectory of urban planning today, and a questioning of its spirit and purpose. During a period of immense change and added complexity within planning, it is worthwhile considering the bigger picture. The academic literature is rich in attempts to provide this bigger picture of planning in the past, including the work of Bruton (1974), Buchanan (1972), Brindley et al (1989), Cherry (1974), Healey et al (1988) and Reade (1987). But such portraits have been lacking more recently, perhaps because of a lack of consensus as to the purpose and direction of urban planning politically and professionally, and constant and ongoing waves of planning reform that make pausing for assessment problematic.

The ongoing trade-offs in the position and purpose of urban planning further removes the discipline from its historic roots. Increasingly, the form urban planning takes today appears increasingly divorced from the objectives of either the town planning movement of a hundred years ago or the modernist movement. Given political responses to changing social, economic and environmental concerns over the decades, this is not surprising. However, parts of the academy have failed to acknowledge the ways in which the principles and tools of urban planning have been remolded. There is also an increasing separation of proactive policy planning from regulatory planning, employing different mechanisms and different objectives. And there has been an increasing tendency to utilise shadow, ad hoc or temporary delivery mechanisms by a range of agencies and actors, often in place or to the side of formal planning tools of elected government. Furthermore, reflecting Massey's (2005) contention that older forms of urban planning always attempted to order chaos, there has been an increase in the use of policy and delivery mechanisms that transcend administrative and sectoral boundaries, features that formerly characterised planning territories. And all these evolving processes are aside from the continual use – at least in England – of economic growth and competition as the language of planning, simultaneous to government policy documents stressing a broader sustainable development remit. The two aspects of planning in its old guise that are completely absent from any of these changes are the social agenda and the position of place.

THE CONDITION OF URBAN PLANNING: DEVOID OF A HEART?

There can be little doubt that the purpose of planning has been broadened out dramatically over the last 80 years. In the postwar planning system, the emphasis was on rebuilding cities and the economy, decentralising the population from overcrowded and bomb-damaged inner-city areas, preventing urban sprawl, providing sufficient quantity of housing and controlling new development. Buchanan (1972) identified the purpose of planning in 1947 as:

- ensuring equality of opportunity, prosperity and standards;
- getting urban areas into shape;
- ensuring a sufficient and economic transport system for people and goods;
- conserving natural resources; and
- conserving the nation's heritage.

These are the elements of urban planning that featured so prominently within filmic depictions of change in the postwar period right through to the 1970s, and which we discussed in

Liverpool

Part Two of this book. Writing in the mid-1970s, Bruton (1974) viewed planning as a rational, single-minded, conformist approach to resolving urban problems, seeking public control of land use, decentralising activities within a loose urban form. This form of planning had taken root in the 1940s with increasing centralisation of decision making, and the wartime task had brought the desire for more planning to a head. But it was the need to tackle the economic and social conditions within a strong regional and national planning framework that catalysed formal planning, albeit with a noticeable caveat: urban planning would be set within a democratic context, answerable at national level through ministers to Parliament, and through elected local councillors in local authorities. Bruton (1974) identified this as a bulwark against totalitarianism, such that planning became a matter for central government, but to be made operational and effective through the medium of local government. Gaps in this system opened up in the 1960s and 1970s, particularly in relation to authoritarian prescriptions (which increasingly became questioned), and community needs, leading to a variety of styles of planning and responses locally. At this point, centrally led planning should have become less important, if new forms of regional planning had taken root but, even at this time, the idea of regional policy making and authority was fiercely opposed.

By the 1970s, a one-style type of planning to fit all circumstances was inappropriate. As Cherry (1974, p 79) remarked, foretelling pluralist and communicative thoughts on planning in the following years:

> The fact was that there was not simply one way of doing things, not just one sense of action for the future, but a variety. A pluralist society implied that there are alternative solutions to a particular problem and these depend on the different assumptions and values held by the groups concerned, and the way that problem is perceived.

Planning had moved from a period of disjointed attempts of urban government in the first part of the 20th century, through a process of coordinated and committed planning as a state activity by the 1950s and 1960s, to a locally determined process shaped by national parameters after the 1970s. In the 1970s, urban planning was characterised as a comprehensive corporate government process, managed by objectives. The reforms to planning of the late 1960s sought to allow the development of large-scale, long-term spatial policies as well as ensuring that physical development planning and implementation could be carried out. But the reforms to planning in the late 1960s and 1970s were allied to political contention over local government reorganisation against a backdrop of a failing state and economic decline. As political parties disagreed fundamentally over the most appropriate boundaries of policy making at a sub-national level and the appropriateness of state planning, the revised urban planning system became, essentially and not for the first time, a compromised process (Cross and Bristow, 1983; Bruton and Nicholson, 1987). It has followed this pattern ever since.

The planning system took on an altogether different form and appearance during the 1980s and most of the 1990s, and those debates have been well rehearsed and discussed elsewhere (see Thornley, 1991). But by the time of the election of the Labour Party into government in 1997, urban planning returned as a valid activity, albeit one transformed by the experiences of the previous three decades, and set within a much more plural state. There is no greater indication of this renaissance for planning than a check on the recently set out purposes of planning which are in marked contrast to the 1947 purposes of planning. According to all the various policy statements of government, in 2008 planning had the following objectives:

Manchester

- enabling the building of healthy, thriving, sustainable communities;
- supporting economic development vital to create jobs and ensuring continuing national prosperity;
- protecting the natural and historic environment, ensuring everyone has access to green space;
- enabling the delivery of essential infrastructure;
- supporting individual citizens to improve their homes and protecting people from obtrusive development;
- assisting in resolving differences in opinion towards the way land is used;
- supporting the involvement of local communities in voicing opinions about the future;
- contributing to the prevention of terrorism by designing out crime; and
- supporting the provision of public transport, and healthy and sustainable alternatives to the use of the private car.

Interestingly enough, this list of objectives had to be derived from various statements contained on the Department for Communities and Local Government website since there is no definitive overview of urban planning's purpose in one single document at the present time. These additional expectations to planning reflect the changed expectations of government, but also the fact that planning sits across a complex governmental and policy arrangement, with vertical and horizontal axes, a function of public and private sectors, and employing simultaneously components of authoritarianism and communitarianism. In the last two years, these objectives are being changed yet again by the 2010 Coalition government. As such, the postwar centralised more authoritarian top-down approach to urban planning can no longer be valid even if there are vested national interests and priorities at stake. There is also a spatial and geographical dimension to planning which now actively encourages planning difference and divergence. And there exists a commitment toward the idea of spatial planning alongside land use planning, which we may also recognise as bearing some of the hallmarks of the 1960s model of planning as a comprehensive, well-managed corporate governance process, managed by objectives and attempting to achieve integration between various actors and strategies. Furthermore, there are proposals to implement planning

Surveillance society

Bucklersbury Lane

and other policy areas at the sub-national scale, perhaps through city-region and sub-regional models, an idea not that far away from the late 1960s attempt to reorganise local government boundaries.

There is a considerable literature available on the varying forms and trajectories of UK planning, where planning is:

■ a facilitator, regulator or barrier on a whole host of measures (Allmendinger, 2006);

■ a coordinating or choreographic tool for regional and local public bodies (Bianconi et al, 2006); and

■ an access point for wider stakeholders to get involved not only in planning but local and regional governance and strategy making (Healey, 2007).

Planning, in England at least, appears to be splitting up in many ways that suggests both continuity with the past (development control management, for example) and radical reform (spatial planning, that emphasises governance, integration and delivery). The problems around these emerging forms of planning and their interrelationships rest on a number of core issues, the most prominent of which is the rights and responsibilities of the state to shape and determine nationally significant issues. Within a changed government structure that emphasises devolved, regional or local governance, how can a UK-wide government ideologically and procedurally 'control' the planning process(es) to assist in action on national priorities when the very definition of 'national' in planning terms has changed over the last 10 years? Successive governments are facing this challenge in the debate on the role of the state and public sector against a continual suspicion or dislike of planning politically and an acknowledged need still to provide national infrastructure (such as new energy sources and high speed rail links). But the principle applies equally well on questions of national policy within planning and how this filters down to other layers of planning that are based on an ideological commitment to localism, enhanced local and regional participation, discretion and subsidiarity. Assessment of future land use needs can occur at the national scale, but the key question is how action will be achieved through the legal and administrative machinery in an increasingly multi-agency policy and spatial fluid decision context.

Healey et al (1988) identified urban planning as a mix of processes: bureaucratic-legal, techno-rational, semi-judicial, consultative and politico-rational. Brindley et al (1989) additionally identified a temporal and spatial dimension to planning. In the 21st century, we might say that the revised components of planning indicate that UK planning is: bureaucratic-legal, semi-judicial, participative and negotiable, integrative and coordinative, political, spatial and temporal, fluid, diverse and adaptable and outcome-focused. Urban planning is now concerned with efficient and integrative planning decisions, and is the most effective when it utilises a range of tools and processes, and harnesses actors and resources to deliver outcomes. It remains a regulatory mechanism but is also a fluid supportive and facilitating process. It remains a function of the state and of the market, intended to bring about sustainable development. Encompassing its democratic roots, it operates in the interests of a range of public and private concerns, and is achieved through negotiation and partnership. Above all, planning is concerned with managing the externalities arising from taking sustainable development decisions. Twenty-first century urban planning encompasses a variety of state

The City

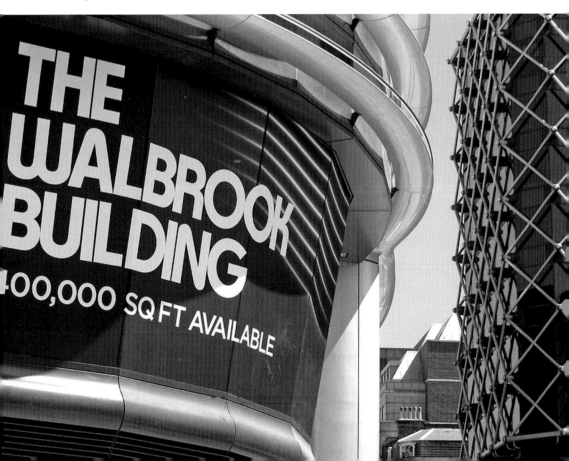

and non-state activities that are now labelled 'planning' but to the extent that its true historic intentions can either be viewed as largely absent or else weighed down by multifarious and contradictory expectations.

Urban planning has always had to face considerable challenges and difficulties in addressing the problems of today and the burdens of tomorrow, and planning has always been adapted to meet those needs. The problems for urban planning today are how to resolve problems within a complex environment on issues that are rarely discrete in nature and not resolved by one set of actors. The increased number of purposes of planning may stretch it to the point that it deals with everything and solves nothing. Take the environment, for example; the government provides planning policy guidance on issues such as flood risk and climate change but these are policy advisory tools, and take their place alongside a range of other policy advice issued by government on such matters as infrastructure provision, housing development, retail change and economic development. In many ways, this ability for urban planning to transform and adapt to suit changing needs and conditions is the crux of the problem; over decades successive governments have told planners, predominantly at the local level, to take account of a range of national policy issues in formulating their own strategies but have rarely prioritised one issue over another. While this may seem a sensible approach, particularly in tackling climate change, governments are notoriously reluctant to state this explicitly within planning for fear of upsetting politically other parts of the planning equation – and perhaps, more pertinently, property and development interests. Similarly, the government is reluctant to impose a direction in a particular substantive policy area for fear of being accused of riding roughshod over other democratically elected tiers, an issue made even sharper as planning has embraced stakeholder participation at the grassroots level and appears in 2011 to be heading towards a localism steer. We therefore have an endless list of issues for planners to address locally and regionally, all of which are proclaimed by government to be relevant and important, and that planning has to incorporate.

A FUTURE FOR URBAN PLANNING: SPACES, PLACES AND SOCIAL ACTION

A review of the urban planning system at the beginning of the 21st century in Britain only adds substance to the view of planning lacking direction and a philosophical purpose. There is now greater concern with planning as performance, for speedy and efficient administration, for the generation of league tables of the most efficient planning authorities nationally, for the publication of benchmarks showing the public and businesses the rights they should expect from the administration of planning locally, and for ensuring that planning decisions are made in accordance with plans and policies. Although important to a degree, in demonstrating value for money and efficient use of public monies, these are all issues relating to technical competence and administrative discretion. In fact, they should not be thought of as planning at all. The technocratic dominance of planning under the Major–Blair–Brown administrations should be regarded as a new proceduralism; central government keeps local authorities occupied by doing this and it is nothing more than the continued commodification of planning without broader debate on the strategic objectives or political and philosophical purpose of planning in socioeconomic and environmental change.

There is a danger that the same bureaucratic preoccupation of planning will be true today and tomorrow as we enter a new administration period and with further reform to urban planning on the horizon. The threat and uncertainty in the 1980s emanated from a government eager to reduce the role of the state and with it the red tape of planning. The 1990s and 2000s have witnessed a renaissance in planning's fortunes with a legitimate role to play in generating evidence bases, encouraging participation, producing plans and ensuring the delivery of development. The threats and uncertainty over the last 15 years have been the intellectual void created by little or no discussion of planning's political purpose in achieving social benefits or in contributing towards a sense of place and space.

This is an opportunity for urban planning, or at least the disparate group of activities within government and governing pertaining to place and space, to be reasserted socially and geographically in broader intellectual discussion concerning the future strategic direction of places. I make no prescription here to insist that planners do this, merely to encourage planners to consider whether they want to alter their roles, and to debate the advantages and disadvantages of proactive change. One of the most serious shortcomings of urban planning and for that matter recent planning education has been its continued evasion of the emotional and the human in matters concerning territory and identity. The tendency has been to think of the personal, the social and the community as unimportant or too nebulous. Many planning schools believed that we should abandon the personal and concentrate on facts, procedures and rules: we must show students what occurs at the workplace, show them how the planning system operates, show them how modern planning is organised. Even I have contributed to this literature in the past. But the structures, institutions and procedures of planning affect people as much as the land. It is not possible to understand planning without a deeper appreciation of both aspects. Planning degree programmes have rarely and sufficiently shown students how people perceive of or feel about planning and about places. The only true meaning of the word 'planning' for me is true to life, observable, experiential and a positive force for societal development and change.

It has not all been negative. A renaissance of urban planning has occurred in the UK over the last 15 years but behind a continual wave of legislative reform, new policy guidance, strategy and new management talk, over-zealous bureaucratic requirements from

Albert Embankment

central government and passive professionalism. This has been in line with and led by successive governments' continued commodification of the planning system. Planners themselves have failed to seize the opportunity by discussing much more fundamental notions about local democracy, contributing to eradicating social disadvantage, supporting well-being and engaging people in big conversations about places on terms the public understand and appreciate. This failure has, in turn, affected how planning and planners are viewed by members of the public and individual communities. To all intents and purposes, despite the urban planning renaissance, planners have become *them*, the bureaucrats, the pen-pushers, the people who get in the way, the arrogant professionals who do not have to experience the effect of their own local planning decisions, whether they represent the public sector or private sector. Governments of all political persuasion continue to criticise planning for its failure to deliver development to the timescales the market appears to crave for. I am not at all convinced that large sections of the planning market necessarily possess a problem with timescales at the present time. But the peddling of the myth appears to be a useful hook on which the Treasury can justify its continued vilification of local planning authorities' work. Neither the Treasury nor planning ministers seem to possess the capacity to be able to pause for a moment, and acknowledge the wider purpose of planning. Yes urban planning, by its very nature, is supposed to be an impediment, a respite, a chance to take stock, to consider the wider impacts and externalities of a proposed change. Planning operates in this way in the name of democracy and community. Politicians who crave faster decisions are doing nothing more than undermining the very existence of a process they claim to believe in. Perhaps it is the case that politicians are embarrassed by the potential power of planning to hold back the market, in a political era where neoliberalism has, ideologically, triumphed over socialism. For in essence, to campaign for and champion the democratic and community role of planning might be to place a question mark over planning's automatic role in delivering development.

One would like to think, in the light of the New Labour regime and on the back of strong ideological and political manifesto commitment towards social inclusion, that a more balanced ideological stance for urban planning would have developed, between facilitating development and supporting public and community desires, and the disadvantaged. Reading the rhetoric of government statements on the purpose of planning, one could almost be fooled into thinking

The Brunswick, WC 1

that that balance has been achieved. But the reality is, planning is still a subject matter caught between two very different political perspectives within government, championed by the Treasury on the one hand, and the Communities and Environment ministries on the other. Perhaps one of the reasons for planning's current unpopularity, particularly within government, is that its historical context – socialism, modernism and a deep-rooted political conviction to assist wider societal interests – has been expunged. Planning is therefore swimming in a sea without any obvious means of support. The 'p' word – planning – has become almost as dirtier a word as socialism. As one Labour minister remarked to me, "That's the trouble with planning. Sounds rather Soviet." But the loss of a visionary purpose of planning is somewhat strange if you consider that governments are able to (and frequently do) make a societal and moral case for setting out a visionary direction for, let's say, health and education. Of course it is also possible to view planning, certainly at the local level, with the same degree of crusade. After all, we are increasingly witnessing the influence of planning in shaping and possibly determining local election results.

It is doubtful whether politicians at Westminster feel it appropriate to even consider that fact; planning, as so many politicians within the Coalition government remind us regularly, with its push to localism and the big society, is a predominantly local matter. In other words, so long as local planning disputes are not blown up to

Weekend leisure

Leadenhall Building construction

become national political problems, there is absolutely no need for politicians to defend the retention of planning or to set out a grander, more inclusive, vision of what planning could actually do to benefit communities, beyond its narrow regulatory role. That, they would argue, is a matter for local democrats and local people, although I doubt they would add to that response two factual statements: the degree to which local agendas continue to be constrained by a centralised bureaucratic polity within planning, and by a checklist mentality imposed by central government that has deprived local authorities of resources and incapacitated visionary zeal ability.

To expect a national government today to set out a moral justification for planning should not be met with a snigger. The creation of the modern planning system in 1947, following the wartime devastation of cities, was hailed as a central plank of both the nationalisation agenda and the means by which cities and towns would rise from the ashes to become not only economic growth engines, but also places where people wanted to live and enjoy their surroundings. Planning certainly possessed vision in those days and, bound up with the modernist movement and, unfortunately, a desperate need to build quickly and often insensitively, quickly became established politically. The reasons why the modernist movement failed in the 1960s and 1970s had as much to do with cheap building materials, brutal designs and a period where speed outclassed vision, quality and community, as questions over the appropriateness of having a planning process. Planning, like architecture, survived this period, although both activities suffered major setbacks. It is really only in the last 15 years or so that architecture has managed to recreate itself as an attractive discipline with signature architects able to convince politicians and the public that their equally radical designs should be welcomed. Planning's renaissance as a proactive radical activity has simply not occurred, partly because there has not been a call to arms from either the planning profession or a political party.

In my view, urban planning can no longer be expected to do it all. The restructuring of governance, constitutional change and a push towards localism, whatever that means practically, provides a new opportunity to determine the future form of urban planning, its role and representation, and – indirectly – its status and relevance with the public. In fact, the public and politicians will expect planners to react to change. Public sector planning has become bogged down with bureaucracy and has lost some visionary ideal. The climate change agenda, a renaissance in the interest of the public towards matters that planning has to intervene in, and higher local interest in places and how they change, could prove to be the catalysts for

East Manchester stadium

urban planning to respond positively. This is also an opportunity for urban planning to reassert itself in the eyes of the public, the media and popular culture, as a governmental activity and scientific endeavour to focus people's attention and prompt debate on the need for change and to consider the future of places. That is exactly what film was attempting to communicate in the 1930-79 period, as illustrated in Part Two of the book.

Urban planning will always imply economic development, of course, in addition to environmental protection. Given the changes occurring and about to occur in governance within the UK, and the prominence of the private sector in promoting development and master planning, should public sector planning abandon its neutrality and positively discriminate for social justice, community development, and the disadvantaged. The reorientation of public sector urban planning towards social justice and local environmental matters (reflecting the need to protect the interests of a broader set of people) is distinctly possible. What could be envisaged here is a new philosophy for planning as a localised community and place-focused activity, in which place lies at the centre of debate and discourse, and on which policies and decisions rest, rather than pigeonholing community and history into minor, inconvenient facets along the inevitable road to development. These, and other subject matters devoted to reconsidering the planning system across Britain, require a great deal of debate, not least by politicians, analysts and planners themselves. I am not advocating the adoption of my own sketchy ideas as a complete panacea for planning; this book is merely an attempt to encourage planning to focus on places, place meaning and people's emotions towards change as principal concerns.

CONCLUSIONS

> Large-scale planning of any reasonable and positive kind is shamefully absent here.... It is the negation of true planning. It is mere opportunism, and a dull, shifty opportunism at that. And as a result we have muddle, waste, frustration, mess. Nothing at all that the imagination can catch hold of; nothing to stimulate and inspire; only dullness, disorder, pettiness and a dreary depressing inefficiency. (Sharp, 1940, p 142)

Thomas Sharp's call to arms for a radical planning system reflects a frustration that had developed in the first half of the 20th century for a more comprehensive and visionary basis to manage land use change. Mindful of being accused of a form of authoritarianism just at the time when fascism was spreading across Europe, Sharp also makes the point that refusal to plan properly is inhuman, in the context of depressed regions, poverty, decay and unemployment: 'It is no overstatement to say that the simple choice between planning and non-planning, between order and disorder, is a rest-choice for English democracy' (Sharp, 1940, p 143). With the wartime devastation of towns and cities, the need to rebuild infrastructure and the dire need to build houses for people immediately after these sentiments were expressed, planning did indeed become a visionary, bold and comprehensive activity in a new political and ideological movement as part of the reconstruction of the country. Times have changed markedly over 80 years and we may not have such an urgent requirement to overcome disaster and the ravages of war, but the country, indeed the state, still needs to address housing need, employment creation, improvements to the transport network, infrastructure requirements, the affect of climate change and degradation to the environment, poverty and deprivation, the future of places and the democratic right for people to get involved in political decisions.

Urban planning has been through the doldrums but continues to exist in part because there is a need for it, even if it clashes with neoliberal ideology, dominant economic growth agendas, a reliance on the market, a reluctance of national politicians to take bold visionary decisions and a suspicion that it is somehow unfair and a threat to individual liberties. It continues despite politicians from all parties peddling a right-wing media perspective that it is Stalinist. It continues even though the form of urban planning today is totally divorced from its garden cities, suburbia, the modernist movement and deregulation predecessors. It continues because, in truth, people and politicians rely on it to mediate and manage conflicts in our expectations on the future use of land and it is one of the few areas of the state's public activity that engages directly with individuals.

A renaissance of policy and strategy making in planning has occurred across the UK since the 2000s and is also being mirrored at the local level in local planning processes and in community involvement although, naturally enough, this optimism remains patchy at the moment. Should people be concerned about whether this is called urban planning, spatial planning, integrative governance or localism? The fact of the matter is that these processes are still occurring today in a fragmented and very diverse state, yet devoid of the very ideological elements that gave rise to urban planning in the first place.

Perhaps we should celebrate the fact that planning continues even without a core philosophical purpose, and with contradictory forces pulling for and against it. But aspects of urban planning politically and practically, and the way places are considered and managed by the state today, resemble nothing more than a process of what Charles Lindblom might describe as muddling through. Politically, of course, this is advantageous; it allows ad hoc and pragmatic responses to problems as and when they occur without political ideology being a bind on decision making. It also allows those with the most power and resources to influence that political choice of direction. And it only serves to undermine any intellectual or scientific base to considered and measured intervention. Much of urban planning in the UK has reached a point where it is no longer planning in the historic sense of the phrase at all, but rather pragmatism. There is much evidence of governments being more than willing to parachute in delivery mechanisms that stand outside elected tiers of government, and indeed the formal planning tools, in order to provide expedited arrangements for change. The Thames Gateway is one obvious example, but so were the new towns, urban development corporations, enterprise zones, urban regeneration companies, business improvement districts and local strategic partnerships. These are set up with a short-term specific political purpose.

The spirit and purpose of urban planning in the 21st century is in danger of collapsing from its remarkable ability to transform itself and to take on so many divergent policy expectations; it is in danger of having too many bolt-ons added to its agenda caused by governments not willing to provide strong direction for fear of upsetting entrenched political forces. This is particularly evident in the context of the spatial planning agenda that is supposed to be more about balancing and integrating competing agendas and policy, but is also increasingly locally shaped. Places need to renew, to be economically buoyant, to be efficient in transport networks and infrastructure, to be sustainable, to be secure, to provide sufficient and quality housing, accessible to all, and to be, above all, exciting places for people. Urban planning has always been associated with making difficult choices between competing demands on the land, but those choices – and more significantly the *implications* of those choices – have escalated over the last 25 years, taking into account democratic necessities, in addition to national, regional and local interests, economic, environmental and social needs, infrastructure provision, protection of the best landscapes and the provision of new homes and sustained economic growth. It could be argued that we have arrived at the present form of planning – integrating, negotiating, compromising between scores of vested interests and overlapping and contradictory policy expectations – directly as a result of 80 years of government and policy unclear steer and the planning system's ability to adapt to changing circumstances. Facing so many directions simultaneously is a useful planning trick but it is in danger of undermining its own credibility. Sooner or later, priorities for action need to be set. And this will be bound to have implications for democratic involvement in planning, for directions for change and for levels of responsibility. The questions of who decides in future, for what sort of planned future, within an agreed and shared set of planning principles, are bound to become increasingly pertinent.

The end of the line

References

Abercrombie, P. (1944) *Greater London plan*, London: HMSO.

Aitken, I. (1990) *Film and reform: John Grierson and the documentary film movement*, London: Routledge.

Aldridge, M. (1979) *British new towns: A programme without a policy*, London: Routledge and Kegan Paul.

Allen, S. (1999) *News culture*, Buckingham: Open University Press.

Allmendinger, P. (2001) *Planning in postmodern times*, London: Routledge.

Allmendinger, P. (2006) 'Zoning by stealth? The diminution of discretionary planning', *International Planning Studies*, vol 11, no 2, pp 137-43.

Allmendinger, P. and Haughton, G. (2007) 'The fluid scales and scope of UK spatial planning', *Environment and Planning A*, vol 39, no 6, pp 1478-96.

Allmendinger, P. and Tewdwr-Jones, M. (2000) 'New Labour, new planning? The trajectory of planning in Blair's Britain', *Urban Studies*, vol 37, no 8, pp 1379-402.

Andrew, G. (1997) 'Robinson in space', *Time Out*, 8-15 January, p 69.

Anstey, E. (1970) 'British transport films roll for twenty one years', *Film User*.

Ashworth, W. (1954) *The genesis of modern town planning*, London: RKP.

Attenborough, D. (2002) *Life on air*, London: BBC Books.

Audit Commission (2006) *The planning system: Matching expectations and capacity*, Wetherby: Audit Commission Publications.

Barker, K. (2004) *Delivering stability: Securing our future housing needs*, London: The Stationery Office.

Barker, K. (2006) *Barker Review of land-use planning: Interim report*, London: The Stationery Office.

Barr, C. (1993) *Ealing Studios* (2nd edn), London: Studio Vista.

Beauregard, R. (1990) 'Bringing the city back in', *Journal of the American Planning Association*, vol 56, no 2, pp 210-14.

Bendixson, T. and Platt, J. (1992) *Milton Keynes: Image and reality*, Cambridge: Granta Editions.

Berman, M. (1982) *All that is solid melts into air: The experience of modernity*, London: Verso.

Betjeman, J. (1931a) *Mount Zion*, London: The James Press.

Betjeman, J. (1931b) 'The death of modernism', *Architectural Review*, December.

Betjeman, J. (1933) *Ghastly good taste*, London: Chapman and Hall.

Betjeman, J. (1935a) 'Film clips', *Evening Standard*, 13 May.

Betjeman, J. (1935b) 'Film clips', *Evening Standard*, 20 August.

Betjeman, J. (1937) 'Swindon', BBC Home Service Broadcast, 8 May.

Betjeman, J. (1939a) 'The country town', BBC Home Service Broadcast, 27 June.

Betjeman, J. (1939b) 'Antiquarian prejudice', Pamphlet, London: Hogarth Press.

Betjeman, J. (1952) *First and last loves: Essays on towns and architecture*, London: John Murray.

Betjeman, J. (1955) 'Interview with John Betjeman', *Illustrated London News*.

Betjeman, J. (1956) *The English town in the last hundred years*, Cambridge: Cambridge University Press.

Betjeman, J. (1960) *Summoned by bells*, London: John Murray.

Betjeman, J. (1966) *High and low*, London: John Murray.

Betjeman, J. (1973) 'Obituary: Arthur Elton', *North Somerset Mercury*, January.

Betjeman, J. (1974) *A nip in the air*, London: John Murray.

Betjeman, J. (1979) *Collected poems* (4th edn), London: John Murray (first published 1958).

Betjeman, J. (1981) *Church poems*, London: John Murray.

Betjeman, J. (1982) *Uncollected poems*, London: John Murray.

Betjeman, J. and Clarke, B. (1964) *English churches*, London: Vista Books.

Bianconi, M., Gallent, N. and Greatbatch, I. (2006) 'The changing geography of subregional planning in England', *Environment and Planning C: Government and Policy*, vol 24, no 3, pp 317-30.

Brindley, T., Rydin, Y. and Stoker, G. (1989) *Remaking planning*, London: Unwin Hyman.

British Railways Board (1963) *Re-shaping of British Railways*, London: British Transport Commission.

Bruegmann, R. (2005) *Sprawl: A compact history*, Chicago: University of Chicago Press.

Bruton, M.J. (ed) (1974) *The spirit and purpose of planning*, London: Hutchinson.

Bruton, M.J. (1984) *The spirit and purpose of planning* (2nd edn), London: Hutchinson.

Bruton, M.J. and Nicholson, D.J. (1987) *Local planning in practice*, London: Hutchinson.

Bryson, B. (1995) *Notes from a small island*, London: Black Swan.

BTC (British Transport Commission) (1955) *Modernisation and the re-equipment of British Railways*, London: BTC.

Buchanan, C.D. (1972) *The state of Britain*, London: Faber and Faber.

Bullock, N. (2002) *Building the post-war world*, London: Routledge.

Burgess, J. (1990) 'The production and consumption of environmental meanings in the mass media: a research agenda for the 1990s', *Transactions of the Institute of British Geographers*, NS 15, pp 139-61.

Burgess, J. and Gold, J.R. (1985) 'Place, the media and popular culture', in J. Burgess and J.R. Gold (eds) *Geography, the media and popular culture*, Beckenham: Croom Helm, pp 1-32.

Burns, R.W. (1986) *British television: The formative years*, London: Peter Peregrinus.

Calvino, I. (1974) *Invisible cities*, New York: Harcourt Brace Jovanovich.

Campbell, H. and Marshall, R. (2005), 'The changing conception of professionalism in planning', *Town Planning Review*, vol 76, no 2, pp 191-214.

Castells, M. (1989) *The informational age: Information technology, economic restructuring and the urban regional process*, Oxford: Blackwell.

Chapman, J. (2006) 'Ealing and national identity', Paper presented to the 'Ealing Revisited' Conference, Department of Film Studies, University of Hull, 4 November. [Copies available from the author, Professor James Chapman, Department of the History of Art and Film, University of Leicester, University Road, Leicester LE1 7RH.]

Cherry, G.E. (1974) 'The development of planning thought', in M.J. Bruton (ed) *The spirit and purpose of planning*, London: Hutchinson, pp 66-84.

Childs, D. (2001) *Britain since 1945: A political history* (5th edn), London: Routledge.

Clarke, D.B. (ed) (1997) *The cinematic city*, London: Routledge.

Clifford, B.P. (2006) '"Only a town planner would run a toxic waste pipeline through a recreational area": planning and planners in the British press', *Town Planning Review*, vol 77, no 4, pp 404-23.

Cloke, P. (2002) 'Deliver us from evil? Prospects for living ethically and acting politically in human geography', *Progress in Human Geography,* no 26, pp 587-604.

Collard, J. (2003) 'Tomorrow's people', *The Times*, 27 December, p 22.

Conservative Party (2010) *Open source: Planning Green Paper,* London: Conservative Party.

Cross, D.T. and Bristow, M.R. (eds) (1983) *English structure planning: A commentary on procedures and practice in the seventies*, London: Pion.

Crow, S. (1996) 'Development control: the child that grew up in the cold', *Planning Perspectives*, vol 11, no 4, pp 399-411.

Cullingworth, B. and Nadin, V. (2002) *Town and country planning in the UK* (13th edn), London: Routledge.

Cullingworth, J.B. and Nadin, V. (2006) *Town and country planning in the UK,* 14th edn, London: Routledge.

Dave, P. (2000) 'Representations of capitalism history and nation in the work of Patrick Keiller', in J. Ashby and A. Higson (eds) *British cinema past and present*, London: Routledge, pp 339-51.

Davies, A.R. (2001) 'Hidden or hiding? Public perceptions of participation in the planning system', *Town Planning Review*, vol 72, no 2, pp 193-216.

Dennis, N. (1970) *People and plans: The sociology of slum clearance*, London: Faber and Faber.

Docter, R. (2000) 'Post-war town planning in its mid-life crisis: dilemmas in redevelopment from a policy point of view', in T. Deckker (ed) *The modern city*, London: Spon Press, pp 197-213.

DoE (Department of the Environment) (1992) *Attitudes toward town and country planning*, London: HMSO.

DTLR (Department for Transport, Local Government and the Regions) (2001) *Planning: Delivering a fundamental change*, London: The Stationery Office.

Durning, B. and Glasson, J. (2004) *Skills base in the planning system: A literature review*, London: Local Government Association.

Easthope, A. (1999) *Englishness and national culture*, London: Routledge.

Egan, J. (2004) *The Egan Review: Skills for sustainable communities*, London: Office of the Deputy Prime Minister.

Enticknap, L. (2000) 'This modern age and the British non-fiction film', in J. Ashby and A. Higson (eds) *British cinema: Past and present*, London: Routledge, pp 207-20.

Enticknap, L. (2001), 'Post-war urban development, the British film industry, and The Way We Live', in Shiel, M. and Fitzmaurice, T. (eds), *Cinema and the city*, Oxford: Blackwells, pp 233-44.

Eversley, D. (1973) *The planner in society: The changing role of a profession*, London: Faber and Faber.

Finnegan, R. (1998) *Tales of the city: A study of narrative and urban life*, Cambridge: Cambridge University Press.

Fishman, R. (1977) *Urban utopias in the twentieth century: Ebenezer Howard, Frank Lloyd Wright and Le Corbusier*, New York: Basic Books.

Games, S. (2006) *Trains and buttered toast: Selected radio talks of John Betjeman*, London: John Murray.

Gans, H.J. (1972) *People and plans: Essays on urban problems and solutions*, Harmondsworth: Pelican.

Garside, P. (1988) '"Unhealthy areas": town planning, eugenics and the slums 1890-1945', *Planning Perspectives*, vol 3, pp 24-46.

Geraghty, C. (2000) *British cinema in the fifties: Gender, genre and the 'new look'*, London: Routledge.

Giddens, A. (1990) *The consequences of modernity*, Cambridge: Polity Press.

Gilbert, M. (1990) *Second World War*, London: Weidenfeld & Nicholson.

Glancey, J. (2006) 'Introduction', in J. Davies, *The English landscape*, London: Chris Boot, pp 5-7.

Gold, J. (1997) *The experience of modernism: Modern architects and the future city 1928-1953*, London: Spon Press.

Gold, J. (2007) *The practice of modernism: Modern architects and urban transformation 1954-1972*, London: Routledge.

Gold, J. and Ward, S. (1994) '"We're going to do it right this time": cinematic representations of urban planning and the British new towns 1939-1951', in S.C. Aitken and L.E. Zonn (eds) *Place, power, situation and spectacle: A geography of film*, Lanham, MD: Rowman & Littlefield, pp 229-58.

Gold, J. and Ward, S. (1997) 'Of plans and planners: documentary film and the challenge of the urban future 1935-52', in D.B. Clarke (ed) *The cinematic city*, London: Routledge, pp 59-82.

Goodman, R. (1972) *After the planners*, Harmondsworth: Pelican.

Gormley, A. (2007) 'Foreword', in S. Penrose, *Images of change: An archaeology of England's contemporary landscape*, Swindon: English Heritage, pp 7-9.

Government Office for Science (2010) *Land use futures: Making the most of the land in the 21st century*, London: Government Office for Science.

Grant, M. (1999) 'Planning as a learned profession', unpublished paper to the Royal Town Panning Institute, London.

Green, L.L. (1997) *John Betjeman: Coming home: An anthology of prose*, London: Methuen.

Grierson, J. (1948) 'Prospect for documentary: what is wrong and why', *Sight & Sound*, vol 17, p 66.

Grierson, J. (1979) 'The documentary idea: 1942' in F. Hardy (ed) *Grierson on documentary*, London: Faber (abridged version; originally published 1946).

Grierson, J. (1981a) '*New Clarion* 11 June 1932', collected in F. Hardy (ed) *Grierson on the movies*, London: Faber.

Grierson, J. (1981b) 'Documentary (2): Symphonies', *Cinema Quarterly*, vol 1, 1933, reprinted in F. Hardy, *Grierson on documentary*, London: Faber (abridged version; originally published 1946).

Hall, P. (1978) *Great planning disasters*, London: Weidenfeld.

Hall, T. (1997), '(Re)placing the city: cultural relocation and the city as centre", in S. Westwood. and J. Williams, J (eds) *Imagining cities: Scripts signs and memories*, Routledge, London.

Hall, P. (2002) *Cities of tomorrow: An intellectual history of urban planning and design in the twentieth century*, Oxford: Wiley-Blackwell.

Hall, P. and Tewdwr-Jones, M. (2011) *Urban and regional planning* (5th edn), London: Routledge.

Hardy, D. (1991) *From garden cities to new towns: Campaigning for town and country planning 1899-1946*, London: Spon Press.

Harvey, D. (1985) *The urbanization of capital*, Oxford: Blackwell.

Harvey, D. (1988), 'Urban places in the "global village"', in Mazza, L (ed), *World cities and the future of the metropolis*, Milan: Electra, pp 21-33.

Harvey, D. (2000) *Spaces of Hope*. Berkeley: University of California Press.

Haughton, G. and Counsell, D. (2004) *Regions, spatial strategies and sustainable development*, London: Routledge.

Hay, I. and Israel, M. (2001) '"Newsmaking geography": communicating geography through the media', *Applied Geography*, vol 21, pp 107-25.

Healey, P. (2006a) *Collaborative planning* (2nd edn), Basingstoke: Palgrave.

Healey, P. (2006b) 'Territory, integration and spatial planning', in M. Tewdwr-Jones and P. Allmendinger (eds) *Territory, identity and spatial planning: Spatial governance in a fragmented nation*, London: Routledge, pp 64-79.

Healey, P. (2007) *Urban complexity and spatial strategies: Towards a relational planning for our times*, London: Routledge.

Healey, P., McNamara, P., Elson, M. and Doak, A. (1988) *Land use planning and the mediation of urban change*, Cambridge: Cambridge University Press.

Hennessey, P. (1994) *Never again: Britain after 1945*, London: Vintage Publishing.

Hennessey, P. (1995) *Post war Britain 1946-51*, London: Jonathan Cape.

Higson, A. (1984) 'Space, place, spectacle', *Screen*, vol 25, pp 4-5, October.

Higson, A. (1986) 'Britain's outstanding contribution to film: the documentary-realist tradition', in C. Barr (ed) *All our yesteryears: 90 years of British cinema*, London: British Film Institute, pp 72-97.

Higson, A. (1995) *Waving the flag: Constructing a national cinema in Britain*, Oxford: Oxford University Press.

Higson, A. (2000) 'The instability of the national', in J. Ashby and A. Higson (eds) *British cinema: Past and present*, London: Routledge, pp 35-47.

Hill, J. (1986) *Sex, class and realism: British cinema 1956-1963*, London: British Film Industry.

Hillier, B. (2004) *Betjeman: The bonus of laughter*, London: John Murray.

HM Government (1940) *The Barlow Commission, Report of the Royal Commission on the Distribution of the Industrial Population*, Cmnd 6153, London: HMSO.

HM Government (1942a) *The Scott Report. Report of the Committee on Land Utilisation in Rural Areas*, Cmnd 6378, London: HMSO.

HM Government (1942b) *The Uthwatt Report. Report of the Expert Committee on Compensation and Betterment*, Cmnd 6386, London: HMSO.

HM Government (1963) *Traffic in towns*, Report by C.D. Buchanan, London: HMSO.

Hogenkamp, B. (1976) 'Film and the Workers' Movement in Britain 1929-39', *Sight & Sound*, vol 45, no 2, Spring.

Hood, S. (1983) 'John Grierson and the documentary film movement', in J. Curran and V. Porter (eds) *British cinema history*, London: Barnes and Noble.

Hopkins, H. (1964) *The new look: A social history of the forties and fifties in Britain*, London: Readers Union and Secker and Warburg.

Howard, E. (1898) *To-morrow: A peaceful path to real reform*, London: Routledge (reprinted 2003).

Humphries, S. and Hopwood, B. (2000) *Green and pleasant land*, Basingstoke: Macmillan.

Kaniss, P. (1991) *Making local news*, Chicago, IL: University of Chicago Press.

Jacobs, J. (1962) *The death and life of great American cities*, New York: Random House.

Jay, A. (1968) *Bird's Eye View of Britain: An outline of sixteen possible programmes*, 1 February, BBC Written Archives, Caversham Park.

Jennings, C. (1995) *Up north*, London: Abacus.

Jervis, J. (1998) *Exploring the modern*, Oxford: Blackwell.

Jordison, S. and Kieran, D. (2003) *Crap towns: The 50 worst places to live in the UK*, London: Boxtree.

Jordison, S. and Kieran, D. (2004) *Crap towns II: The nation decides*, London: Boxtree.

Kynaston, D. (2007) *Austerity Britain 1945-51*, London: Bloomsbury.

Lambton, L. (1996) *A-Z of Britain*, London: HarperCollins.

Lawless, P. and Brown, F. (1986) *Urban growth and change in Britain*, London: Harper and Row.

Lawrence, D.H. (1929) *The English*, cited in Sharp, T. (1940), op.cit.

Lefebvre, H. (1974 [1991]) *The production of space*, Oxford: Blackwell.

Legard, J. (1998) 'Introduction', *BTF Recollections*, BTF Archive, London: British Film Institute.

Levin, B. (1970) *The pendulum years: Britain in the sixties*, Cambridge: Icon Books, cited in B. Hillier (2004) *Betjeman: The bonus of laughter*, London: John Murray, p 126.

Light, A. (1991) *Forever England: Femininity, literature and conservation between the wars*, London: Routledge.

Lochner, J. (1998) 'Out on production', *BTF Recollections*, BTF Archive, London: British Film Institute.

Lowenstein, A. (2000) 'Under the skin horrors: social realism and classlessness in "Peeping Tom"', in J. Ashby and A. Higson (eds) *British cinema: Past and present*, London: Routledge, pp 221-32.

Lovell, T. (1990) 'Landscapes and stories in the 1960s: British realism', *Screen*, vol 31, no 4, October.

Lowe, P., Murdoch, J. and Cox, G. (1995) 'A civilized retreat? Anti-urbanism, rurality and the making of an Anglo-centric culture', in P. Healey et al (eds) *Managing cities: The new urban context*, Chichester: Wiley, Chapter 3.

Lycett Green, C. (1997) *John Betjeman coming home: An anthology of prose*, London: Methuen.

Lyons, Sir M. and HM Government (2006) *Well placed to deliver? Shaping the pattern of government service*, Final Report of the Independent Review of Public Sector Relocation, London: HM Treasury.

McNeill, D. (2005) 'Skyscraper geography', *Progress in Human Geography*, vol 29, no 1, pp 41–55.

Marr, A. (2009) *The making of modern Britain*, London: Pan.

Mason, M. (2001) 'Naked: social realism and the urban wasteland', in M. Shiel and T. Fitzmaurice (eds) *Cinema and the city: Film and urban societies*, Oxford: Blackwell, pp 244–53.

Massey, D. (1992) 'Double articulation: a place in the world', in A. Bammer (ed) *Displacements: Cultural identities in question*, Bloomington, IN: Indiana University Press, pp 110–21.

Massey, D. (1999) 'Space-time, "science" and the relationship between physical geography and human geography', *Transactions of the Institute of British Geographers,* vol 24, pp 261–76.

Massey, D. (2005) *For space*, London: Sage Publications.

Matless, D. (1998) *Englishness and landscape,* London: Reaktion Press.

Matless, D. and Short, B. (eds) (1998) *Geographies of British modernity: Space and society in the twentieth century*, Oxford: Blackwell.

Mowl, T. (2000) *Stylistic cold wars: Betjeman versus Pevsner*, London: John Murray.

Mingay, G.E. (1991) *A social history of the English countryside*, London: Routledge.

Mirzoeff, E. (2003) 'John Betjeman and Bird's Eye View', Transcript of an interview with Eddie Mirzoeff, conducted by Mark Tewdwr-Jones, 7 August, available from the author.

Morphet, J. (2010) *Effective practice in spatial planning*, London: Routledge.

Morphet, J., Tewdwr-Jones, M., Gallent, N. and Deloitte (2007) *Shaping and delivering tomorrow's places: Effective spatial planning in practice*, London: RTPI/CLG.

Mullan, B. (1980) *Stevenage Ltd: Aspects of the planning and politics of Stevenage New Town*, London: Routledge and Kegan Paul.

Murphy, R. (1989) *Realism and tinsel: Cinema and society in Britain 1939-1949*, London: Routledge.

Observer (1969) 'Television', 30 March.

Orwell, G. (1941) 'England, your England', Pamphlet, London: Ministry of Information (reprinted 2001).

O'Shea, A. (1996) 'English subjects of modernity', in M. Nava and A. O'Shea (eds) *Modern times: Reflections on a century of English modernity*, London: Routledge.

Nadin, V. (2007) 'The emergence of the spatial planning approach in England', *Planning Practice and Research*, vol 22, no 1, pp 43–62.

Nairn, I. (1955) *Outrage*, London: Architectural Press.

Nowell-Smith, G. (2001) 'Cities: real and imagined', in M. Shiel and T. Fitzmaurice (eds) *Cinema and the city: Film and urban societies*, Oxford: Blackwell, pp 99–108.

NPF (2007) *Culture Change Action Plan*, London: National Planning Forum.

Pahl, R.E. (1975) *Whose city?*, Harmondsworth: Penguin.

Paxman, J. (1998) *The English: A portrait of a people*, London: Michael Joseph.

Pendlebury, J. (2009) *Conservation in the age of consensus*, London: Routledge.

Phelps, N.A. and Tewdwr-Jones, M. (2008) 'If geography is anything, maybe it's planning's alter ego? Reflections on policy relevance in two disciplines concerned with place and space', *Transactions of the Institute of British Geographers*, vol 33, issue 4, pp 566–84.

Potter, C. (1998) 'Nationalisation and British transport films 1946-1977', *BTF Recollections*, BTF Archive, London: British Film Institute.

Priestley, J.B. (1979) *English journey*, London: Penguin.

Prince of Wales, The (1987) Speech to the Corporation of London Planning and Communication Committee's Annual Dinner, Mansion House, London, 1 December.

Prince of Wales, The (1989) *A vision of Britain*, London: Doubleday.

Raco, M., Parker, G. and Doak, J. (2006) 'Reshaping spaces of local governance? Community strategies and the modernisation of local governance in England', *Environment and Planning C: Government and Policy*, vol 24, no 4, pp 475-96.

Radio Times (1969) Thursday 25 December, Christmas and New Year edition.

Reade, E. (1983) 'If planning is anything, maybe it can be identified', *Urban Studies*, vol 20, pp 159-171.

Reade, E. (1987) *British town and country planning*, Buckingham: Open University Press.

Reed, J. (1990) *Moving images: Commemorating 40 years of British Transport Films*, Middlesex: Capital Transport.

Richards, J. (1997) *Films and British national identity: From Dickens to 'Dad's Army'*, Manchester: Manchester University Press.

Rose, E.A. (1984) 'Philosophy and purpose in planning', in M.J. Bruton (ed) *The spirit and purpose of planning*, London: Hutchinson, pp 31-66.

Rotha, P. (1949) 'A survey of recent film literature in Britain', in A. Higson (1995) *The year's work in the film*, London.

Rotha, P. (1952) *Documentary film*, London: Faber (originally published in 1936).

RTPI (Royal Town Planning Institute) (2003) *A New Vision for Planning*, London: RTPI.

Sandercock, L. (2003) *Mongrel cities: Cosmopolis II*, London: Continuum Press.

Savage, M. and Ward, A. (1993) *Urban sociology, capitalism and modernity*, Macmillan, Basingstoke.

Sayer, A. and Storper, M. (1997) 'Ethics unbound: for a normative turn in social theory', *Environment & Planning D., Society & Space,* vol 15, pp 1-17.

Scott, J.C. (2000) *Seeing like a state: How certain schemes to improve the human condition have failed*. London: Yale University Press.

Scott, A.J. and Roweis, S.T. (1977) 'Urban planning in theory and practice', *Environment and Planning A*, vol 9, pp 1097-119.

Scott, E. (1998) 'Random thoughts', *BTF Recollections*, BTF Archive, London: British Film Institute.

Sharp, T. (1940) *Town planning*, Harmondsworth: Penguin Pelican.

Shiel, M. (2001) 'Cinema and the city in history and theory', in M. Shiel and T. Fitzmaurice (eds) *Cinema and the city: Film and urban societies*, Oxford: Blackwell, pp 1-18.

Sked, A. (1979) *Post-war Britain: A political history*, London: Rowman and Littlefield.

Skeffington, A.M. (1969) *People and planning: Report of the Committee on Public Participation in Planning*, London: HMSO.

Soja, E. (1989) *Postmodern geographies*, Brooklyn, NY: Verso Press.

Stead, P. (1990) *Film and the working class*, London: Routledge.

Stedall, J. (2002) 'From John Betjeman to Michael Portillo', *Camera: Cambridge University Film Quarterly*, Winter, Cambridge.

Sutcliffe, A. (1981) 'Introduction: British town planning and the historian', in A. Sutcliffe (ed) *British town planning: The formative years*, Leicester: Leicester University Press, pp 2-15.

Swain, C. and Tait, M. (2007) 'The crisis of trust and planning', *Planning Theory and Practice*, vol 7, no 2, pp 229-47.

Swann, P. (1983) 'John Grierson and the GPO Film Unit 1933-1939', *Historical Journal of Film, Radio and Television*, vol 3, no 1.

Taylor, P.J. (1999) 'Places, spaces and Macy's: place-space tensions in the political geography of modernities', *Progress in Human Geography*, vol 23, pp 7-26.

Tewdwr-Jones, M. (1999) 'Reasserting town planning: challenging the image and representation of the planning profession', in P. Allmendinger and M. Chapman (eds) *Planning beyond 2000*, Chichester: John Wiley and Sons, pp 123-50.

Tewdwr-Jones, M. (2002) *The planning polity: Planning, government and the policy process*, London: Routledge.

Tewdwr-Jones, M. (2004) 'Spatial planning: principles, practice and culture', *Journal of Planning and Environment Law*, vol 57, no 5, pp 560-9.

Tewdwr-Jones, M. (2005) 'Oh the planners did their best: the planning films of John Betjeman', *Planning Perspectives*, vol 20, no 4, pp 389-411.

Tewdwr-Jones, M., Gallent, N. and Morphet, J. (2010) 'An anatomy of spatial planning: coming to terms with the spatial element in UK planning', *European Planning Studies*, vol 18, no 2, pp 239-57.

Thornley, A. (1991) *Urban planning under Thatcherism*, London: Routledge.

Wadley, D. and Smith, P. (1998) 'If planning is about anything, what is it about?', *International Journal of Social Economics,* vol 25, pp 1005-29.

Walker, J. (1993) *Arts TV: A history of arts television Britain*, Luton: Luton University Press.

Ward, S.V. (1994) *Planning and urban change*, London: Paul Chapman.

Ward, S.V. (2002) *Planning the twentieth century city: The advanced capitalist world*, Chichester: John Wiley and Sons.

Watkin, D. (1998) *Why is there only one word for thesaurus?*, London: Beulah.

Wells, H.G. (1900) *Anticipation of the reaction of the mechanical and scientific progress upon human life and thought,* London: Chapman and Hall.

While, A. (2006) 'Modernism versus urban renaissance: negotiating post-war built heritage in English city centres', *Urban Studies*, vol 43, no 13, pp 2399-419.

While, A. (2007) 'The state and the controversial demands of cultural built heritage: the origins and evolution of post-war listing in England', *Environment and Planning B*, vol 34, no 4, pp 645-63.

While, A. and Tait, M. (2009) 'Exeter and the question of Thomas Sharp's physical legacy', *Planning Perspectives*, vol 24, no 1, pp 77-97.

Williams, R. (1985 [1973]) *The country and the city,* London: Hogarth Press.

Williams-Ellis, C. (1928) *England and the octopus*, London: Geoffrey Bles.

Wright, P. (1985) *On living in an old country*, London: Verso.

Wyver, J. (1989) 'Representing arts or representing culture? Tradition and innovation in British television coverage of the arts (1950-87)', in P. Hayward and W. Bell (eds) *Picture this: Media representations of visual art and visual artists*, Luton: Luton University Press.

index